THE

50 GREATEST PLAYERS

IN

NEW YORK GIANTS

HISTORY

THE
50 GREATEST PLAYERS
IN
NEW YORK GIANTS
HISTORY

ROBERT W. COHEN

GUILFORD, CONNECTICUT

An imprint of The Rowman and Littlefield Publishing Group, Inc.
4501 Forbes Blvd., Ste. 200
Lanham, MD 20706
www.rowman.com

Distributed by NATIONAL BOOK NETWORK

British Library Cataloguing in Publication Information Available

Library of Congress Cataloging-in-Publication Data

Names: Cohen, Robert W., author.
Title: The 50 greatest players in New York Giants history / Robert W. Cohen.
Other titles: 50 greatest players in New York Giants football history | Fifty
    greatest players in New York Giants history
Description: Guilford, Connecticut : Lyons Press, [2018] | "Distributed by
    NATIONAL BOOK NETWORK"—T.p. verso. | "A previous hardcover edition
    was published by Rowman & Littlefield in 2014"—T.p. verso. | Includes
    bibliographical references.
Identifiers: LCCN 2018015735 (print) | LCCN 2018017332 (ebook) | ISBN
    9781493035663 (e-book) | ISBN 9781493035656 (alk. paper)
Subjects: LCSH: New York Giants (Football team)—Biography. | Football
    players—Rating of—United States.
Classification: LCC GV956.N4 (ebook) | LCC GV956.N4 C64 2018 (print) | DDC
    796.332/64097471—dc23
LC record available at https://lccn.loc.gov/2018015735

— CONTENTS —

ACKNOWLEDGMENTS

wish to thank Richard Albersheim of Albersheims.com, Joseph Umphlett of SportsMemorabilia.com, Troy Kinunen of MearsonlineAuctions.com, Kate of RMYAuctions.com, Pristineauction.com, CollectAuctions.com, AmericanMemorabilia.com, NearMintCards.com, FootballCardGallery .com, EACGallery.com, George Kitrinos, Mike Morbeck, and Rick Sparacino, each of whom supplied me with several photos included in this book.

I would also like to express my appreciation to Erica Wines, Scott Mecum, John J. Shelmet, Michael Cassella, Andy Kronen, Alexa Scordato, Erik Drost, Tony Mangia, and Dave Kopp for contributing to the photographic content of this work.

— INTRODUCTION —

THE GIANT TRADITION OF WINNING

The New York Giants, one of the National Football League's flagship franchises, first came into existence in 1925, when bookmaker (a legal profession at the time), raconteur, and sportsman Timothy J. Mara paid NFL president Joe Carr the $2,500 entrance fee that made him sole owner of New York's first representative in the infant circuit. Merely five years old at the time, the NFL, which spent most of its formative years operating in the shadows of baseball, boxing, and college football, knew that it needed to place a successful franchise in a large market such as New York if it had any hope of surviving. Although the Giants struggled—along with every other team in the league—to make ends meet throughout the first decade of their existence, they nevertheless managed to win their first NFL title in just their third season, compiling a record of 11–1–1 in 1927 that earned them recognition as league champion. (The NFL did not institute a playoff system until 1933.)

The stability of the National Football League became even more tenuous following the stock market crash of 1929, when the nation entered the Great Depression. Having suffered substantial losses that threatened the existence of the Giants, Tim Mara eventually handed over control of the franchise to his two sons, Jack and Wellington, only 22 and 14 years of age, respectively, when they assumed significant roles in the front office. However, before entrusting the team to his offspring, the elder Mara named Steve Owen the Giants coach in 1931. Owen, a huge lineman who remained active as a player his first two years at the helm, continued to coach the Giants until 1953, leading them to eight Eastern Division titles and two NFL championships.

The Giants captured the first of those championships in 1934 when they defeated the Chicago Bears by a score of 30–13, just one year after losing to them in the title game by a score of 23–21. In what eventually became known as the "Sneakers Game," the Giants overcame George Halas's powerful "Monsters of the Midway" by simply outsmarting them. Trailing Chicago by a score of 10–3 at halftime, the Giants combatted New York's Polo Grounds' icy surface (game-time temperature stood at only 9 degrees) by exchanging their football cleats for basketball shoes. Able to find better footing than their physically superior counterparts, the Giants subsequently scored 27 unanswered points in the second half, romping to a 30–13 victory in the process.

The Giants returned to the title game six more times under Owen, capturing their only other championship with him at the helm in 1938, when they defeated the Green Bay Packers 23–17. One of the league's most successful franchises from 1933 to 1944, the Giants posted a combined record of 89–39–9 over that 12-year stretch. Although many other outstanding players—such as quarterback Ed Danowski, running back Tuffy Leemans, end Ray Flaherty, and the extremely versatile Ward Cuff—graced the team's roster at different times during that period, lineman Mel Hein remained the one constant, serving as a rock on both sides of the ball. Anchoring the offense from his center position, while also leading the defense from his linebacking spot, Hein established himself as the Giants' first truly great player, eventually earning Hall of Fame honors with his superb two-way play.

New York struggled somewhat during the latter portion of the 1940s, posting a winning record just once between 1945 and 1949. However, with the development of young defensive back Emlen Tunnell into the team's next great player and the arrival of brilliant defensive mind Tom Landry, who helped Owen install the famed "umbrella defense" in 1950, the Giants once again became one of the NFL's most formidable squads, posting a combined record of 26–9 from 1950 to 1952. Nevertheless, New York's 3–9 finish in 1953 convinced team management that changes in the game such as the split-T formation, the man-in-motion, and the option play had caused Owen's "down in the dirt" coaching philosophy to become outdated. Choosing to end its long association with Owen, ownership subsequently elected to replace him as head coach with former assistant Jim Lee Howell prior to the start of the 1954 season.

The hiring of Howell ushered in the next era of greatness for the Giants, who, after finishing a combined 13–10 in their first two seasons under their new head coach, went on to appear in six out of the next eight

NFL championship games, winning the title in 1956. Much of the success New York experienced during that time had a great deal to do with the exceptional abilities of the members of their coaching staff. While Tom Landry devised intricate defensive schemes to thwart opposing offenses, Vince Lombardi did a superb job of coaching the offense. Even after both men left to accept head coaching jobs with other teams and Howell announced his retirement at the conclusion of the 1960 campaign, the Giants continued to thrive under Howell's replacement, Allie Sherman, who took over the top spot after previously doing an expert job of coaching the offensive backfield.

Also key to New York's success throughout the period was the level of talent the team fielded on both sides of the ball, particularly on the defensive end. The Giants' front four of Andy Robustelli, Dick Modzelewski, Rosey Grier, and Jim Katcavage proved to be as dominant as any in the league. Sam Huff established himself as one of the circuit's top linebackers. Meanwhile, Emlen Tunnell, Jimmy Patton, Dick Lynch, and Erich Barnes starred in the secondary.

Although not quite as formidable on offense, the Giants also had their fair share of weapons on that side of the ball. Wide receiver Kyle Rote, fullback Alex Webster, quarterback Charlie Conerly, and the versatile Frank Gifford gave the team talent at the skill positions, while perennial All-Pros Roosevelt Brown and Ray Wietecha provided excellent blocking up front. The offense became significantly more potent when veteran quarterback Y. A. Tittle and speedy wide receiver Del Shofner joined the team prior to the start of the 1961 campaign.

However, a 14–10 loss to the Chicago Bears in the 1963 NFL championship game (their third consecutive defeat in the NFL title game) marked the end of New York's successful run. With much of the team's veteran nucleus aging all at once, the Giants quickly plummeted to the depths of the NFL in 1964, compiling a record of just 2–10–2. A series of ill-advised selections in the annual college draft and frequent attempts at improving the squad via the "quick fix" subsequently relegated the Giants to second-tier status for most of the next two decades. In easily the darkest period in their franchise history, New York posted a winning record just twice between 1964 and 1980, finishing out of the playoffs each year, while compiling an overall mark of only 84–156–4. The Giants also switched homes three times during that period, spending the first several seasons playing at Yankee Stadium, moving briefly to the Yale Bowl in New Haven, Connecticut, and to New York's Shea Stadium, and finally settling in at Giants Stadium in 1976. The team also changed head coaches no fewer than four times, replacing Sherman with longtime fan favorite Alex Webster in 1969, bringing in Bill Arnsparger in 1974, hiring John McVay during the 1976 campaign, and replacing McVay with Ray Perkins at the conclusion of the 1978 season.

Yet, even in mediocrity, those Giant squads featured several outstanding performers. After being acquired from Minnesota for a boatload of draft picks, scrambling quarterback Fran Tarkenton brought excitement to Yankee Stadium for five seasons. Speedy wide receiver Homer Jones developed into one of the NFL's most potent offensive weapons. Bob Tucker became the first tight end to lead the NFC in pass receptions, while halfback Ron Johnson became the first Giants running back to rush for 1,000 yards in a season. On defense, safety Carl "Spider" Lockhart earned multiple trips to the Pro Bowl, while linebackers Brad Van Pelt and Harry Carson each appeared on the All-Pro squad a number of times.

The Giants continued to flounder as a team until they turned the managerial reins over to veteran front office man George Young, who previously held numerous positions with the Baltimore Colts and the Miami Dolphins. Hired as general manager in 1979, Young helped right the ship by naming no-nonsense Ray Perkins as his new head coach. He then set about rebuilding the Giants' roster by drafting such future standouts as quarterback Phil Simms, cornerback Mark Haynes, defensive end Leonard Marshall, running back Joe Morris, tight end Mark Bavaro, and linebackers Lawrence Taylor and Carl Banks. Simms and Taylor proved to be the two most significant figures in New York's resurgence, along with Bill Parcells, who replaced Perkins as head coach when the latter returned to the University of Alabama to coach his alma mater in 1983. With Simms leading the offense and Taylor spearheading an imposing defense, the Giants earned five playoff berths in eight seasons under Parcells, capturing the NFL championship in both 1986 and 1990.

New York experienced another brief period of mediocrity after differences between Young and Parcells prompted the latter to resign as head coach following the conclusion of the 1990 championship campaign. However, after posting a winning record just twice in six seasons under Parcells's successors, Ray Handley and Dan Reeves, the Giants made three playoff appearances in seven years under Jim Fassell, earning a trip to Super Bowl XXXV, where they lost to the Baltimore Ravens, 34–7. Nevertheless, a disastrous 2003 season once again caused team management to change coaches, with the front office this time turning to Tom Coughlin, who previously coached the expansion Jacksonville Jaguars to an appearance in the AFC championship game in just their second year of existence.

Although the Giants struggled in their first season under the somewhat autocratic Coughlin, they eventually discovered that his regimented ways worked well in the NFL, bringing to them a greater sense of structure and purpose. After finishing just 6–10 in their first season under Coughlin, the Giants compiled an overall mark of 77–51 with him at the helm over the course of the next eight years, earning in the process five trips to the playoffs and victories over the New England Patriots in Super Bowls XLII and XLVI. Outstanding players to perform for the team under Coughlin included, at different times, defensive ends Michael Strahan, Osi Umenyiora, and Justin Tuck; running back Tiki Barber; wide receivers Amani Toomer, Plaxico Burress, Victor Cruz, Hakeem Nicks, and Odell Beckham Jr.; and quarterback Eli Manning, who has established himself as arguably the greatest signal-caller in franchise history.

Unfortunately, the successful run the Giants experienced under Coughlin came to an end in 2013, when they began a three-year stretch during which they posted an overall mark of just 19–29, prompting team management to turn over head coaching duties to offensive coordinator Ben McAdoo. After bolstering their porous defense with several expensive free-agent acquisitions during the off-season, the Giants performed well under McAdoo in 2016, earning their first playoff berth in five years by compiling a record of 11–5. However, a disastrous 2017 campaign in which the team went just 3–13 led to the firing of McAdoo and the hiring of Pat Shurmur, who spent the previous two seasons serving as an assistant on the coaching staff of the Minnesota Vikings.

Heading into the 2018 season, the Giants have appeared in 19 NFL championship games—more than any other team. They have also won eight league championships, tying them with the Bears for second place on the all-time list (the Green Bay Packers, with 13 NFL titles to their credit, have won more than any other team). Meanwhile, 26 players who spent at least one full season wearing a Giants uniform have been inducted into the NFL Hall of Fame; 16 of those men spent the majority of their careers playing for the Giants.

FACTORS USED TO DETERMINE RANKINGS

It should come as no surprise that selecting the 50 greatest players ever to perform for a team with such a storied past presented quite a challenge. Even after narrowing the field down to a mere 50 men, I still needed to devise a method of ranking the elite players that remained. Certainly, the names of Lawrence Taylor, Mel Hein, Roosevelt Brown, Harry Carson, Phil

Simms, Eli Manning, Emlen Tunnell, and Michael Strahan would appear at, or near, the top of virtually everyone's list, although the order might vary somewhat from person to person. Several other outstanding performers have gained general recognition through the years as being among the greatest players ever to wear a Giants uniform. Andy Robustelli, Sam Huff, Mark Bavaro, Carl Banks, Frank Gifford, and Brad Van Pelt head the list of other Giant icons. But how does one compare players who lined up on opposite sides of the ball with any degree of certainty? Furthermore, how does one differentiate between the pass-rushing and run-stopping skills of players such as Andy Robustelli, Lawrence Taylor, and Michael Strahan and the ball-hawking and punt-return abilities of an Emlen Tunnell? And, on the offensive end, how can a direct correlation be made between the contributions made by Hall of Fame lineman Rosey Brown and skill position players such as Eli Manning and Odell Beckham Jr.? After initially deciding who to include on my list, I then needed to determine what criteria I should use to formulate my final rankings.

The first thing I decided to examine was the level of dominance a player attained during his time in New York. How often did he lead the NFL in a major statistical category? Did he ever capture league MVP honors? How many times did he earn a trip to the Pro Bowl or a spot on the All-Pro Team?

I also chose to assess the level of statistical compilation a player achieved while wearing a Giants uniform. I reviewed where he ranked among the team's all-time leaders in those statistical categories most pertinent to his position. Of course, even the method of using statistics as a measuring stick has its inherent flaws. Although the level of success a team experiences rushing and passing the ball is impacted greatly by the performance of its offensive line, there really is no way to quantifiably measure the level of play reached by each individual offensive lineman. Conversely, the play of the offensive line affects tremendously the statistics compiled by a team's quarterback and running backs. Furthermore, the NFL did not keep an official record of defensive numbers such as tackles and quarterback sacks until the 1980s. In addition, when examining the statistics compiled by offensive players, the era during which a quarterback, running back, or wide receiver competed must be factored into the equation.

To illustrate my last point, rule changes instituted by the league office have opened up the game considerably over the course of the past two decades. Quarterbacks are accorded far more protection than ever before, and officials have also been instructed to limit the amount of contact defensive backs are allowed to make with wide receivers. As a result, the game has experienced an offensive explosion, with quarterbacks and receivers posting numbers players from prior generations rarely even approached. That being the case, one must place the numbers Eli Manning has compiled during his career in their proper context when comparing him to other outstanding Giant quarterbacks such as Phil Simms and Fran Tarkenton. Similarly, Odell Beckham Jr.'s huge receiving totals must be viewed in moderation when comparing him to previous Giant wide-outs Homer Jones and Del Shofner.

Other important factors I needed to consider were the overall contributions a player made to the success of the team, the degree to which he improved the fortunes of the club during his time in New York, the manner in which he impacted the team both on and off the field, and the degree to which he added to the Giant legacy of winning. While the number of championships the Giants won during a particular player's years with the team certainly entered into the equation, I chose not to deny a top performer his rightful place on the list if his years in New York happened to coincide with a lack of overall success by the club. As a result, the names of players such as Brad Van Pelt and Ron Johnson will appear in these rankings.

One other thing I should mention is that I only considered a player's performance while playing for the Giants when formulating my rankings. That being the case, the names of truly exceptional players such as Y. A. Tittle and Fran Tarkenton, both of whom had most of their best years while playing for other teams, may appear lower on this list than one might expect. Meanwhile, the names of other standout performers such as Ottis Anderson and Fred Dryer are nowhere to be found.

Having established the guidelines to be used throughout this book, we are ready to take a look at the 50 greatest players in Giants history, starting with number 1 and working our way down to number 50.

1

LAWRENCE TAYLOR

Although Harry Carson, Emlen Tunnell, Roosevelt Brown, Mel Hein, and Michael Strahan all proved to be worthy contenders, the enormous impact that Lawrence Taylor made on the Giants and the NFL as a whole after he entered the league in 1981 made him the only possible choice for the top spot in these rankings. Featuring a rare combination of power, speed, and intensity, Taylor turned the Giants into perennial contenders after they failed to make the playoffs in any of the previous 17 seasons. At the same time, LT, as he came to be known, helped revolutionize the game of football by changing the position of linebacker from a "read and react" spot to one that attacked opposing offenses. In the process, Taylor developed a reputation second to none among NFL defenders, gaining general recognition as arguably the greatest defensive player in league history.

Born in Williamsburg, Virginia, on February 4, 1959, Lawrence Julius Taylor spent most of his early years in sports concentrating primarily on baseball, failing to play organized football until he joined his Lafayette High School squad at the age of 16. Proving to be a natural at his newfound love, Taylor subsequently went on to star at the University of North Carolina at Chapel Hill, where he found a home as linebacker after originally being recruited as a defensive lineman. Accumulating 16 sacks in his final year of collegiate ball, Taylor earned consensus first-team All-American and Atlantic Coast Conference Player of the Year honors in 1980. Although Taylor's extraordinary play prompted most pro teams to rank him as the top prospect heading into the 1981 NFL Draft, the New Orleans Saints instead made Heisman Trophy–winning halfback George Rogers the first overall selection, enabling the Giants to nab Taylor with the second pick.

After initially balking at the idea of playing in Giants Stadium for a team that finished the previous campaign with a record of just 4–12, Taylor grew increasingly enthusiastic as his first professional training camp approached. However, he often found himself at odds with New York's defensive coordinator at the time, Bill Parcells, who frequently agitated

Lawrence Taylor helped revolutionize the game of football with his extraordinary play as outside linebacker.
Courtesy of MearsOnlineAuctions.com

his players in the hope of getting them to reach their maximum potential. Unhappy over Parcells's constant derision, Taylor finally told his coach, "I've had enough. You either cut me or trade me, but get the __ck off my back."[1]

Meanwhile, Taylor made an extremely favorable impression on his new teammates. Harry Carson later recalled, "The first play that he went in during his rookie training camp we knew that this guy was something special. You could tell that this guy was like from another planet."[2]

Safety Beasley Reece, Taylor's teammate in New York from 1981 to 1983, offered his recollections from that first training camp: "You saw things that made you go, 'My God, did you just see that?'"[3]

The 6'3", 242-pound Taylor soon began creating a stir around the entire league as well. Before long, opposing teams began devising complicated blocking schemes to prevent LT from destroying their quarterback and demolishing their running backs. Taylor's size, speed, agility, and intensity made him the NFL's most dominant defensive player—one capable of completely disrupting the offenses of opposing teams.

Former Washington Redskins quarterback Joe Theismann revealed, "You walk into an offensive meeting and you sit down, and the first thing that comes out of the coach's mouth is, 'How do we block number 56?'"[4]

Legendary coach and television commentator John Madden believed that any such meetings invariably ended in futility, saying, "I don't care who you bring—guard, tackle, center—you weren't going to block Lawrence Taylor."[5]

Dick Butkus, perhaps the greatest middle linebacker ever to play the game, expressed his admiration for Taylor by mentioning the qualities LT possessed that made him such a difficult player for opposing offenses to prepare for: "When you get a guy like Lawrence, who's got the size, the speed, the intensity, and everything else, and then you add his heart, then you've got a superman on your hands."[6]

Taylor's immense talent enabled him to make the other players around him better. His ability to rush the passer, run down ball carriers from behind, and confuse and intimidate his opponents inspired confidence in his teammates, raising their level of play as well. Furthermore, Taylor's intensity and enthusiasm for the game became contagious, greatly altering the losing mind-set that previously pervaded the Giants' locker room. Reflecting back on the manner in which he impacted the Giants from a psychological perspective, Taylor stated, "I think I brought enthusiasm back to the game of football. If you get excited by a play, then, all of a sudden, the next guy gets excited! I think that's one of the things I brought to the Giants."[7]

Taylor's spirited play and great talent helped lead the Giants into the playoffs for the first time in 18 years in his first NFL season. New York's defense, which surrendered 425 points to the opposition one year earlier, allowed only 257 points in 1981. The Giants concluded the regular season with a record of 9–7 and upset the favored Philadelphia Eagles in the first round of the postseason tournament, before losing to the eventual world champion San Francisco 49ers 38–24 in the NFL divisional playoffs. For his efforts, Taylor earned AP Defensive Rookie of the Year and AP Defensive Player of the Year honors. He also was selected to appear in the Pro Bowl for the first of 10 consecutive times, and he was named First-Team All-Pro for the first of eight times.

Former Chicago Bears linebacker Mike Singletary entered the NFL the same year as Taylor. The Bears great later recalled, "There were times when you saw him play that you thought, 'Wait a minute . . . the guy can't be that good!'"[8]

Discussing the style of play that made him so successful from the time he first entered the league, Taylor commented, "I feel I have enough ability that, if I get into trouble, I can get out of it pretty well. You know, some guys have to play the technique, and the technique is what gets them by in the league. I play more on instinct than technique-wise."[9]

Although changes in the Giants' coaching staff caused them to struggle as a team in both 1982 and 1983, Taylor continued to perform at an extremely high level, earning First-Team All-Pro honors each year and being named AP Defensive Player of the Year for the second consecutive time in 1982.

The Giants began to come together as a team in 1984, beginning a stretch during which they advanced to the playoffs in five of the next seven years. With Carl Banks joining Taylor and Harry Carson in the linebacking corps, New York fielded arguably the finest trio of backers in NFL history. Taylor had solid seasons in 1984 and 1985, compiling a total of 24½ sacks, en route to earning Pro Bowl and First Team All-Pro honors for the fourth and fifth consecutive times. Nevertheless, LT's off-field transgressions, which included drug abuse and overindulging in liquor and women, adversely affected his overall performance to some extent, leaving him feeling disappointed at the end of each season, especially when the Giants came up short in the playoffs both times.

Focusing more on football than perhaps ever before in 1986, Taylor put together his finest season, leading the Giants to a regular-season record of 14–2, the NFC championship, and, eventually, their first Super Bowl victory. Taylor led the NFL with a career-high 20½ sacks, en route to earning Pro Bowl and First-Team All-Pro honors for the sixth straight time, AP Defensive Player of the Year honors for the third time, and recognition as the NFL's Most Valuable Player. By being named league MVP, Taylor became the first defensive player in 17 years to be so honored.

Commenting on his star linebacker's amazing season, Giants head coach Bill Parcells stated, "I know Lawrence Taylor very well. He's a catalyst. He can provide a lot of things to a team. He told me before the season what he was gonna do, so I really didn't make any predictions. I knew what he was gonna do because he told me."[10]

Meanwhile, other coaches around the league found themselves envying Parcells, wishing they had an opportunity to coach someone with Taylor's extraordinary talent.

Dan Reeves, head coach of the Denver Broncos, whom the Giants defeated in Super Bowl XXI by a score of 39–20, proclaimed, "He [Taylor] is, without question, the most dominating player that we've seen on defense. I've never seen anybody as big as he is, as fast as he is, and as relentless as he is."[11]

Washington Redskins assistant head coach Joe Bugel said of LT, "He's relentless. He has a motor that never goes off. He plays the game at 1,000 miles an hour, and he's really the most prolific football player that we have to face, year-in and year-out."[12]

Taylor also left a lasting impression on Redskins quarterback Jay Schroeder, who described his adversary as "a phenomenal blitzer. He comes from everywhere all the time, and, when he hits you, you have to take inventory. You have to see if everything is still hooked up, and you get up and you start shaking—make sure your legs are there, your arms are there, and everything else; and, hopefully, he doesn't get there too often over the course of a game."[13]

Even though Taylor posted 12 quarterback sacks in the 12 games he played over the course of the strike-shortened 1987 campaign, he failed to perform at the same lofty level. After causing strife in the locker room by crossing the picket line when New York's replacement players lost their first three contests, Taylor missed the first game of his career with a hamstring injury, ending his consecutive-games-played streak at 106. The Giants ended the season with a record of just 6–9, before failing to make the playoffs again in 1988 despite posting a mark of 10–6. Taylor played well in 1988, compiling 15½ sacks in only 12 games. However, the Giants lost his services for the first four contests after the league suspended him for 30 days for violating the NFL's substance abuse policy for the second time by testing positive for cocaine. The Giants went 2–2 in Taylor's absence.

Despite being forced to play the latter portion of the 1989 campaign with a fractured tibia, suffered during a 34–24 loss to the 49ers in week 12, Taylor had another big year, recording 15 sacks en route to earning his ninth straight Pro Bowl selection and the last of his eight First-Team All-Pro nominations. The Giants returned to the playoffs for the first time since winning the Super Bowl three years earlier, concluding the regular season with a record of 12–4. However, they subsequently found themselves eliminated by the Rams in the first round of the postseason tournament, losing in overtime by a final score of 19–13.

Taylor earned his final trip to the Pro Bowl in 1990, helping the Giants capture their second championship in four years by recording 10½ sacks over the course of the regular season. After a less successful 1991 campaign, he suffered a ruptured Achilles tendon in a November 8, 1992, game against Green Bay that sidelined him for the season's final seven contests. Healthy again in 1993, Taylor returned to the team for one final run, helping the Giants advance to the playoffs with a record of 11–5 under new head coach Dan Reeves. However, his career ended on a sour note, with the Giants losing to the 49ers by a score of 44–3 in the second round of the playoffs. Taylor announced his retirement at the postgame press conference, telling the assembled media, "I think it's time for me to retire. I've done everything I can do. I've been to Super Bowls. I've been to playoffs. I've done things that other people haven't been able to do in this game before. After 13 years, it's time for me to go."[14]

Lawrence Taylor ended his career with 1,088 tackles and 132½ "official" quarterback sacks (he registered another 9½ sacks in his rookie season of 1981, one year before the NFL began recording sacks as an official statistic). Taylor's sack total placed him second on the NFL's all-time list at the time of his retirement (he has since slipped to 13th). He also intercepted nine passes, scored two touchdowns, forced 33 fumbles, and made 11 fumble recoveries. Taylor earned a spot on the NFL's 75th Anniversary Team in 1994, leaving behind him a legacy of being perhaps the greatest defensive player in league history. Both the *Sporting News* and the NFL Network have recognized him as such, with the former ranking him behind only offensive players Jim Brown, Jerry Rice, and Joe Montana on its list of greatest players, while the latter placed him third, behind only Rice and Brown, on its Top 100 Players of All Time list.

Taylor continued to draw praise from those closely associated with the game following his retirement. Speaking of LT, who constantly harassed his quarterbacks whenever the Giants played Washington, former Redskins head coach Joe Gibbs stated, "He's changed the game of football because he's just so dominating. It used to be that you'd say 'our back blocks him,' and you'd go ahead and throw the pass. If you get a back blocking Lawrence Taylor, you'll lose."[15]

Longtime Philadelphia Eagles quarterback Ron Jaworski suggested, "Lawrence Taylor was one of those guys that revolutionized the game. When you played against the Giants with Lawrence Taylor, you had to game-plan for him. Throughout my 17 years, there were a lot of great

Many people consider Taylor to be the greatest defensive player in NFL history.
Courtesy of George A. Kitrinos

players, and a lot of great teams, but, first and foremost, he stands out in my mind, and the Giant defense, because of him; because you did not execute a play without knowing where he was, not only as a quarterback, but as a complete offense."[16]

Bill Parcells supported Jaworski's contention, noting, "He [Taylor] changed the way the game was played on offense. They had to do something different. He may have invented the one-back offense. Joe Gibbs started using the one-back offense to deal with Lawrence Taylor."[17]

Parcells added, "I think you're talking about one of the best guys that's ever played. I don't think there's any question about that. Maybe *the* best guy, in deference to all the other great players that have come before him. I'm not saying he is the best, but he certainly has to be among the top handful of players that ever played in this league."[18]

Yet, in spite of Taylor's greatness as a player, a considerable amount of uncertainty surrounded his candidacy when he became eligible for the Pro Football Hall of Fame in 1999. Taylor's hard-partying lifestyle, multiple suspensions, and involvement with drugs and prostitutes created doubt in the minds of many as to whether the voters would be able to overlook his many vices. Any concerns proved to be ill-founded, however, since Taylor was voted in the first time his name appeared on the ballot.

With his ex-wife, three children, and parents all in attendance at his induction ceremony, Taylor acknowledged each of them, saying, "Thank you for putting up with me for all those years."[19] He also credited former Giants owner Wellington Mara for being so supportive of him, stating, "He [Mara] probably cared more about me as a person than he really should have."[20]

Although he has since run afoul of the law on numerous occasions for displaying a lack of judiciousness at times, Taylor ingratiated himself to the general public during a 2003 television interview with Mike Wallace. Speaking candidly about his time in the NFL, Taylor made numerous soul-wrenching admissions, describing the drug-abusing stages of his life as the "L.T." period of his life. He described "L.T." as an adrenaline junkie who lived life on a thrill ride. Displaying a great deal of emotion, Taylor stated that "L.T. died a long time ago, and I don't miss him at all . . . all that's left is Lawrence Taylor."[21]

CAREER HIGHLIGHTS

Best Season

Although Taylor had a number of exceptional seasons for the Giants, the 1986 campaign would have to be considered his finest. In addition to leading the NFL with a career-high 20½ sacks and earning Pro Bowl, First-Team All-Pro, and AP NFL Defensive Player of the Year honors, LT became the first defensive player since Minnesota's Alan Page in 1969 to be named the league's Most Valuable Player.

Memorable Moments/Greatest Performances

Several great games and memorable plays highlighted Taylor's career, one of which took place in his second year in the league. Playing in front of a national television audience on Thanksgiving Day, November 25, 1982, the Giants and Detroit Lions remained tied at 6–6 early in the fourth quarter, when the host Lions drove deep into Giants territory. Detroit quarterback Gary Danielson threw a short pass out to the left flat that appeared to have touchdown written all over it. However, Taylor, playing on a bad knee, ran in front of the intended receiver, intercepted the pass, and jetted down the sidelines for a 97-yard TD interception return that ended up giving the Giants a 13–6 win.

In another notable play, Taylor made a stop that essentially ended the career of Redskins quarterback Joe Theismann. Once again playing before a national audience, this time in a 1985 *Monday Night Football* game, Taylor registered a clean sack of Theismann that resulted in a compound fracture of the quarterback's right leg. Realizing the severity of the injury, a distraught Taylor spent the next several moments screaming for paramedics to attend to Theismann, who never blamed the Giants linebacker for the injury.

Just one year later, Taylor turned in one of his finest performances against the Redskins and Jay Schroeder, Theismann's replacement in Washington. Facing the Redskins in a critical week 14 NFC East showdown, the Giants defeated their primary competitors for divisional supremacy by a score of 24–14, with LT registering three sacks of Schroeder.

One month later, Taylor all but sealed New York's 49–3 victory over San Francisco in their first-round playoff matchup by intercepting a Joe Montana pass late in the first half and returning it 34 yards for a touchdown that gave the Giants an insurmountable 28–3 lead.

Taylor made another memorable play against the 49ers in the NFC Championship Game four years later that enabled the Giants to register a stunning upset of the two-time defending Super Bowl champions. With San Francisco clinging to a 13–12 lead and trying to run out the clock late in the fourth quarter, New York defensive tackle Erik Howard stopped 49er running back Roger Craig, dislodging the ball in the process. Ever the opportunist, Taylor plucked the ball out of midair, giving the Giants possession with only 2 minutes 30 seconds left on the clock. The Giants subsequently drove the ball downfield, enabling placekicker Matt Bahr to put them in the Super Bowl by kicking a game-winning 42-yard field goal as time expired.

However, Taylor's signature game would have to be considered the performance he turned in against the Saints in New Orleans on November 27, 1988. With Phil Simms injured and backup quarterback Jeff Hostetler making his first NFL start, the Giants knew heading into the contest that points were likely to be at a premium. A wounded LT, wearing a harness to protect his badly injured right shoulder, willed his team to a hard-fought 13–12 win by making 10 tackles, recording three quarterback sacks, and forcing two fumbles. After witnessing Taylor's performance, sportswriter Dave Anderson later said, "He was so great that night that that's one of the few games I ever saw that I felt a defensive player won the game. Lawrence Taylor that night won that game."[22] Phil Simms, who watched the game from the sidelines, suggested, "I think it was his greatest moment ever."[23]

NOTABLE ACHIEVEMENTS

- Finished in double-digits in sacks seven times.
- Compiled at least 15 sacks three times, surpassing the 20-mark once.
- Led NFL with 20½ sacks in 1986.
- Ranks 13th all-time in NFL in sacks.
- Ranks second all-time on Giants with 132½ "official" sacks.
- Nine-time NFC Defensive Player of the Week.
- Ten-time Pro Bowl selection.
- Ten-time All-NFC selection.
- Eight-time First-Team All-Pro selection.
- Two-time Second-Team All-Pro selection.
- 1981 Associated Press NFL Defensive Rookie of the Year.
- Three-time Associated Press NFL Defensive Player of the Year (1981, 1982, 1986).
- 1986 NFL MVP.
- NFL 1980s All-Decade Team.
- Named to NFL's 75th Anniversary Team in 1994.
- Fourth on the *Sporting News* 1999 list of 100 Greatest Players in NFL History.
- Third on the NFL Network's 2010 list of Top 100 Players of All Time.
- Two-time NFC champion.
- Two-time Super Bowl champion.
- Elected to Pro Football Hall of Fame in 1999.

2

EMLEN TUNNELL

After seriously considering slotting either Roosevelt Brown or Mel Hein just ahead of him in these rankings, I ultimately decided to award the number 2 spot to Emlen Tunnell due to his extraordinary list of accomplishments. The first black player in Giants history proved to be a trailblazer in many other ways as well, ultimately becoming the first person of African American descent to serve as both a scout and an assistant coach at the NFL level. The former defensive back also became both the first black player and the first defensive player to be inducted into the Pro Football Hall of Fame. More than just a pioneer, though, Tunnell established himself over the course of his career as one of the greatest defensive backs and punt returners in NFL history, retiring at the conclusion of the 1961 campaign with league records for most career interceptions (79), most punt returns (262), and most punt-return yardage (2,217). Although each of those marks has since been broken, Tunnell remains a legendary figure, particularly among Giants fans, for whom he performed for 11 of his 14 NFL seasons.

Born in Bryn Mawr, Pennsylvania, on March 29, 1925, Emlen Lewis Tunnell excelled as an all-around athlete throughout his youth, starring in football, baseball, and basketball in high school and college. In fact, Tunnell later admitted that he likely would have pursued a career in baseball had he ultimately not found a home in the NFL, stating, "I'd have gone into pro baseball because I was a better baseball player than I was a football player. But I didn't like it."[1]

Tunnell's sports career nearly ended prematurely when he broke his neck while playing football for the University of Toledo. Although Tunnell recovered, the injury prevented him from joining the U.S. Army and Navy during World War II. However, the U.S. Coast Guard ultimately accepted him, allowing him to fulfill his desire to serve his country.

After spending two years in the Coast Guard, Tunnell attended the University of Iowa, where he resumed his athletic career, starring at

11

Emlen Tunnell retired in 1961 as the NFL's all-time leader in
interceptions and punt-return yardage.
Courtesy of NearMintCards.com

quarterback, halfback, and on defense in his two years as a Hawkeye. Subsequently left undrafted by the NFL, the 23-year-old free agent elected to
hitchhike a ride to New York, where he met with Giants owner Tim Mara,
requesting a tryout with the ball club.

Eventually signed to a contract by Mara, Tunnell spent the first part of
his rookie season of 1948 playing both offense and defense. However, after
intercepting three passes in a game against the Green Bay Packers, Tunnell
moved to the safety spot full time, remaining there for the rest of his career.

He concluded his first year in the league with a total of seven interceptions, returning one of those for a touchdown.

Rapidly developing into one of the game's top defenders, Tunnell recorded a career-high 10 interceptions in 1949, returning two of those for touchdowns. He also finished second in the league with a total of 315 punt-return yards, averaging just over 12 yards per return. Tunnell earned Pro Bowl honors for the first of nine times the following year, when he intercepted seven passes and once again placed second in the league in punt-return yards, this time with a total of 305.

Standing 6'1" and weighing close to 210 pounds, Tunnell possessed outstanding size and strength for a defensive back. However, his greatest attribute may well have been his marvelous instincts. Former linebacker Harland Svare, who played alongside Tunnell on the Giants defense for six years, stated emphatically, "Emlen Tunnell was one of the great football players of all time . . . of all the weak-side safeties I ever saw, he's probably got the best instincts on the ball I've ever seen."[2]

Tunnell's ability to make plays on the ball made him a veritable interception machine in the secondary. He intercepted at least six passes in each of his first 10 seasons in New York, compiling a total of 73 during that time. Teaming up with fellow safety Tom Landry his first several years with the Giants, Tunnell gave New York's coaching staff the confidence to install its famed "umbrella" defense, which helped to shut down opposing offenses.

Giants coach Jim Lee Howell once told the *New York Times*, "Emlen changed the theory of defensive safeties. He would have been too big for the job earlier, and they'd have made him a lineman. But he had such strength, such speed, and such quickness I'm convinced he was the best safety ever to play."[3]

Not given to false modesty, the extremely forthright Tunnell agreed with Howell's assessment, taking it one step further by saying, "I'm the greatest defensive back ever to play the game."[4]

The numbers Tunnell posted his first 10 years with the Giants would certainly seem to support his contention. Considering that most teams rarely passed the ball more than 25 times per game when Tunnell played, his 73 interceptions during that time are a true indication of his greatness. Yet longtime teammate Frank Gifford found himself equally impressed by Tunnell's punt-returning ability, stating, "I used to love to watch him catch a punt. He caught it like Willie Mays. He had the softest hands I've ever seen, and he wasn't all that fast, and yet he had those incredible returns of punts and kickoffs. He just had a great instinct of knowing where he was on the field at all times."[5]

Tunnell's superb all-around skills were never more apparent than in 1951 and 1952. In the first of those campaigns, he intercepted nine passes, led the NFL with 489 punt-return yards, and averaged 37.8 yards on six kickoff returns, returning one of those 100 yards for a touchdown. He followed that up in 1952 by intercepting seven passes, recovering a league-leading six fumbles, accumulating 364 yards on kickoff returns, and leading the NFL with 411 punt-return yards. The 924 total yards Tunnell compiled that year on interception, kickoff, and punt returns surpassed by 30 the total number of yards amassed by the NFL's leading rusher.

Tunnell continued his exceptional play from 1953 to 1957, annually finishing among the league leaders in interceptions and punt returns, en route to earning a Pro Bowl selection in each of those five seasons. His six interceptions and veteran leadership helped the Giants win the NFL Championship in 1956.

A true iron man as well, Tunnell appeared in 158 consecutive games at one point during his career. Speaking of his amazing streak, Tunnell said, "You play when you're hurt—in the hospital up until Sunday morning any number of times. They brought you in to play and you played 'cause you wanted to play—I didn't have to play."[6]

In addition to his toughness and extraordinary all-around ability, Tunnell proved to be an outstanding leader, with his easygoing demeanor helping to pave the way for other African American players to enter the almost all-white NFL that existed when he first joined the Giants in 1948.

Longtime Giants teammate Andy Robustelli once told the *New York Times*, "One of the reasons we never had problems was because of Em Tunnell. Emlen was good to all people. He was a hell of a decent person who meant a lot to young ballplayers."[7]

After intercepting just one pass for the Giants in 1958, Tunnell joined Vince Lombardi in Green Bay following New York's 23–17 defeat at the hands of the Baltimore Colts in that year's NFL Championship Game. Tunnell spent his final three seasons with the Packers, earning one final trip to the Pro Bowl in 1959 and helping Green Bay defeat his former team 37–0 for the NFL title in 1961. He retired at the end of the 1961 season with more career interceptions, punt returns, and punt-return yards than any other player in NFL history. Although more than half a century has passed since Tunnell played his last game, he remains second on the all-time list in interceptions, while his total of 1,282 interception return yards places him fifth all-time.

Following his retirement, Tunnell became a scout, first for the Packers and then for the Giants. He continued to serve in that capacity in New York

Tunnell holds franchise records for most interceptions and interception-return yards.
Public domain (author unknown)

until 1965, when the Giants made him the first black assistant coach in the NFL. Tunnell remained in that position until he died from a heart attack during a practice session on July 22, 1975. He was only 50 years old at the time of his passing.

Just a few years earlier, the always candid Tunnell told an interviewer, "Not pattin' myself on the back—but they have never compared any defensive back with me. And I kind of dig that more than the Hall of Fame. And they won't compare anybody to me in my day, 'cause I won't listen to them!"[8]

GIANT CAREER HIGHLIGHTS

Best Season

Although Tunnell played exceptionally well for the Giants throughout his time in New York, he proved to be particularly effective from 1949 to 1952, intercepting at least seven passes in each of those seasons, while also accumulating more than 300 punt-return yards all four years. He had perhaps his finest defensive season in 1949, intercepting a career-high 10 passes and returning them for 251 yards and two touchdowns. Two years later, he intercepted nine passes, registered the only touchdown of his career on a kickoff return, averaged a career-best 14.4 yards per punt return, and led the league with a career-high 489 punt-return yards.

Still, the feeling here is that Tunnell had his finest all-around season in 1952 when, in addition to intercepting seven passes and returning them for 149 yards, he amassed 364 yards on kickoff returns and led the NFL with 411 punt-return yards and six fumble recoveries. His 924 total return yards that year gave him 30 more than Rams running back Dan Towler, who led the league in rushing. Tunnell's extraordinary performance that year earned him First-Team All-Pro honors for one of four times in his career.

Memorable Moments/Greatest Performances

Tunnell played perhaps his greatest game against the Green Bay Packers on November 21, 1948, recording three interceptions and returning one of them 43 yards for a touchdown, in helping the Giants register a lopsided 49–3 victory over their overmatched opponents.

Yet he made arguably the biggest play of his career some eight years later in the 1956 NFL Championship Game. With the Giants holding a 13–0 lead over the Bears early in the second quarter and Chicago in possession of the ball near midfield, Bears head coach George Halas elected to go for the first down on 4th and 1. Tunnell burst across the line of scrimmage and stopped Chicago running back J. C. Caroline for a one-yard loss. The Giants subsequently drove down the field and scored on an Alex Webster three-yard run, en route to posting a convincing 47–7 win over the Bears that gave them their last championship of the pre–Super Bowl era.

NOTABLE ACHIEVEMENTS

- Intercepted at least six passes 10 times, finishing in double-digits once (10 in 1949).
- Returned four interceptions for touchdowns.
- Returned five punts for touchdowns.
- Returned one kickoff for a touchdown.
- Led NFL in punt returns twice, punt-return yardage twice, TD interceptions once, fumble recoveries once, and non-offensive touchdowns twice.
- Ranks second all-time in NFL with 79 interceptions (74 as a Giant).
- Ranks fifth all-time in NFL in interception return yardage.
- Ranks first all-time on Giants in career interceptions (74), career interception return yardage (1,240), single-season interception return yardage (251 in 1949), career punt returns (257), career punt return yardage (2,206), single-season punt return yardage (489 in 1951), career punt return TDs (5), single-season punt return TDs (3 in 1951).
- First African American to play for Giants.
- First African American scout in NFL.
- First African American assistant coach in NFL.
- First African American to be inducted into Pro Football Hall of Fame.
- First defensive player to be inducted into Pro Football Hall of Fame.
- Eight-time Pro Bowl selection.
- Four-time First-Team All-Pro selection.
- Four-time Second-Team All-Pro selection.
- NFL 1950s All-Decade Team.
- Number 70 on the *Sporting News* 1999 list of 100 Greatest Players in NFL History.
- Number 79 on the NFL Network's 2010 list of Top 100 Players of All Time.
- Two-time NFL Eastern Division champion.
- 1956 NFL champion.
- Elected to Pro Football Hall of Fame in 1967.

ROOSEVELT BROWN

elected by the Giants in the 27th round of the 1953 NFL Draft with the 321st overall pick, Roosevelt Brown turned out to be one of the greatest "sleeper" picks in league history. The greatest offensive lineman ever to play for the Giants, Brown gained general recognition as the NFL's first pulling tackle, using his quickness and agility to earn nine Pro Bowl selections and six First-Team All-Pro nominations. In so doing, he provided ample blind-side protection for quarterbacks Charlie Conerly and Y. A. Tittle, while also opening up gaping holes for legendary running backs Frank Gifford and Alex Webster. Yet Brown likely never even would have been drafted by the Giants had a newspaper article in the *Pittsburgh Courier* not brought him to the attention of Giants owner Wellington Mara.

Born in Charlottesville, Virginia, on October 20, 1932, Roosevelt Brown Jr. began his football playing career at the behest of one of the coaches at Jefferson High School, who, Brown later recalled, "thought I was too big to be playing trombone in the school band, so he made me go out for football."[1]

After graduating from Jefferson High, Brown went on to star in football, baseball, and wrestling at Morgan State University, eventually earning himself a write-up in the *Pittsburgh Courier*, an African American newspaper that named him to its 1952 Black All-American team. Subsequently selected by the Giants in the 27th round of the 1953 NFL Draft (the draft featured 30 rounds at that time) without anyone from the team's organization ever having seen him play, Brown appeared ill-equipped to compete at the professional level when he joined the squad for his first training camp. Al DeRogatis, another member of the team's offensive line at the time, later noted, "He [Brown] didn't even know how to take a proper stance."[2]

Meanwhile, former Giants general manager Ernie Accorsi said that Brown once related the following story to him: "I was playing against Len Ford of the Browns, and I couldn't block him. He would jump over me. Steve Owen was the head coach then, and he said, 'If you can't block him,

Roosevelt Brown starred for the Giants at left tackle for 13 seasons.
Courtesy of RMYAuctions.com

we're going to cut you.' So I tackled Ford two straight plays. He said, 'If you do that again, I'm going to kill you.' I said, 'Well, if I don't stop you, I'm going to get cut, so what's the difference if you kill me?'"[3]

Despite his lack of refinement, Brown impressed Owen with his strength, quickness, and outstanding athleticism. Even though he stood 6'3" and weighed close to 255 pounds, Brown boasted a 29-inch waistline and exceptional foot speed that few men of his proportions could match. He also possessed a solid work ethic and the ability to learn things quickly.

Before long, Brown found himself starting at left tackle—a position he manned for the remainder of his 13-year career in New York. Perhaps the most athletic offensive lineman of his era, Brown developed into a classic left tackle, using his foot speed and long arms to impede the progress of opposing pass-rushers, while also employing his quickness to lead Giants ball carriers on end sweeps and halfback options.

Considered by many to be the greatest pass blocker of his time, Brown had the size, strength, and agility to compete in any era. Frank Gifford, for whom Brown opened many a hole, said of his former teammate, "I wouldn't be in the Hall of Fame if it weren't for him." Referring to a 79-yard run he made from the line of scrimmage, Gifford continued, "The longest run of my career was on a pitchout against Washington. Rosie made a block at the line of scrimmage. I cut it up, and then I'm running downfield and I look up and I see No. 79 in front of me, and he wiped out another guy."[4]

Legendary Giants linebacker Sam Huff revealed that Brown made an extremely favorable impression on him the first time the two men met in Giants training camp in 1956. Seeing the huge offensive lineman sitting outside the team's dormitory in a T-shirt and shorts, Huff stated, "He was a big Jim Brown. I wanted to turn around and go back to West Virginia. I said, 'Are they all built like this?'"[5]

The Giants defense and skill-position players on offense received most of the praise for the success the team experienced during Brown's tenure with them. Nevertheless, perhaps no other player proved to be more indispensable to the Giants during that period. Serving as an anchor on the left side of the offensive line, Brown helped lead New York to six division titles over an eight-year stretch, including the NFL Championship in 1956. He earned Pro Bowl and All-NFL honors virtually every year, even being named Lineman of the Year by the Associated Press at the conclusion of the Giants' 1956 championship campaign. Brown played at such a high level that he eventually became just the second player to be elected to the Pro Football Hall of Fame on the merits of his offensive line play alone.

Unfortunately, chronic phlebitis forced Brown to retire at the end of the 1965 season, bringing to an end a playing career that spanned 162 games over 13 years. However, he subsequently remained with the organization another 38 years, serving the team in various capacities during that time. Hired as assistant offensive line coach immediately following his retirement, Brown became the offensive line coach in 1969. He remained in that position until 1971, when he became a scout, scouring the countryside for the top offensive and defensive line prospects in the nation.

Successful in whatever role he assumed within the Giants organization, Brown urged the team to draft such eventual standouts as John Mendenhall and Leonard Marshall. Ernie Accorsi recalled how the Hall of Fame tackle once shared his knowledge of the game with the other front-office members present in the Giants draft room: "Rosie gave a spontaneous, philosophical talk. If it was recorded, it would be a manuscript for how to conduct a draft; a manuscript on scouting; on how to get these kids to become a finished product. He was a very wise man."[6]

Roosevelt Brown's 51-year association with the Giants ended on June 9, 2004, when he passed away at age 71 after suffering a heart attack while gardening at his home in Columbus, New Jersey. Years earlier, Brown, who never earned more than $20,000 in any single season, revealed his love of the game when he said, "Nobody plays this game for the money. You have to enjoy it. You have to have the game in your heart. They can't pay us enough for what we go through on the field."[7]

Brown earned nine trips to the Pro Bowl and nine All-Pro selections
during his time in New York.
Courtesy of MearsOnlineAuctions.com

CAREER HIGHLIGHTS

Best Season

Although Brown earned First-Team All-Pro honors six times between 1956
and 1962, the first of those campaigns would have to be considered his finest. In addition to helping the Giants win the NFL Championship, Brown
was named NFL Lineman of the Year by the Associated Press.

Memorable Moments/Greatest Performances

In discussing the 1958 NFL "sudden death" title game between the Giants and Colts during an interview that took place in the early 1970s, Brown stated, "Not only was the '58 game the greatest game I ever played in, it was the greatest game ever played."[8]

While there may be a great deal of merit in Brown's assertion, he perhaps played *his* greatest game against the Chicago Bears two years earlier. Doing an exceptional job against the Chicago Bears' vaunted defense in the 1956 NFL Championship Game, Brown ended up walking away with Lineman of the Game honors.

NOTABLE ACHIEVEMENTS

- Nine-time Pro Bowl selection.
- Six-time First-Team All-Pro selection.
- Three-time Second-Team All-Pro selection.
- 1956 NFL Lineman of the Year.
- NFL 1950s All-Decade Team.
- Named to NFL's 75th Anniversary Team in 1994.
- Number 57 on the *Sporting News* 1999 list of 100 Greatest Players in NFL History.
- Six-time NFL Eastern Division champion.
- 1956 NFL champion.
- Elected to Pro Football Hall of Fame in 1975.

4

MEL HEIN

Although a valid case could certainly be made for slotting either Harry Carson or Michael Strahan just ahead of Mel Hein in these rankings since both Carson and Strahan competed against superior athletes than the players Hein typically faced during the 1930s and 1940s, I ultimately decided to award the number four spot to Hein due to the tremendous impact he made on both sides of the ball. Rivaling Roosevelt Brown as the greatest offensive lineman in Giants history, Hein manned the center position for New York from 1931 to 1945. Still considered to be one of the greatest centers ever to play the game, Hein remains the only offensive lineman ever to capture league MVP honors, doing so in 1938, when he led the Giants to the NFL Championship for the second time in five years. An outstanding middle linebacker as well, the 6'2", 230-pound Hein also led the Giants on defense, applying pressure to opposing quarterbacks and bringing down ball carriers with bone-crunching tackles. Playing 60 minutes a game throughout his career, Hein established himself as a true iron man, never missing a single game due to injury and calling a timeout for himself just once, in order to allow the people on the sidelines to repair a broken nose so that he could return to the fray. Hein's brilliant play on both offense and defense earned him All-NFL honors 11 straight times from 1931 to 1941, a spot on the *Sporting News* list of the 100 greatest players of all time, and a place in Canton, Ohio, when the Pro Football Hall of Fame first opened its doors in 1963.

Born in Redding, California, on August 22, 1909, Melvin Jack Hein first made a name for himself at Washington State University, where he earned All-American honors as a senior by leading the Cougars to an undefeated record and a spot in the Rose Bowl against Alabama. Although the Crimson Tide defeated Washington State 24–0 in Hein's final collegiate game, the Cougars ended up posting an overall mark of 26–6 in the center/linebacker's three varsity seasons.

Mel Hein starred on both sides of the ball for the Giants for 15 seasons.
Courtesy of CollectAuctions.com

In spite of the success Hein experienced at the collegiate level, he garnered little interest from the NFL after he graduated in 1931. Finally, after
failing to receive a single offer from any pro team, Hein decided to take
matters into his own hands, writing to four different teams to notify them
of his availability. Ray Flaherty, an assistant coach with the Giants, was
among the first to respond, showing up at Hein's doorstep with a contract
that offered the former All-American $150 a game.

Hein began to display his wide array of skills and tremendous leadership ability shortly after he joined the Giants for his first pro training camp. Establishing himself as the team's starting center on offense and starting middle linebacker on defense in his rookie season, Hein began an extremely successful 15-year run in New York that ties him with Phil Simms for the longest in franchise history. Hein served as Giants captain his final 10 seasons, leading them into the playoffs a total of eight times, and to the NFL title in both 1934 and 1938.

Considered by many to be the greatest two-way center ever to play professional football, Hein excelled on both sides of the ball. On offense, he provided exceptional protection for his quarterback and opened up huge holes for Giant running backs. In addition to blocking like a demon, Hein's flawless centering allowed the Giants to run from a tricky formation that gave him the option of snapping the ball to any one of three men in the backfield. Meanwhile, his great strength and surprising speed made him a veritable tackling machine on defense. Known for his aggressive, hard-hitting style of play on the defensive end, Hein also possessed the quickness to cover opposing pass receivers. One of the few NFL players who had the speed and agility to contain Green Bay's Don Hutson, the era's premier receiver, Hein typically did so by bottling him up along the sidelines so that he could not maneuver into the open.

Former Giants coach Jim Lee Howell, who earlier spent six years playing alongside Hein on New York's defense, had this to say about his former teammate: "He played all of the time, hardly ever hurt, and was a great linebacker and a great blocker. He played right behind me. I used to tell him I made him look good because I turned loose the blockers and runners at him, and he had to stop the whole works."[1]

Longtime Giants owner Wellington Mara, who followed Hein closely during his formative years as a member of the team's front office, once called the longtime Giants captain the greatest player to perform for them in their first 50 years, adding that only Lawrence Taylor has perhaps equaled him since.

Considered to be virtually indestructible, Hein appeared in more than 200 regular-season, championship, and exhibition games without missing a single contest, going the full 60 minutes most of the time. The combination of his durability, mental alertness, leadership, and playing ability made Hein a legend to Giants players, coaches, fans, and opponents alike throughout his playing career.

After earning First-Team All-Pro honors five times and a spot on the Second Team on six other occasions, Hein elected to call it a career at

Hein captured league MVP honors in 1938, when he led the Giants to the NFL title.
Courtesy of AlbersheimsStore.com

the conclusion of the 1945 campaign—one in which the Giants finished out of the playoffs for the first time in three years with a record of just 3–6–1. Following his retirement, Hein served as line coach for several pro teams, including the Yankees and Rams, before spending 15 seasons coaching at the University of Southern California. In 1965, he accepted

Al Davis's offer to serve as the director of officials in the American Football League, continuing to serve in the same capacity in the AFC after the two leagues merged in 1968. After 10 years in that post, he left the game for good, announcing his retirement at the end of the 1974 season. Hein died 18 years later, passing away from stomach cancer at the age of 82 on January 31, 1992.

Asked about his longtime friend and associate, former Raiders owner and coach Al Davis stated, "He was truly a football legend and a giant among men. Mel was one of the greatest football players who ever lived."[2]

Meanwhile, Steve Hirdt of the Elias Sports Bureau revealed that Hein's longtime coach with the Giants, Steve Owen, once suggested, "No man played more for the Giants but needed to be coached less than Mel Hein."[3]

GIANT CAREER HIGHLIGHTS

Best Season

Although Hein earned First-Team All-Pro honors four other times as well, the 1938 campaign proved to be the most satisfying of his career. In addition to leading the Giants to the NFL Championship for the second time, Hein was named league MVP, making him the only offensive lineman ever to be so honored.

Memorable Moments/Greatest Performances

Hein experienced two of his most memorable moments against the Green Bay Packers late in the 1938 season. During a key 15–3 win over the Packers that helped propel the Giants into the playoffs, Hein intercepted a pass and raced 50 yards down the sidelines to score the only touchdown of his pro career. Just three weeks later, Hein led the Giants to a 23–17 victory over the Packers in the NFL title game. However, almost as notable as New York's win in the championship contest was Hein's first-half departure after suffering a broken nose. Knocked out briefly, Hein had to be carried off the field before returning a few minutes later to help the Giants nail down the victory. The incident marked the only time in Hein's career that an injury forced him to call a timeout.

NOTABLE ACHIEVEMENTS

- Holds share of Giants team record for most seasons played (15).
- Played in 172 consecutive games.
- Four-time Pro Bowl selection.
- Five-time First-Team All-Pro selection.
- Six-time Second-Team All-Pro selection.
- 1938 NFL MVP.
- NFL 1930s All-Decade Team.
- Named starting center on NFL's 50th Anniversary Team in 1969.
- Named to NFL's 75th Anniversary Team in 1994.
- Number 74 on the *Sporting News* 1999 list of 100 Greatest Players in NFL History.
- Number 96 on the NFL Network's 2010 list of Top 100 Players of All Time.
- Seven-time NFL Eastern Division champion.
- Two-time NFL champion (1934, 1938).
- Elected to Pro Football Hall of Fame in 1963.

5

MICHAEL STRAHAN

Although he has since gone on to perhaps even greater fame as a television personality, Michael Strahan first made a name for himself as a member of the Giants, establishing himself over the course of his 15 seasons in New York as one of the greatest players in franchise history. New York's all-time "official" sack leader, Strahan ranks sixth in NFL history in quarterback sacks, with 141½ to his credit. He also is the league's single-season record holder in that category, having recorded 22½ sacks in 2001. More than just an outstanding pass-rusher, Strahan excelled against the run as well, proving to be one of the league's best run-stuffers from his left defensive end position. Strahan's exceptional all-around play earned him seven trips to the Pro Bowl, four First-Team All-Pro selections, and two Second-Team nominations. He also earned NFL Defensive Player of the Year honors once and NFC Defensive Player of the Year honors twice. An outstanding team leader as well, Strahan spent his final several years with the Giants grooming fellow defensive ends Osi Umenyiora and Justin Tuck, while also serving as one of Coach Tom Coughlin's most trusted locker-room spokesmen.

Born in Houston, Texas, on November 21, 1971, Michael Anthony Strahan lived a somewhat nomadic existence during his formative years, traveling back and forth between two countries, on two different continents. The son of a U.S. Army major, Strahan moved with his parents and five older siblings to an army base in Mannheim, Germany, after he turned nine years of age. He became involved in organized football for the first time while attending school in Germany, playing linebacker for the Mannheim Redskins in 1985. Strahan returned to the United States prior to his senior year of high school when his father sent him to live with his uncle in Houston so he could attend Westbury High School. While at Westbury, Strahan played one season of football, excelling to such a degree that he received a scholarship offer from Texas Southern University. He then flew

Michael Strahan recorded more sacks than anyone else in franchise history.
Courtesy of SportsMemorabilia.com

back to Germany for the spring term, where he graduated from Mannheim Christian Academy.

Back in the States by 1989, Strahan enrolled at Texas Southern, where he moved to the defensive line. Quickly establishing himself as a dominant defensive end, Strahan drew constant double teams, turning himself into an NFL prospect by his junior year, when he led the Southwest Athletic Conference (SWAC) with 14½ quarterback sacks. As a senior the following year, he recorded 62 tackles and set a new school record by registering 19 quarterback sacks. Strahan's total of 41½ career sacks at Texas Southern remains a school record.

Subsequently selected by the Giants in the second round of the 1993 NFL Draft with the 40th overall pick, Strahan began his professional career slowly, appearing in only nine games as a rookie due to injuries, and recording just one sack. Although he showed gradual improvement over the course of the next three seasons, he failed to play at the lofty level the Giants hoped he would reach when they first drafted him, compiling a total of only 17 sacks from 1994 to 1996. However, Strahan finally developed into an elite defensive end in 1997, when he earned Pro Bowl and First-Team All-Pro honors for the first time by finishing third in the NFL with 14 sacks. He followed that up with another outstanding year in 1998, recording 15 quarterback sacks and returning an interception 24 yards for the first touchdown of his career, en route to making the Pro Bowl and First-Team All-Pro for the second straight time.

Strahan experienced somewhat less success over the course of the next two seasons, failing to compile the lofty sack totals he posted in 1997 and 1998. Nevertheless, he managed to get to opposing quarterbacks a total of 15 times, return another interception for a touchdown, and continue to play the run extremely well, taking part in a total of 123 tackles. Strahan also took on more of a leadership role, serving as mentor to some of his younger teammates on the Giants squad that captured the NFC Championship in 2000.

Strahan truly stepped to the forefront, though, in 2001, when he established a new single-season NFL record by registering 22½ quarterback sacks. His extraordinary performance earned him NFC and NFL Defensive Player of the Year honors. After another solid season in 2002 in which he recorded 11 sacks, Strahan again led the NFL in sacks in 2003, getting to the quarterback 18½ times, en route to winning his second NFC Defensive Player of the Year trophy.

A torn pectoral muscle limited Strahan to only eight games and four sacks in 2004, prompting him to alter his training regimen at season's end. The 6'5" defensive end spent most of his career playing at close to 275 pounds. Strahan possessed outstanding strength and surprising quickness at that weight. However, in an effort to improve his quickness even more and put less stress on his aging legs, Strahan entered the 2005 campaign some 20 pounds lighter, at approximately 255 pounds. The change seemed to agree with the 33-year-old veteran, who returned to his previous Pro Bowl form by recording 11½ sacks.

A contract holdout forced Strahan to miss the entire 2006 preseason, and, when he returned to the team at the start of the regular season, he didn't appear to be his old self. Strahan recorded only three sacks in the first nine contests, before suffering a Lisfranc fracture against the Houston Texans that kept him out for the remainder of the year.

After contemplating retirement at the end of the 2006 campaign, Strahan ultimately elected to return to the Giants for one more shot at the Super Bowl. As it turned out, the 35-year-old defensive end made the right choice since he helped the Giants capture the NFC title by recording nine sacks in his final season. Strahan subsequently joined the rest of his Giant

Strahan earned NFC Defensive Player of the Year honors twice.
Courtesy of Rick Sparacino

defensive line-mates in applying constant pressure to New England quarterback Tom Brady throughout the Super Bowl, as the Giants stunned the
football world by handing the previously unbeaten Patriots a 17–14 loss.
Strahan contributed three tackles and one sack to the Giant cause.

A little over four months later, on June 9, 2008, Strahan announced
his retirement. He ended his playing career with 141½ sacks, 854 tackles
(667 of them solo), four interceptions, 24 forced fumbles, 15 fumble recoveries, and three defensive touchdowns. Strahan appeared in 216 games as a
member of the Giants—tying him with Eli Manning for the most in team
annals. Meanwhile, his 15 years with the team tie him with Mel Hein and
Phil Simms for the most in franchise history.

Following Strahan's announcement, Giants general manager Jerry
Reese said, "I'm happy for him, in a lot of ways. He's going out on top,
which every athlete dreams of doing. He's one of the all-time greats, and
we'll miss him."[1]

Former Giants GM Ernie Accorsi, who served as general manager for
three teams, including the Giants for nine seasons, stated, "I have been
with six NFL Hall of Famers in my career. Michael will be the seventh.
He played the run better than any great pass-rusher I have ever seen, and I
really feel he is the greatest defensive player I have ever been with."[2]

Blessed with a gregarious and outgoing nature, Strahan has become a media personality since he retired as an active player. In addition to providing analysis on *Fox NFL Sunday*, he spent more than 3½ years cohosting the highly rated television morning talk show *Live! With Kelly and Michael* before accepting a position on *Good Morning America*.

CAREER HIGHLIGHTS

Best Season

Strahan played exceptionally well for the Giants in 1997 and 1998, combining for 29 sacks and 135 tackles those two seasons. He also had an outstanding year in 2005, recording 11½ sacks and making a career-high 82 tackles (61 of them solo). Nevertheless, he had his two best seasons in 2001 and 2003, earning NFC Defensive Player of the Year honors both times. In the second of those campaigns, Strahan led the NFL with 18½ sacks, made 75 tackles, forced three fumbles, and recovered one himself. That would be a career-year for most defensive ends. However, in addition to recording a NFL-record 22½ sacks in 2001, Strahan made 73 tackles (62 of them solo), forced six fumbles, and recovered another, en route to earning NFL Defensive Player of the Year honors. It's a close call, but Strahan had his best season in 2001.

Memorable Moments/Greatest Performances

Strahan turned in his first dominant performance for the Giants on September 17, 1995, sacking Green Bay quarterback Brett Favre three times during a 14–6 loss to the Packers. Six weeks later, on October 29, Strahan helped the Giants defeat Washington 24–15 by intercepting a Gus Frerotte pass and returning it 56 yards, for the longest interception return of his career.

Strahan scored the first touchdown of his career in the 1998 season opener, returning an interception 24 yards for a TD during a 31–24 victory over the Washington Redskins. He also recorded two sacks during the contest. Strahan scored his second touchdown on October 31, 1999, giving the Giants a 23–17 overtime victory over Philadelphia by returning a Doug Pederson pass 44 yards for the winning score.

As one might expect, Strahan turned in a number of memorable performances over the course of his record-setting 2001 campaign, with his most dominant efforts coming against the Rams on October 14 and the Eagles on December 30. Strahan recorded a season-high four sacks during a 15–14 loss to St. Louis, before making another 3½ sacks during a 24–21 loss to Philadelphia.

However, Strahan made his most famous play in the season finale against Green Bay. With the Packers comfortably in front by a score of 34–25 and less than three minutes remaining in the game, it seemed as if Strahan's quest to break Mark Gastineau's record of 22 sacks in a season would fall just a bit short. Although Strahan needed just one more sack to establish a new mark, the Packers appeared content to just run out the clock in the game's closing moments. However, Brett Favre surprised everyone by rolling out to his right and falling at the feet of Strahan, who simply touched the Green Bay quarterback to set a new record. Although Favre later said that he attempted to catch the Giants off guard by changing the running play called in the huddle to a pass, most observers felt that he intentionally allowed his good friend Strahan to surpass Gastineau in the record books.

Five years later, on October 23, 2006, Strahan tied Lawrence Taylor for the most "official" sacks in Giants history (132½) by bringing down Dallas quarterback Drew Bledsoe behind the line of scrimmage during a 36–22 win over the Cowboys. Early the following year, on September 30, 2007, he sacked Philadelphia's Donovan McNabb during a 16–3 victory over the Eagles to set a new franchise record (although Taylor's "official" sack total does not include the 9½ sacks he recorded as a rookie in 1981, one year before sacks became an official NFL statistic).

Strahan made his final NFL game a memorable one, recording a sack, three tackles, two quarterback hurries, and four hits during New York's stunning 17–14 victory over New England in Super Bowl XLII.

NOTABLE ACHIEVEMENTS

- Finished in double-digits in sacks six times.
- Compiled at least 15 sacks three times, surpassing the 20-mark once (22½ in 2001).
- Led NFL in sacks twice (2001, 2003).
- Scored three defensive touchdowns.
- Ranks sixth all-time in NFL in sacks.
- Giants all-time leader with 141½ "official" sacks.

- NFL's single-season record holder with 22½ sacks in 2001.
- Tied for first all-time on Giants in games played (216) and seasons played (15).
- Five-time NFC Defensive Player of the Week.
- Seven-time Pro Bowl selection.
- Five-time All-NFC selection.
- Four-time First-Team All-Pro selection.
- Two-time Second-Team All-Pro selection.
- 2001 Associated Press NFL Defensive Player of the Year.
- Two-time NFC Defensive Player of the Year (2001, 2003).
- NFL 2000s All-Decade Team.
- Number 99 on the NFL Network's 2010 list of Top 100 Players of All Time.
- Two-time NFC champion (2000, 2007).
- Super Bowl XLII champion.
- Elected to Pro Football Hall of Fame in 2014.

6

HARRY CARSON

An exceptional player and outstanding team leader, Harry Carson spent his entire 13-year career with the Giants, serving as team captain in his final 10 years with the club. After excelling on some of the worst squads in franchise history, Carson ended up leading the Giants into the playoffs in three of his final five years in New York. Along the way, he established himself as one of the greatest inside linebackers in NFL history, earning nine trips to the Pro Bowl, six All-Pro selections, and two nominations as NFC Linebacker of the Year.

Born in Florence, South Carolina, on November 26, 1953, Harold Donald Carson played high school football at Wilson High before transferring to McClenaghan High School, from which he graduated. After enrolling at South Carolina State University, Carson spent the next four years starring at defensive end for the Bulldogs, becoming the first Mid-Eastern Athletic Conference player to win Defensive Player of the Year honors in consecutive seasons, en route to leading his team to back-to-back conference championships. As a senior in 1975, he set school records with 117 tackles and 17 sacks, finishing his four-year college career without having missed a single game. Excelling off the field as well, Carson earned a bachelor of science degree in education, winning awards for the highest academic average among Black College All-Americans.

After the Giants selected Carson in the fourth round of the 1976 NFL draft with the 105th overall pick, they immediately moved him to middle linebacker. Carson saw limited action during the early stages of the 1976 campaign, but he became a starter by midseason, after which he went on to earn a spot on the All-NFL Rookie Team. Carson quickly developed into one of the league's top players at his position. At 6'2" and 237 pounds, he had good size for a middle linebacker. However, he also possessed several other attributes that soon made him one of the most feared and respected defenders in the league. A fierce hitter and ferocious tackler, Carson had the agility and range to track down opposing ball carriers, as well as the

Harry Carson served as captain of the Giants for 10 seasons.
Courtesy of SportsCollectibles.com

intensity, intelligence, and leadership skills needed to provide direction to his teammates, both on and off the field.

Unfortunately, the Giant teams of the late 1970s surrounded Carson with a poor supporting cast. Although Brad Van Pelt and Brian Kelley combined with Carson to give the Giants one of the NFL's top linebacking units, the club lacked talent at virtually every other position. As a result, New York posted a combined record of just 24–52 over the course of Carson's first five seasons. Nevertheless, he continued to perform at an extremely high level, building a reputation as the NFL's premier run-stopping linebacker of his day. After earning Pro Bowl, All-NFC, and All-NFL honors for the first time in 1978, Carson was named captain of the Giants in 1979, a distinction he held for the remainder of his career. Thriving in his new role, Carson went on to amass a career-high 185 tackles in his first year as captain.

Yet, in spite of the great individual success Carson experienced his first several years in New York, the Giants' failures as a team often left him feeling dejected. Carson later admitted to parking his car on the opposite side of the players' entrance at Giants Stadium, revealing, "I didn't want people to recognize me as a player."[1] He even saw a psychologist to deal with his embarrassment at being a Giant.

Carson's shame became such that he nearly retired on two separate occasions. After a particularly humiliating 35–3 Monday night loss to Philadelphia in 1980, Carson packed his bags in the locker room and had to be talked out of leaving by head coach Ray Perkins. He also asked to be traded after the Giants finished just 3–12–1 in 1983. However, second-year head coach Bill Parcells knew which buttons to push when Carson left New York's 1984 preseason training camp. Furious with the captain of his team, Parcells told the media that Carson didn't know the meaning of the word *leadership*, and that he should stop by a library to look it up. Carson later noted, "That was pretty smart of him [Parcells]. He knew I would read that. He knew how I'd react."[2] Carson eventually returned to the Giants, leading them to the playoffs in each of the next three seasons.

Of course, Carson was not solely responsible for New York's resurgence. The wise drafting of General Manager George Young also played a huge role in the team's improvement, with players such as Phil Simms, Lawrence Taylor, Leonard Marshall, Carl Banks, Mark Bavaro, and Joe Morris all contributing greatly to the success the Giants experienced in Carson's last several years in New York. Taylor, in fact, quickly established himself as the team's preeminent figure and the NFL's most dominant defender after he joined the Giants in 1981. However, while Carson spent his last eight years playing in Taylor's shadow, he remained consistently brilliant on the inside, leading the team in tackles every year.

After Carson missed the second half of the 1980 campaign with an injury, he returned the following year to give the Giants one of the NFL's stingiest run defenses. The Giants' defense, which completely fell apart in Carson's absence during the latter stages of the 1980 season, allowed opposing ball carriers only 3.59 yards per rushing attempt from 1981 to 1987—well below the league average. Although the NFL did not begin recording tackles as an official statistic until after Carson retired, he received credit for 856 "unofficial" tackles during that seven-year period, including 627 unassisted stops.

Carson persevered through some of the darkest days in franchise history
to lead the Giants to their first Super Bowl win.
Courtesy of PristineAuction.com

Carson's superb play on the inside prompted well-known football writer
Peter King to state on one occasion, "Carson did the one thing no defensive player ever gets enough credit for, even though it's the first thing every
defensive coach talks about with his team every week: he defended the run."[3]

Meanwhile, Carson drew praise from two assistants on Bill Parcells's
coaching staff who later went on to greater fame as head coaches of their
own teams. Bill Belichick stated on more than one occasion that he considered Carson to be the best all-around linebacker he ever coached. Marty
Schottenheimer, a member of the Giants' defensive staff when they drafted
Carson in 1976, later said, "He [Carson] was the best athlete that size I had
ever seen."[4]

More than just an outstanding player, Carson was the heart and soul of the Giants in many ways. Bill Parcells once revealed, "I don't think a day goes by when I don't talk to him about something. I burden him with a lot of things. In all honesty, I probably shouldn't. Sometimes I ask him to fix things he doesn't even know are broken. But I do it anyway because he can take it. He's an amazing guy."[5]

Parcells added, "You don't accomplish what he has without being someone special."[6] After leading the Giants in tackles in four of the previous five seasons, Carson finished second to Carl Banks in stops in 1986, making 118 tackles for the eventual NFL champions. He spent two more years captaining New York's defense, before retiring at the conclusion of the 1988 campaign. In addition to leading the Giants in tackles in six of his 13 seasons, Carson recorded 17 sacks, 11 interceptions, and 14 fumble recoveries, one of which he returned for a touchdown. He also forced seven fumbles. Among Carson's nine Pro Bowl selections were seven consecutive nominations, from 1982 to 1988. He also earned two First-Team All-Pro selections and four Second-Team nominations. Carson's 173 games in a Giants uniform tie him with Keith Hamilton for eighth place on the team's all-time list.

Yet, in spite of his many accomplishments, it took Carson several years to gain induction into the Pro Football Hall of Fame. A finalist each year from 2000 to 2005, Carson finally received the necessary votes in 2006, 13 years after he first became eligible. Growing increasingly agitated as he continued to be bypassed year after year, Carson criticized the Hall of Fame selection process, finding fault with its practice of placing the vote in the hands of the media instead of the players and coaches. At one point, he even asked to have his name removed from the ballot. Nevertheless, Carson graciously accepted his induction in 2006, although he also stated:

> The Hall of Fame will never validate me. I know my name will be in there, but I take greater pride in the fact that my teammates looked at me as someone they could count on. I still remember, and I will remember this for the rest of my life, the Super Bowl against Denver. We had three captains—me, Phil Simms, and George Martin. But, when it came time for the coin toss before the game, I started to go out and looked around for those guys. Bill Parcells said to me, "No. You go . . . just you." And that was about the coolest feeling I've ever had in the world—going out to midfield for the Super Bowl, as the lone captain. There were nine Denver Broncos out there, and me. Just me. An awesome responsibility. The greatest respect.[7]

Since retiring from the game, Carson has remained closely involved with the Giants, serving for a while as color commentator for the team's preseason broadcasts, and currently cohosting *Giants Access Blue* on TV with Bob Papa. He also founded his own company, Harry Carson, Inc., which deals mainly in sports consulting and promotions.

Having spent much of his retirement battling various physical maladies brought on by injuries he incurred during his playing days, including post-concussion syndrome, Carson has become an outspoken advocate of providing for the welfare of his National Football League brethren. Instead of focusing on his own career achievements, he used his 2006 Pro Football Hall of Fame induction speech as an opportunity to discuss the issues of inadequate pensions and the need for improved benefits for retired NFL players.

CAREER HIGHLIGHTS

Best Season

Carson played exceptionally well in both 1981 and 1984, earning First-Team All-Pro honors for the only two times in his career. Nevertheless, the feeling here is that he had his finest season in 1979, when he made a career-high 185 tackles en route to earning unanimous First-Team All-NFC honors.

Memorable Moments/Greatest Performances

Carson scored two regular-season touchdowns during his career, both of which rank among his most memorable moments. He crossed the goal line for the first time on October 21, 1979, returning a recovered fumble 22 yards for the winning fourth-quarter score in a 21–17 victory over the Kansas City Chiefs. Carson scored the only offensive touchdown of his career almost exactly seven years later, on October 12, 1986, when he collaborated with backup quarterback Jeff Rutledge on a fake field goal attempt to haul in a 13-yard TD pass during a 35–3 win over the Philadelphia Eagles. Carson also recorded one touchdown in postseason play, intercepting a Joe Montana pass and returning it 14 yards for the Giants' only TD in a 21–10 playoff loss to the 49ers in 1984.

Carson saved his greatest individual performance for a 1982 Monday night contest against Green Bay, making 20 solo tackles and assisting on five others during a 27–19 loss to the Packers.

An outstanding big-game player, Carson always seemed to be at his best when the stakes were highest. He recorded an interception and made 12 solo tackles during a key 24–14 victory over Washington on December 7, 1986, that practically guaranteed the Giants the NFC East title. Later in the year, he also made one of the biggest plays of Super Bowl XXI, when he stopped Denver running back Gerald Willhite for no gain during New York's first-half goal-line stand against the Broncos. Carson concluded the contest with seven tackles.

NOTABLE ACHIEVEMENTS

- Averaged 122 tackles per year from 1981 to 1987.
- Led Giants in tackles six times.
- Served as captain of the Giants from 1979 to 1988.
- Nine-time Pro Bowl selection (1978, 1979, 1981–1987).
- Two-time First-Team All-Pro selection (1981, 1984).
- Four-time Second-Team All-Pro selection (1978, 1982, 1985, 1986).
- Five-time First-Team All-NFC selection (1978, 1979, 1981, 1982, 1986).
- 1985 Second-Team All-NFC selection.
- Pro Football Reference Second-Team All-1980s Team.
- 1986 NFC champion.
- Super Bowl XXI champion.
- Elected to Pro Football Hall of Fame in 2006.

7
ELI MANNING

Since having his abilities questioned by the New York media, Giants fans, and even some of his own teammates during the early stages of his career, Eli Manning has gone on to establish himself as the greatest quarterback in franchise history. The holder of virtually every team passing record, Manning has passed for more than 51,000 yards and thrown 339 touchdown passes over the course of his career, earning in the process four Pro Bowl nominations. Yet when Manning eventually hangs up his cleats, he is likely to be remembered most for his outstanding postseason play that has earned him Super Bowl MVP honors twice. One of the NFL's best big-game quarterbacks, Manning has displayed an uncanny ability during his time in New York to perform his best when the stakes are highest, leading the Giants to a pair of NFL championships, with his brilliant play against the previously unbeaten New England Patriots in Super Bowl XLII enabling the Giants to record one of the biggest upsets in NFL history.

Born in New Orleans, Louisiana, on January 3, 1981, Elisha Nelson Manning has had football in his blood virtually from the time he took his first step. The son of former NFL quarterback Archie Manning, who spent his best years calling signals for the hapless New Orleans Saints during the 1970s, Eli spent most of his youth following in the footsteps of older brother Peyton, who went on to star for the Indianapolis Colts, before joining the Denver Broncos in 2012. After attending prep school at Isidore Newman School in New Orleans, the youngest Manning played his college football at the University of Mississippi, where he demonstrated that he possessed many of the same qualities previously displayed by his father and older brother. Eli set or tied 45 single-game, season, and career records while at Ole Miss, leading the Rebels to a 10–3 record and a 31–28 victory over Oklahoma State in the Cotton Bowl as a senior. Manning's outstanding performance in his final year at Mississippi enabled him to win the Maxwell Award as the nation's best all-around player. He also finished third in the Heisman Trophy voting, coming in just behind Oklahoma quarterback Jason White and University of Pittsburgh wide receiver Larry Fitzgerald.

Manning made a strong impression on his two head coaches at Ole Miss, both of whom greatly admired the young quarterback's intelligence and natural football instincts. Former head coach David Cutcliffe stated, "Eli has what I call 'fast-twitch' mental fibers. He has great football-thinking ability. He has instant recall and is able to use it. In that three to five seconds of play, he can have 45 seconds' worth of thoughts go through his head."[1]

Meanwhile, Johnny Vaught, Manning's other head coach at Mississippi, noted, "Eli can recognize defenses and knows where the weaknesses are. He has studied football. He studies the opposition. He studies the defense. I just like to see him go out there and pick it to death. I think Eli probably knows more football than either his father or Peyton did at this time of their careers."[2]

Manning's pedigree and exceptional football intellect made him the most coveted player heading into the 2004 NFL Draft. However, with the San Diego Chargers slated to make the first overall pick, Manning began his professional career in controversial fashion by announcing that he had no intention of going to San Diego if the Chargers drafted him. The Giants and Chargers subsequently worked out a deal in which San Diego selected Manning, then traded him to the Giants for quarterback Philip Rivers, whom New York tabbed with the fourth overall pick. The Chargers also received two other draft picks from the Giants.

Although many people felt the Giants overpaid for Manning, New York general manager Ernie Accorsi remained adamant in defending the move, saying of his prize acquisition, "He's unflappable, and it's not phony. I'm sure it's his whole upbringing. Nothing bothers this kid."[3]

Nevertheless, Accorsi often found his judgment being questioned over the course of the next few seasons as Manning failed to play at the lofty level that had been predicted for him. After replacing Kurt Warner as the starter in New York midway through his rookie season, Manning led the Giants to only one victory in their final seven games, completing fewer than 50 percent of his passes, while throwing six touchdown passes and nine interceptions. He improved significantly his second year in the league, leading the Giants to a record of 11–5 by throwing for 3,762 yards, completing nearly 53 percent of his passes, and tossing 24 TD passes and 17 interceptions. Particularly effective against the Chargers in front of a hostile San Diego crowd that jeered him throughout the contest for the manner in which he snubbed them earlier, Manning threw for 352 yards and two touchdowns during a 45–23 loss. Nevertheless, he continued to play erratically at other times, throwing four interceptions during a 24–21 home loss to Minnesota.

Manning started off the 2006 season well, but he struggled during the second half of the campaign, prompting questions to once again arise as to whether the Giants made the right decision when they targeted him in the first round of the 2004 NFL draft, instead of either sticking with Rivers or selecting Ben Roethlisberger, whom Pittsburgh nabbed a few picks later. Manning finished the year with 3,244 passing yards, 24 touchdown passes, 18 interceptions, and a 57.7 completion percentage. Meanwhile, despite making the playoffs as a wild card, the Giants compiled a record of just 8–8 during the regular season.

Eli Manning holds virtually every team passing record.
Courtesy of Mike Morbeck

Manning posted similar numbers in 2007, throwing for more than 3,300 yards and 23 touchdowns. However, he continued to struggle with his consistency, also tossing a league-high 20 interceptions. After being outplayed by Dallas quarterback Tony Romo during one particularly disheartening loss to the Cowboys in week 9, Manning found his ability to lead the Giants going forward being publicly questioned by Giants co-owner John Mara, who stated, "The only thing we evaluate is 'Can we win with this guy?' That's the one thing. When we talk about any player at the end of the season, the number one question is 'Will he help us win?' And, to take it one step further, 'Can we win a championship with this guy?'"[4]

Former Giants teammate Tiki Barber, who began a career in broadcasting shortly after he played his last game in 2006, also questioned Manning's leadership ability, stating during an interview he did prior to the start of the 2007 season that the quarterback's motivational pregame speeches sounded "almost comical."

Yet not everyone on the team had as little confidence in Manning as Mara and Barber. Center Shaun O'Hara defended his quarterback by saying, "I don't think Eli's trying to win anybody over in this locker room. We've had faith in him since he took over the reins."[5]

Meanwhile, Giants offensive coordinator Kevin Gilbride spoke of the pressure placed on the young quarterback's shoulders, stating, "The standards for him are very high. The city asks a lot of him. That's the nature of the New York audience."[6]

The Giants finished 2007 with a record of 10–6 and advanced to the playoffs as a wild card. Manning, who nearly led his team to victory over the previously unbeaten New England Patriots in the regular season finale by passing for 251 yards and four touchdowns during a 38–35 loss, subsequently played his best ball during the postseason. In directing the Giants to wins over Tampa Bay, Dallas, and Green Bay in the NFC playoffs, Manning threw four touchdown passes and no interceptions. He then led the Giants to a stunning 17–14 upset of New England in the Super Bowl, earning game MVP honors by completing 19 of 34 passes, for 255 yards and two touchdowns, including the game-winner to Plaxico Burress with less than one minute left to play in the contest.

Giants head coach Tom Coughlin, who remained firmly in Manning's corner while others continued to question his ability, took the opportunity to praise his quarterback's leadership skills by proclaiming, "He leads by example. When he speaks, they listen."[7]

Coughlin added, "He has really taken control of the game, control of himself, control of the offense."[8]

Showing renewed confidence following his MVP performance in Super Bowl XLII, Manning compiled the best overall numbers of his five-year career in 2008, leading the Giants to a 12–4 record by passing for 3,238 yards and 21 touchdowns, tossing only 10 interceptions, and establishing new career highs by completing 60.3 percent of his passes and posting a quarterback rating of 86.4. For his efforts, Manning received his first Pro Bowl nomination at season's end. Although the Giants finished just 8–8 the following year, Manning improved upon his numbers in every major statistical category, throwing for 4,021 yards and 27 touchdowns, completing just over 62 percent of his passes, and compiling a quarterback rating of 93.1. The Giants rebounded in 2010 to finish 10–6, with Manning throwing for 4,002 yards, tossing 31 touchdown passes, and completing 62.9 percent of his passes. However, he also threw a league-high 25 interceptions.

The usually guarded Manning subsequently created a considerable amount of controversy prior to the start of the 2011 season, when he gave an honest answer to a loaded question during a radio interview. Asked by sports talk-show host Michael Kay if he considered himself to be an elite "Top 10, Top 5" quarterback in the same class as Tom Brady, Manning responded, "I consider myself in that class. Tom Brady is a great quarterback. . . . I think now he's grown up and gotten better every year, and that's what I'm trying to do. I kind of hope these next seven years of my quarterback days are my best."[9]

Even though any quarterback who truly believed in himself likely would have responded in similar fashion, Manning soon found himself being criticized for trying to inflate his own status and skills, with his detractors pointing to his inconsistent numbers, including the 25 interceptions he threw the previous season. Perhaps motivated even more than usual by the criticism he received, Manning had

Manning has led the Giants to a pair of NFL titles.
Courtesy of Mike Morbeck

the finest season of his career. In addition to completing 61 percent of his passes, throwing 29 touchdown passes, and posting a quarterback rating of 92.9, he established a new Giants record by throwing for 4,933 yards, en route to earning his second Pro Bowl selection.

Despite finishing the regular season just 9–7, the Giants ended up winning the NFC East, after which they defeated Atlanta, Green Bay, and San Francisco in the playoffs. They then upset the Patriots again in the Super Bowl, with Manning outplaying Tom Brady and capturing game MVP honors for the second time. Manning performed brilliantly throughout the postseason, completing 65 percent of his passes, for 1,219 yards and nine touchdowns. He also threw only one interception, with his 1,219 passing yards setting a new NFL record for a single postseason.

Manning's exceptional play afforded Giants offensive lineman David Diehl the opportunity to address the quarterback's critics. Speaking after the team's victory in Super Bowl XLVI, Diehl stated, "People mocked him [Manning] earlier this year when he said he was an elite quarterback. And people challenged him. Well, go ahead and say that stuff now, and see how that goes. Talk about a guy who deserves it and, most important, earned it. There's no other quarterback I'd want behind me."[10]

Although the Giants failed to return to the playoffs in 2012 and Manning performed somewhat less spectacularly, he had another very solid season, throwing 26 touchdown passes and nearly reaching 4,000 yards passing (3,948) for the fourth consecutive year. Manning subsequently suffered through a horrific 2013 campaign in which he tossed a league-high 27 interceptions for a Giants team that finished just 7–9. Even though the Giants continued to struggle in each of the next two seasons, posting identical 6–10 records, Manning raised his level of play considerably, passing for 4,410 yards and tossing 30 touchdown passes in 2014, before earning his fourth trip to the Pro Bowl the following year by throwing for 4,432 yards and establishing new career highs with 35 TD passes and a quarterback rating of 93.6.

Unfortunately, Manning has failed to perform nearly as well in either of the last two seasons, with the Giants' weak offensive line and inability to establish anything in the way of a running game contributing greatly to his lackluster play. Nevertheless, he still managed to throw for 4,027 yards and complete 26 touchdown passes for a Giants team that earned a spot in the playoffs with a record of 11–5 under new head coach Ben McAdoo in 2016. But after the Giants won just two of their first 11 games in 2017, McAdoo elected to replace Manning behind center with Geno Smith, who previously had failed to distinguish himself in his two seasons as a starter with the New York Jets. Although very much hurt by McAdoo's decision, Manning chose not to criticize his coach in the media, instead merely expressing his disappointment at seeing his streak of 210 consecutive regular season starts come to an end. However, with former Giants players and coaches subsequently speaking out against the organization's shoddy treatment of the veteran quarterback, Manning regained his starting job just a few days later when team ownership relieved McAdoo of his duties.

Although Manning spent the final few weeks of the 2017 campaign calling the signals for the Giants, it remains to be seen how much longer the team's new coaching staff plans to entrust the offense to him. Certainly, rebuilding the offensive line and developing a running game will go a long way toward helping him recapture his earlier form. But, at 37 years of age as of this writing, Manning is considered by many to be well past his prime. Only time will tell if that assessment is accurate. He will enter the 2018 season with career totals of 51,682 yards passing, 339 touchdown passes, and 228 interceptions, a pass completion percentage of 59.8 percent, and a passer rating of 83.5.

CAREER HIGHLIGHTS

Best Season

Manning played very well in 2009, passing for 4,021 yards, throwing 27 touchdown passes and only 14 interceptions, completing 62.3 percent of his passes, and posting a quarterback rating of 93.1. He also put up outstanding numbers in 2015, concluding the campaign with 4,432 yards passing, 35 TD passes and just 14 interceptions, a pass completion percentage of 62.6 percent, and a career-high quarterback rating of 93.6. Nevertheless, Manning had his finest all-around season in 2011, when he tossed 29 TD passes and 16 interceptions, completed 61 percent of his passes, compiled a quarterback rating of 92.9, and passed for a franchise record 4,933 yards. Manning established a new single-season NFL record by tossing 15 fourth-quarter touchdown passes, and he also led all league quarterbacks by directing the Giants to eight game-winning drives and seven comeback wins. Manning punctuated his fabulous season by leading the Giants to victory in Super Bowl XLVI.

Memorable Moments/Greatest Performances

Manning has turned in a number of exceptional performances and experienced several memorable moments during his career. After passing for 352 yards and two touchdowns during a 45–23 loss to San Diego one week earlier, Manning led the Giants to a 44–24 win over the St. Louis Rams in week 4 of the 2005 campaign by throwing for nearly 300 yards and tossing four touchdown passes for the first time in his young career. Two games later, he directed a last-minute drive against Denver that netted the Giants a 24–23 victory over the Broncos. The drive culminated in a two-yard TD pass to Amani Toomer with only five seconds remaining on the clock.

In week 2 of the 2006 season, Manning led the Giants to a stunning fourth-quarter comeback against the Philadelphia Eagles that saw them turn a 24–7 deficit into a 30–24 overtime victory. Despite being sacked eight times by Philadelphia's defense, Manning completed 31 of 43 passes on the day, for 371 yards and three touchdowns. He ended the game with a 31-yard TD strike to Plaxico Burress nearly 12 minutes into overtime.

Manning played extremely well for a prolonged period of time in 2008, capturing NFC Offensive Player of the Month honors for November by throwing for 1,036 yards, tossing 10 touchdown passes, and compiling a 94.9 passer rating, while leading the Giants to a perfect 5–0 record.

Manning turned in two of the most prolific passing performances of his career in 2009, leading the Giants to a 34–31 overtime victory over Atlanta on November 22 by throwing for 384 yards and three touchdowns, before failing to deliver a win against Philadelphia three weeks later despite completing 27 of 38 passes for 391 yards and three touchdowns during a 45–38 home loss.

Manning came up big both times the Giants defeated the rival Dallas Cowboys in 2011, leading his team to a pair of late scores that enabled New York to come away with a 37–34 come-from-behind victory the first time the two teams met on December 11. Manning tossed two touchdown passes and threw for 400 yards on the day, reaching the 400-yard plateau for the third time during the season. When the Giants defeated the Cowboys 31–14 in the regular season finale three weeks later, Manning passed for 346 yards and three touchdowns, enabling New York to win the NFC East title and advance to the playoffs for the first time in three years.

Manning also turned in a pair of epic performances in 2012, passing for three touchdowns and a career-high 510 yards during a 41–34 come-from-behind victory over Tampa Bay in week 2, before leading the Giants to a 42–7 win over Philadelphia in the regular season finale by tossing five TD passes for the first time in his career.

Performing extremely well in 2014 even though the Giants finished just 6–10, Manning engineered a 45–14 blowout of Washington in week 4 by passing for 300 yards, throwing four touchdown passes, three of which went to tight end Larry Donnell, and running for one score himself. He had another huge game on December 28, 2014, leading the Giants to a 37–27 win over the St. Louis Rams by completing 25 of 32 passes for 391 yards and three touchdowns, with his longest completion of the day being an 80-yard scoring strike to Odell Beckham Jr. Although the Giants lost the regular season finale to Philadelphia one week later by a score of 34–26, Manning starred in defeat, throwing for 429 yards and completing a 63-yard TD pass to Beckham.

Continuing his strong play in 2015, Manning completed 41 of 54 pass attempts for 441 yards and three touchdowns during a 30–27 win over San Francisco on October 11, with his 12-yard TD pass to Larry Donnell with only 21 seconds remaining in regulation providing the margin of victory. Although a porous Giants defense surrendered 505 passing yards and seven touchdown passes to Drew Brees during a 52–49 loss to the Saints three weeks later, Manning had one of the finest statistical days of his career, throwing for 350 yards and tossing a career-high six TD passes, with three of those going to Odell Beckham Jr. Manning had another big game later in the year, leading the Giants to a 31–24 win over Miami on December 14 by completing 27 of 31 pass attempts for 337 yards and four touchdowns, with the last of those being an 84-yard connection with Odell Beckham Jr. early in the fourth quarter that proved to be the game's decisive score.

Although the Giants lost their December 17, 2017, meeting with the Philadelphia Eagles by a score of 34–29, Manning turned in easily his finest performance of the campaign. Just one week after being inserted back into the starting lineup, Manning nearly led the Giants to an upset win over the eventual Super Bowl champions by passing for a season-high 434 yards and three touchdowns.

Still, Manning may well have played his very best game against San Francisco when the Giants faced the 49ers in the 2011 NFC title game. Although Manning posted solid numbers, completing 32 of 58 passes for 316 yards and two touchdowns, he compiled a far more impressive stat-line several other times in his years with the Giants. However, Manning ended up leading New York to a 20–17 overtime win over San Francisco even though the 49ers sacked him six times, knocked him down many other times, and harassed him practically every time he dropped back to pass. Showing tremendous poise and toughness, Manning stood tall against the NFL's top defense, never appearing flustered or intimidated in the least. Manning's effort against the 49ers likely will go down as one of the finest performances of his career.

Yet Giant fans are likely to look back even more fondly on Manning's performances in Super Bowls XLII and XLVI, both of which earned him game MVP honors. In the first of those contests, the Giants put an end to New England's hopes for a perfect season by defeating their AFC counter-parts by a final score of 17–14. Trailing 14–10 with 2:42 left in the game, Manning led the Giants on an 83-yard touchdown scoring drive that fea-tured one of the most memorable plays in Super Bowl history. With the Giants in possession at their own 44-yard line, Manning connected with David Tyree on a critical third-down-and-5 play in which he avoided sev-eral near sacks before flinging the ball deep downfield to the receiver, who made the catch by pinning the ball to his helmet. The play, which has since become known simply as "The Catch," covered 32 yards. Four plays later, Manning found a wide-open Plaxico Burress in the corner of the end zone for the game-winning touchdown.

Manning again led the Giants on a late touchdown march in Super Bowl XLVI, directing them on an 88-yard drive that gave them a 21–17 win over New England. He finished the game with 30 completions in 40 attempts, for 296 yards and one touchdown.

NOTABLE ACHIEVEMENTS

- Has passed for more than 4,000 yards six times.
- Has surpassed 30 touchdown passes three times.
- Has completed more than 60 percent of passes eight times.
- Has posted quarterback rating in excess of 90.0 four times.
- Has led all NFL quarterbacks in game-winning drives and comeback wins two times each.
- Finished second in NFL with 35 touchdown passes in 2015.
- Tied for first all-time on Giants in games played (216).
- Holds Giants records for: most career passing yards (51,682); most career completions (4,424); most career touchdown passes (339); most passing yards in a season (4,933 in 2011); and most consecutive pass completions in a game (21 in 2011).
- Holds NFL record for most passing yards in a single postseason (1,219 yards in 2011).
- Holds NFL record for most fourth-quarter touchdown passes in a season (15 in 2011).
- Holds share of NFL record for most game-winning drives in a season (eight in 2011).
- Ranks among NFL's all-time leaders in: pass completions (6th); passing yards (6th); and touchdown passes (8th).
- Owns second-longest consecutive starts streak by a quarterback in NFL history (210 games).
- Four-time NFC Offensive Player of the Week.
- NFC Offensive Player of the Month for November 2008.
- 2016 NFL Walter Payton Man of the Year.
- Four-time Pro Bowl selection (2008, 2011, 2012, 2015).
- Two-time NFC champion (2007, 2011).
- Two-time Super Bowl champion (XLII, XLVI).
- Two-time Super Bowl MVP.

8

ANDY ROBUSTELLI

One of the premier defensive ends of his era, Andy Robustelli served as a key figure on a Giants team that appeared in six NFL Championship Games between 1956 and 1963. An emotional leader both on and off the field, Robustelli is considered by many to be the glue that held the Giants together during that period. Admired and respected by all his teammates, Robustelli inspired everyone around him with his incredible work ethic and cerebral approach to the game. Meanwhile, his tenacity, fierceness, and quickness made him a terror to opposing quarterbacks, whom he sacked with great regularity. Robustelli's many outstanding attributes combined to make him a seven-time Pro Bowler, six-time First-Team All-Pro selection, and four-time Second Team All-Pro nomination over the course of his career, which he split between the Rams and Giants. Indeed, the Giants were quite fortunate to obtain the services of a player with Robustelli's ability, doing so primarily because of the timing of his first child.

Born in Stamford, Connecticut, on December 6, 1925, Andrew Richard Robustelli enlisted in the U.S. Navy to join the war effort shortly after he graduated from Stamford High School in 1944. Following the war, Robustelli enrolled at Arnold College, a tiny school with only a few hundred students that has since been absorbed by the University of Bridgeport in Connecticut. While at Arnold, Robustelli starred in both baseball and football, prompting baseball's New York Giants to offer him a minor league contract when he graduated, and football's Los Angeles Rams to select him in the 19th round of the 1951 NFL Draft.

Choosing football over baseball, Robustelli signed with the Rams, whom he helped win the NFL title as a rookie by starting at defensive end. He remained in Los Angeles four more years, appearing in one more NFL Championship Game, and earning two Pro Bowl nominations and three All-Pro selections during that time. However, when the birth of Robustelli's first child prompted him to request a week's delay in reporting to the Rams'

Andy Robustelli helped lead the Giants to six NFL Championship Game appearances and one league title.
Courtesy of MearsOnlineAuctions.com

training camp facility prior to the start of the 1956 campaign, Los Angeles head coach Sid Gillman elected to trade the star defensive end to the Giants for a first-round draft pick.

Bringing his winning ways with him to New York, Robustelli helped the Giants capture the NFL championship in his first year with his new team. Thriving in the new 4–3 alignment devised by defensive coordinator Tom Landry, Robustelli used his quickness, strength, determination, and ferocity to wreak havoc on opposing offenses. Standing barely 6'1" and weighing only 230 pounds, Robustelli lacked the size of a prototypical defensive end—even one who played during his era. But his heart and intelligence enabled him to overcome any physical advantages his adver-saries held over him. Although the NFL did not record sacks as an official statistic until well after Robustelli retired, the right defensive end was con-sidered to be the premier pass-rusher of his time.

Speaking of his former teammate, Frank Gifford said, "He was far and away above the other defensive ends of his era. Andy was not all that big, but he was very quick. With Andy and Tom Landry, it was almost scary the anticipation that they had of what was going to be run. He and Tom were very, very close. Whereas Tom was the overall defensive coach, Andy basi-cally ran the defensive line along with the linebackers. He was the leader. Everyone knew that. He was the leader in the clubhouse. He was quiet, but when Andy talked, everyone listened."[1]

Gifford added, "Andy was a great leader. When he came to us from the Rams, it turned everything around defensively. He fit perfectly into Tom Landry's defense. Tom Landry was such a leader in putting defense into pro football, and Andy was one of the key components of that."[2]

The empathy that Robustelli and Landry shared helped New York's defense reach new heights. With Robustelli leading the way, the Giants' defense developed into the best in the league, enabling the team to advance to the NFL Championship Game six times over an eight-year stretch. Although New York's offense played well in some of those years, it found itself assuming a supporting role to the defense much of the time. Chants of "De-fense, De-fense!" frequently rang out from the stands at Yankee Stadium during this period, with the names of Robustelli, Huff, Grier, and Katcavage superseding those of Gifford, Conerly, Rote, and Webster in the minds of most fans. Gifford, in fact, later admitted, "They used to boo our offense when it came on the field. It was embarrassing."[3]

Commenting years later on the success New York's defense experienced during that time, Robustelli said, "We had a lot of pride. We weren't kids, and we weren't looking to get out of the game when we were hurt. We were mature enough to realize you could cuss each other out and still have a well-balanced group of guys. I don't think we had more talent than anybody else—we may have had less. We wanted it, and we really didn't care about anybody else. Maybe we were selfish in that respect."[4]

Tom Landry agreed with Robustelli's assessment of New York's defense, suggesting, "They played together probably as well as any team I've ever coached. They had just a sense and feel between each other. . . . It was good talent, but it really wasn't any better than some of the other teams in those days. But their ability to play together and believe in each other was tremendous."[5]

In praising perhaps his favorite player, Landry said of Robustelli, "He put more book time into his work than the others. He thought all the time. Not just on the field, but in his room, and at the dining table."[6]

Robustelli's hard work and dedication helped him earn five Pro Bowl nominations and seven All-Pro selections as a member of the Giants. However, he received his greatest honor in 1962, when he was presented with the Bert Bell Award as the NFL Player of the Year after leading the Giants to an exceptional 12–2 record during the regular season.

Robustelli remained in New York two more years, announcing his retirement at the conclusion of the 1964 campaign. He ended his career having played in 175 out of a possible 176 games over 14 seasons. He recovered 22 fumbles during that time, leaving the game as the NFL's all-time leader in that category. Robustelli played on a winning team in 13 of his 14 seasons, with his club advancing to the NFL title game a total of eight times.

After retiring as a player, Robustelli expanded his business interests, opening a travel agency and a sports marketing business in Stamford. However, he returned to the Giants in 1974 to take over as the team's director of operations, inheriting a squad that had won only two games the previous season. New York didn't fare much better with Robustelli in charge, posting only 21 victories over the course of the next five seasons. The Giants' failures hastened the departure of Robustelli, who returned to his outside business interests at the conclusion of the 1978 campaign, turning over the responsibility of running the team to George Young.

Although Robustelli's five-year reign as general manager in New York would have to be considered a failure, he made a strong impression on many of the players who performed for the Giants during that period. Defensive end George Martin, who spent 14 years in a Giants uniform after being selected by Robustelli in the 11th round of the 1975 NFL Draft, stated years later, "Andy is someone I looked up to fiercely. I think he was legendary among all ballplayers, but especially within the illustrious Giants history. He was the G.M. when I came aboard and I was amazed at his intelligence. Andy had such a regal presence about him and people looked upon him with great admiration for his accomplishments. There were many, many times when I tried to emulate Andy, both on and off the field, which is extremely rare."[7]

Martin added, "Andy was always giving you tips about the game— here's your general manager coming out to give you some words of advice. For a young man, particularly a rookie, those were like words from heaven. Although our styles were different and the eras in which we played in were

Robustelli earned NFL Player of the Year honors in 1962.
Courtesy of MearsOnlineAuctions.com

completely different, one of the things I know I tried hard to copy was the tenacity that Andy had, because it's transferable no matter what era you played in. He had this insatiable drive to get to the ball, whether it was in the possession of the quarterback, or the running back, or the receiver. Andy was relentless in pursuing the ball."[8]

In discussing Robustelli's personality, Martin suggested, "There was no pretense about Andy. He was the same whether you were talking to him as a G.M. or a former ballplayer, or whether he was one of those great icons. He was just Andy. When he was general manager, everyone called him 'Andy,' not 'Mr. Robustelli.' To see how people—I don't want to say 'worship,' but I don't think I'm far off the mark—how they looked up to him and how they were in awe when they were in his presence, you looked at him and said, 'Man, I wish I could have that kind of impact on people.' Andy had that magical aura about him."[9]

Unfortunately, complications resulting from bladder surgery took Andy Robustelli from us on May 31, 2011. He died in his hometown of Stamford at the age of 85.

Reflecting on "The Rich Legacy of Andy Robustelli" in the June 1, 2011, *New York Times*, Andy Barral noted, "Andy Robustelli was modest about his achievements. He only reluctantly, and unsentimentally, reminisced about his football days and seemed genuinely surprised when people recognized him. Like his Connecticut license plate, 'NY81,' Robustelli will be remembered as the right defensive end of the New York Giants in an era when the nation's viewing habits in the fall were dramatically changing and pro football was about to become king."[10]

GIANT CAREER HIGHLIGHTS

Best Season

Robustelli earned First-Team All-Pro honors four times as a member of the Giants between 1956 and 1960. Yet even though he only made it onto the Second Team in 1962, Robustelli had perhaps his finest year at the age of 37, being named the Bert Bell Award winner as the NFL's Player of the Year.

Memorable Moments/Greatest Performances

Although Robustelli built his reputation largely on his ability to pressure opposing quarterbacks, his quickness, athleticism, and extraordinary instincts enabled him to accomplish many other exceptional feats. During a 41–31 victory over the Dallas Cowboys in the final game of the 1962 season, Robustelli set a new NFL record (since broken) by recovering the 21st fumble of his career.

An outstanding punt-blocker as well, Robustelli made perhaps the biggest block of his career against the Chicago Bears in the 1956 NFL Championship Game that New York ended up winning by a score of 47–7. With the Giants already holding a 27–7 lead in the second quarter, Robustelli blocked a punt in the Chicago end zone that enabled the Giants to score a touchdown, giving them in the process an insurmountable 34–7 lead.

NOTABLE ACHIEVEMENTS

- Five-time Pro Bowl selection.
- Four-time First-Team All-Pro selection.
- Three-time Second-Team All-Pro selection.
- 1962 Bert Bell Award winner as NFL Player of the Year.
- Six-time NFL Eastern Division champion.
- 1956 NFL champion.
- Elected to Pro Football Hall of Fame in 1971.

9

FRANK GIFFORD

Perhaps the most recognizable member of the Giants' outstanding teams of the 1950s and early 1960s, Frank Gifford parlayed a Hall of Fame career on the gridiron into an extraordinarily successful sportscasting career that lasted more than three decades. After his playing days ended in 1964, Gifford spent six years broadcasting primarily in the New York market. He then expanded his circle in 1971, becoming the voice of *Monday Night Football*, while also covering several other sports for the ABC network. Prior to venturing into the broadcast booth, though, Gifford established himself as one of the most versatile players in NFL history, earning Pro Bowl honors at three different positions. Starring for the Giants at different times as a defensive back, running back, and wide receiver, Gifford appeared in the Pro Bowl a total of eight times, earned First-Team All-Pro honors on four separate occasions, captured NFL MVP honors in 1956, and helped lead the Giants to five division titles and one world championship. Gifford's athletic ability, outgoing personality, and matinee idol looks ended up making him an iconic figure in New York during his playing days, enabling him to eventually pursue a career that gained him similar recognition in other areas of the country as well.

Born in Santa Monica, California, on August 16, 1930, Frank Newton Gifford got his first taste of football while attending high school in Bakersfield, California. Making the varsity as a 5'7", 120-pound quarterback, he struggled as a student, showing interest in academics for the first time as a junior after his coach told him he had a chance to earn a college athletic scholarship. Nevertheless, even with the additional incentive, Gifford failed to obtain the grades necessary to get into his first choice, USC, until he spent a semester at Bakersfield Junior College, where he earned JC All-American honors.

Although the Trojans recruited Gifford as a quarterback, he spent most of his first two seasons at USC playing in the defensive secondary. However, when Jess Hill took over as the university's head football coach in 1949, he

Frank Gifford proved to be one of the most versatile players in NFL history during his time in New York.
Courtesy of RMYAuctions.com

switched Gifford to tailback. Thriving in his new role, Gifford became the focal point of the team's offense, rushing for 841 yards and seven touchdowns, while also completing 32 of 61 passes, for 303 yards and two scores.

Subsequently selected by the Giants in the first round of the 1952 NFL Draft with the 11th overall pick, Gifford bristled over the idea of coming to New York at first, recalling years later, "I remember I hated the thought of being drafted by the Giants. But, as it happened, it couldn't have worked out better."[1]

Gifford's initial feelings of discontentment worsened when the Giants virtually ignored his offensive skills his first two years in the league. Playing primarily defensive back, Gifford carried the ball only 38 times as a rookie and just 50 times in his second season, although his outstanding play in the secondary earned him the first of his seven consecutive trips to the Pro Bowl in his sophomore campaign of 1953.

After seriously considering quitting prior to the start of his third NFL season, Gifford rediscovered his passion for the game when the Giants hired two new coaches in 1954. With Jim Lee Howell replacing Steve Owen as top man, and Vince Lombardi taking over as his offensive assistant, the Giants shifted Gifford to halfback, hoping that his versatility might add a degree of unpredictability to their somewhat stagnant offense. Commenting years later on his switch in positions, Gifford stated, "In effect, my pro career began that season."[2]

Gifford rushed for 368 yards on 5.6 yards per carry, caught 14 passes for another 154 yards, and scored three touchdowns in his first full year on offense, before a ligament tear in one of his knees ended his season prematurely. Still, he made his second straight Pro Bowl, becoming in the process the first player to earn a Pro Bowl berth on defense and offense in consecutive years.

After another solid season in 1955, Gifford reached his zenith the following year, leading the Giants to the NFL Championship by rushing for 819 yards, making 51 receptions for 603 yards, and scoring nine touchdowns. Gifford's 1,422 yards from scrimmage led the NFL, earning him his second straight First-Team All-Pro nomination and recognition as the league's Most Valuable Player.

Standing 6'1" and weighing 197 pounds, Gifford possessed only average size and strength. He also lacked great breakaway speed. But Gifford's incredible versatility is the thing that ultimately separated him from the other running backs of his era. A true triple-threat on offense, Gifford had the ability to run with the ball, make receptions anywhere on the field, or deliver passes with deadly accuracy via the halfback option. In fact, his 14 career touchdown passes are the most by any non-quarterback in NFL history.

After amassing more than 1,000 total yards from scrimmage in two of the next three seasons as well, Gifford found his 1960 campaign shortened by a vicious hit he received at the hands of Philadelphia Eagles linebacker Chuck Bednarik. Carried motionless from the field on a stretcher, Gifford subsequently suffered severe head trauma, prompting him to retire from football. However, he eventually returned to the Giants after an 18-month

Gifford earned league MVP honors in 1956, when he led the Giants to the NFL championship.
Courtesy of RMYAuctions.com

layoff, displaying his versatility once more by moving to the flanker position. Gifford went on to reach stardom as a wide-out, earning the last of his eight Pro Bowl selections in 1963, before retiring for good following the conclusion of the ensuing campaign. Gifford ended his career with 3,609 yards rushing, averaging 4.3 yards per carry during his 12 years in the league. He also caught 367 passes for 5,434 yards. Gifford ranks among the Giants' all-time leaders in all four categories. He also scored more touchdowns (78) than any other player in team history.

Having gotten his start in broadcasting by doing nightly sports reports for WCBS-TV in New York during the latter stages of his playing career, Gifford transitioned seamlessly into life after football. He spent the next few years working for that same station, covering pro football, college basketball, and golf, before getting his big break in 1971 when he replaced Keith Jackson as the play-by-play announcer on ABC's *Monday Night Football*. Sharing the broadcast booth with Howard Cosell and Don Meredith, Gifford represented the voice of reason, frequently serving as straight man and referee for the two volatile personalities. Although the cast of characters surrounding him changed many times in the years that followed, Gifford remained an integral part of *Monday Night Football*'s broadcast team until 1997, when controversy arose resulting from an affair he had with a former airline stewardess. ABC-TV subsequently gave Gifford a reduced role on the program, assigning him to host its pregame show. After fulfilling his contractual obligations at the end of the year, Gifford elected to leave *Monday Night Football*. Retiring to private life following the conclusion of his broadcasting career, Gifford lived another 18 years, until he died of natural causes on August 9, 2015, just one week shy of his 85th birthday. Studies on Gifford's brain subsequently revealed that he suffered from chronic traumatic encephalopathy, likely brought on by the numerous collisions he endured during his playing days.

Frank Gifford's arrival in New York very much coincided with the incredible run of success the Giants experienced during their glory years of the 1950s and early 1960s. Although many other exceptional players graced the Giants' roster during that period, perhaps none of them made more significant overall contributions to the team than Gifford. He did whatever was asked of him, excelling in whatever role was assigned to him. In doing so, he became a legendary figure in New York sports and a true celebrity.

Joe Namath, another iconic New York sports hero, had this to say about the man whose playing career ended one year before his began: "Frank was always the star to me. My respect for what he had been through and what he brought with him to New York City, and how he performed. Hey, he's a legend."[3]

CAREER HIGHLIGHTS

Best Season

Gifford had a fabulous all-around year in 1959, earning the last of his four First-Team All-Pro selections by finishing second in the league to Jim Brown with 1,308 yards from scrimmage. In addition to rushing for 540 yards and three touchdowns, he caught 42 passes, for 768 yards and four touchdowns. Gifford finished seventh in the NFL in receptions and fifth in receiving yardage, and his 5.1 yard rushing average placed him fifth in the league rankings.

However, Gifford was even better in his MVP season of 1956, rushing for a career-high 819 yards, while also catching 51 passes for 603 yards. His 1,422 yards from scrimmage led the NFL, and he also finished near the top of the league rankings in rushing yardage (fifth), receiving yardage (seventh), and receptions (third). Furthermore, Gifford finished third in yards per rushing attempt (5.2), sixth in touchdowns (9), and tenth in points scored (65).

Memorable Moments/Greatest Performances

Gifford culminated his MVP campaign of 1956 with a strong performance against the Chicago Bears in the NFL Championship Game. After hooking up with quarterback Charlie Conerly on a 67-yard pass play early in the second half of New York's 47–7 victory, Gifford concluded the day's scoring with a 14-yard touchdown reception in the fourth quarter. He finished the day with 30 yards rushing, on only five attempts. He also had four catches for 131 yards.

Three years later, Gifford demonstrated his ability to make big plays during a 21–16 victory over the Steelers in Pittsburgh that improved the Giants' record to 4–1 in late October. Teaming up with quarterback Charlie Conerly on New York's first two plays from scrimmage, Gifford gave the Giants an early 14–0 lead with TD grabs of 77 and 28 yards, en route to compiling a total of 135 yards in receptions on the day.

Later in 1959, Gifford turned in the finest running performance of his career, leading the Giants to a 45–14 home win over the Washington Redskins by rushing for 159 yards on 16 carries. Among Gifford's runs was a 79-yard scamper that proved to be the longest of his career.

The following year, on November 13, 1960, Gifford tied a then-Giants record by scoring three touchdowns against Pittsburgh during a 27–24 New York victory.

Yet, ironically, the two most memorable plays of Gifford's career took place in games the Giants lost. The first of those occurred in the 1958 NFL Championship Game between the Giants and the Colts, which Baltimore ended up winning 23–17 in Sudden Death overtime. After giving New York a 17–14 lead early in the fourth quarter with a 15-yard touchdown reception, Gifford carried the ball in a third-and-four situation from his own 40-yard line, with only two minutes remaining in regulation. Baltimore's Gino Marchetti broke his leg on the play, and, in the confusion that followed, the Giants maintained that the officials incorrectly spotted the ball just short of the first-down marker. Although Gifford argued vehemently that he got the necessary yardage that would have sealed the victory for his team, the Giants found themselves forced to punt. Johnny Unitas subsequently marched the Colts down the field to the tying field goal that sent the game into overtime. He then led them to the game-winning touchdown the first time the Colts touched the ball in the overtime session. Giants linebacker Sam Huff later noted, "If Gifford makes that first down, no one would have heard of the '58 Colts."[4]

Perhaps even more memorable is the play that forced Gifford into temporary retirement. With the Giants and Philadelphia Eagles proving to be the Eastern Conference's two most formidable squads in 1960, the two teams met at Yankee Stadium on November 20 in a pivotal contest with huge playoff implications. The Giants jumped out to an early 10–0 lead, but the Eagles stormed back in the second half to go ahead 17–10. Following a Philadelphia kickoff, the Giants started from deep in their own territory with less than two minutes remaining in the game. A pass to Gifford advanced the ball to near midfield, before Philadelphia linebacker Chuck Bednarik turned in the game's pivotal play. Focusing solely on catching a short pass over the middle, Gifford had no time to look for oncoming danger. With the Giant back headed directly toward him, Bednarik delivered a punishing neck-high tackle that sent Gifford tumbling to the ground, the back of his head hitting the turf as the ball came flying out of his grasp. An alert Eagle scooped up the pigskin, sealing the victory for Philadelphia, as Gifford lay motionless on the field for several minutes before finally being carried into the clubhouse on a stretcher. Although he eventually made a full recovery, Gifford spent 10 days in the hospital with a concussion—an injury that prompted him to announce his retirement from the game (one that lasted 18 months). Meanwhile, the photo of Bednarik standing over his fallen victim with his fist clenched in victory subsequently became one of the most famous pictures associated with American sports.

NOTABLE ACHIEVEMENTS

- Averaged more than five yards per carry three times.
- Caught more than 50 passes once (51 in 1956).
- Returned one interception for a touchdown.
- Led NFL with 1,422 yards from scrimmage in 1956.

- Finished second in NFL in yards from scrimmage twice (1957, 1959).
- Holds NFL record for most TD passes by non-quarterback (14).
- Only NFL player to make Pro Bowl on defense and offense in consecutive seasons (1953, 1954).
- Ranks among Giants' all-time leaders in: touchdowns (1st); rushing touchdowns (7th); touchdown receptions (4th); total points (4th); rushing yardage (8th); yards per carry (4th); receptions (6th); and receiving yardage (2nd).
- 1958 Pro Bowl MVP.
- Eight-time Pro Bowl selection.
- Four-time First-Team All-Pro selection.
- One-time Second-Team All-Pro selection (1958).
- 1956 NFL MVP.
- NFL 1950s All-Decade Team.
- Five-time NFL Eastern Division champion.
- 1956 NFL champion.
- Elected to Pro Football Hall of Fame in 1977.

10

PHIL SIMMS

Those New Yorkers in attendance greeted with derision the words spoken by Pete Rozelle when the former commissioner of the National Football League proclaimed nearly 40 years ago, "With the seventh pick of the 1979 NFL Draft, the New York Giants select quarterback Phil Simms, Morehead State." Viewing New York's selection of the little-known Simms as a continuation of past failures, Giants fans jeered loudly Rozelle's announcement, concluding that the team's new general manager, George Young, knew little more than his immediate predecessors. They continued to express their dissatisfaction with Simms in the years that followed, as the quarterback succumbed to one injury after another, enabling him to appear in only 37 of his team's 73 games over the course of the next five seasons. However, by the time Simms retired in 1993, he had shattered virtually every Giants passing record, leading them to seven playoff appearances and two NFL championships. And even though Simms never received the credit he deserved for being one of the league's top quarterbacks, Giants fans eventually came to appreciate him, recognizing the huge role he played in their team's resurgence.

Born in Lebanon, Kentucky, on November 3, 1954, Philip Martin Simms moved with his family about 60 miles north to Louisville while still in elementary school. He graduated from Southern High School in Louisville in 1974, after which he chose to attend Morehead State University in nearby Morehead, Kentucky. A four-year starter for his college football team, Simms subsequently posted unspectacular numbers in Morehead State's ball-control offense. Nevertheless, he drew a considerable amount of interest from several NFL teams when he graduated in 1979, including the San Francisco 49ers, whose new head coach, Bill Walsh, planned to select him with the team's first pick, the 29th overall, if the quarterback's name remained on the board at that juncture. In fact, Walsh preferred Simms over Joe Montana, whom the 49ers ultimately chose with the 82nd overall

Phil Simms overcame a great deal of adversity during the early stages of his career to lead the Giants to seven playoff appearances and two NFL titles.
Courtesy of MearsOnlineAuctions.com

pick after the Giants surprised virtually everyone by selecting Simms early in the first round.

Simms later recalled, "Even the people back home were shocked when I was drafted in the first round. The next day, the Louisville papers were critical of the Giants. They as much as said I had no right being drafted that high."[1]

Given a cool reception by Giants fans upon his arrival in New York, Simms nonetheless played well as a rookie, winning five of his first six starts and concluding the 1979 campaign with a record of 6–4 as a starter. His 1,743 passing yards and 13 touchdown passes earned him a spot on the NFL All Rookie Team and a runner-up finish to future teammate Ottis Anderson in the Rookie of the Year voting.

However, things quickly went downhill after that, with Simms's next four years being marred by injuries and inconsistent play. After winning only three of his 13 starts in 1980, Simms missed the final three contests with a shoulder separation. A similar injury sidelined him for the final five games the following season, forcing him to sit and watch as his backup, Scott Brunner, quarterbacked the team to its first playoff appearance in 18 years. Simms then missed the entire 1982 campaign after suffering a torn knee ligament in a preseason game against the New York Jets. Bill Parcells elected to make Brunner the starter when he took over as head coach in 1983, inducing a profanity-laced tirade from Simms, who subsequently demanded to be traded. Yet, after pouting for several weeks when team management ignored his request, Simms eventually came to realize that he benefited from his benching, stating years later, "I was probably lucky not to get the job that year. Scott played himself off the team. I might have done the same thing."[2]

With Brunner struggling terribly en route to leading the Giants to an embarrassing 3–12–1 record in 1983, Simms finally got his chance when Parcells turned to him in the sixth game of the season. However, after completing seven of 13 passes, Simms suffered another season-ending injury when the thumb on his throwing hand hit a player's helmet on his follow-through, resulting in a compound fracture.

While recuperating from his latest injury, Simms put a lot of thought into his situation and how he might be able to improve it. Later referring to his benching as "the turning point"[3] of his career, Simms turned the doubts others had in him into a positive, suggesting, "Confidence is a funny thing. You can go around saying you have it, but you really don't until you have some success. There were times I thought I'd never have the chance to show what I thought I could do. There were other times I began to wonder if I was really as good as I thought I was, that I might not have what it takes to play in this league."[4]

During his period of inactivity, offensive coordinator Ron Erhardt convinced Simms that he might benefit from watching more game film, something he had not done regularly in college or the pros. Studying the tendencies of other teams, as well as his own, enabled Simms to gain a better understanding of NFL defenses, his team's formations, and pass-protection schemes, thereby improving his ability to audible at the line of scrimmage. Simms also changed his training regimen, making his body more resistant to injury by working out extensively with weights for the first time. In fact, he developed into more of a team leader by lifting weights with his offensive linemen. As running back Joe Morris noted, "When you got a quarterback out there sweating and working with his offensive linemen, joking with them, you have to know this guy is thinking about one thing: He's trying to win football games."[5]

Returning to the Giants fully healthy in 1984, Simms ended up starting every game for the team over the course of the next three seasons. Establishing himself as one of the league's top quarterbacks in his first full season, Simms passed for 4,044 yards and 22 touchdowns in 1984, en route to leading the Giants to a 9–7 record that earned them a spot in the playoffs.

Simms later recalled that Bill Parcells instructed him to play with reckless abandon, telling him before the team's first game in Philadelphia, "All right, Simms. If you don't throw at least two interceptions today, that means you're not trying enough. I need plays. Make some daring plays. Go for the big plays. Don't be afraid."[6]

The newfound confidence that Parcells placed in him enabled Simms to thrive as never before, with the two men consequently developing a relationship based on trust and mutual respect. Although they continued to share a love–hate relationship through the years, Simms expressed the underlying affection he and Parcells felt for one another when he said, "I knew he was gonna call for me one day . . . I just knew that. I let it go. And, to his great credit, he did too. See? Two stubborn people can make it work."[7]

Simms followed up his outstanding 1984 campaign with an equally productive year in 1985, throwing for 3,829 yards and 22 touchdowns, leading the Giants to a 10–6 record that earned them their second straight trip to the playoffs. Simms made his first Pro Bowl appearance at the end of the year, earning game MVP honors by throwing three touchdown passes during a 28–24 come-from-behind victory by the NFC over the AFC.

Simms compiled slightly less impressive numbers in 1986, passing for 3,487 yards and 21 touchdowns. But, with the Giants establishing themselves as a dominant defensive team that also featured an exceptional running game, Simms found himself playing within the context of a fairly conservative offensive scheme that stressed ball security and time of possession. The Giants also lacked dynamic wide receivers, placing further limitations on the level of creativity they were able to display on the offensive side of the ball. Nevertheless, Simms demonstrated an ability to make big plays when he needed to do so, leading his team to four game-winning drives and two fourth-quarter comebacks. Meanwhile, the Giants posted an NFL-best 14–2 record over the course of the regular season, before going on to win the Super Bowl. Recognizing the outstanding leadership and clutch passing Simms provided to the Giants during the season, the Newspaper Enterprise Association named him its NFL MVP and awarded him First-Team All-Pro honors.

Simms made an equally strong impression on his Giant teammates, who gave him much of the credit for the success they experienced all year long. Lawrence Taylor stated, "There was a time where I felt that the offense didn't have a leader. It was just a bunch of guys out there playing and trying not to lose a game. They really didn't have one person to tie them all together and to lead them anywhere. Phil has really taken on that responsibility, and he has done a very good job."[8]

Phil McConkey proclaimed, "I would rather have no other quarterback behind the center than Phil Simms, especially in those tight situations. The guy's proven over and over again he can get the job done, and, on offense, we have a lot of faith in him."[9]

Nose tackle Jim Burt expressed his admiration for Simms's perseverance by saying, "That's one tough guy. To go through what he's gone through. And the way he's kept his confidence."[10]

Meanwhile, GM George Young, who put his reputation on the line when he drafted the quarterback in the first round several years earlier, stated, "Here's a guy who's had to fight through adversity probably as much, or more, than anybody else . . . with a press that's been on him, and the fans have been on him. But he had to fight through it by himself, and I think that he willed himself into being an outstanding performer."[11]

Simms's mental and physical toughness also earned him the respect of Chicago Bears head coach Mike Ditka, who noted, "He holds the ball to the last second as well as anybody."[12]

After playing extremely well in both of New York's playoff wins, Simms led the Giants to victory in Super Bowl XXI by turning in one of the finest performances in Super Bowl history, completing 22 of 25 pass attempts and throwing for three touchdowns during a 39–20 win over the Broncos. Denver head coach Dan Reeves said after the contest, "The thing that's most impressive about Phil Simms is, when they put pressure on him to do something, he comes through for them."[13]

Although the Giants failed to return to the playoffs in either of the next two seasons, Simms continued to perform extremely well for them, compiling totals of 38 touchdown passes and only 20 interceptions, and

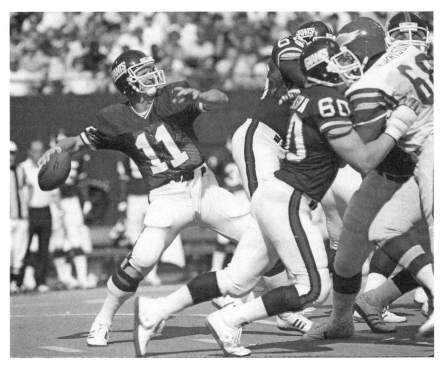

Simms retired as the Giants all-time leader in virtually every statistical category for quarterbacks.
Courtesy of Tony Mangia

ranking among the NFL leaders in quarterback passer rating both years. He subsequently led the Giants to a record of 12–4 that earned them a postseason berth in 1989, topping the 3,000-yard mark in passing for the fifth time in six years in the process. Simms followed that up with one of his finest seasons in 1990, leading the Giants to an 11–3 record in their first 14 contests, and topping all NFC quarterbacks with a 92.7 passer rating, before a broken foot brought his season to a premature end. The Giants, though, ended up beating the Buffalo Bills in Super Bowl XXV, with Jeff Hostetler doing an outstanding job filling in for the team's injured starting quarterback.

The subsequent resignation of Bill Parcells and hiring of Ray Handley as head coach resulted in Simms being relegated to backup duty in 1991. However, after beating out Hostetler for the starting job the following year, Simms suffered a severe arm injury during a week 4 loss to the Raiders, causing him to miss the remainder of the season.

After the Giants fired the unpopular Handley at the end of the 1992 campaign, new head coach Dan Reeves released Hostetler and named

Simms his starting quarterback. The 39-year-old veteran responded by having one of his finest seasons, leading the Giants to an 11–5 record and a spot in the playoffs by completing nearly 62 percent of his passes, throwing for 3,038 yards, and tossing 15 touchdown passes, en route to earning Pro Bowl honors for the second time in his career. Yet, in spite of Simms's outstanding performance, the Giants elected to release him during the off season, replacing him at quarterback with unproven third-year backup Dave Brown, who failed to live up to the team's expectations for him.

Choosing to announce his retirement following his release, Simms ended his playing career as the Giants' all-time leader in virtually every statistical category for quarterbacks, holding franchise records for most pass completions (2,576), most touchdown passes (199), and most passing yardage (33,462). Although Simms spent virtually his entire career being overshadowed by some of the other outstanding quarterbacks of the day, such as Joe Montana, Dan Marino, and John Elway, *Sports Illustrated* ranked him as the Most Underrated Quarterback in NFL History in its August 27, 2001, issue entitled "The Most Overrated and Underrated."

Since retiring as a player, Simms has established himself as one of television's leading football analysts, first working for ESPN, then for NBC, and currently for CBS. He also cohosts *Inside the NFL* on Showtime with James Brown and Cris Collinsworth.

CAREER HIGHLIGHTS

Best Season

Simms had his two most productive seasons in 1984 and 1985, throwing 22 touchdown passes in each of those campaigns, while passing for 4,044 and 3,829 yards, respectively. However, he threw 18 interceptions in 1984, before tossing another 20 the following year. Furthermore, his quarterback rating barely exceeded 78 in each of those years, while his completion percentage ranged from somewhere between 53 and 56 percent. Simms earned NFL MVP honors from the Newspaper Enterprise Association in 1986, when he led the Giants to a 14–2 record and the Super Bowl championship. But he posted extremely comparable numbers to the figures he compiled the previous two seasons, passing for slightly less yardage (3,487), throwing one fewer touchdown (21), tossing 22 interceptions, and finishing with a 55.3 completion percentage and a 74.6 quarterback rating.

Although Simms passed for fewer yards (3,038) and tossed fewer touchdown passes (15), he ironically posted better overall numbers in his final season of 1993. In addition to compiling a career-high 61.8 completion percentage, he threw only nine interceptions and posted a quarterback rating of 88.3. Nevertheless, the feeling here is that Simms had his best overall season in 1990, before a broken foot forced him to sit out the final two regular-season contests and the playoffs. En route to leading the Giants to an 11–3 record in the 14 games he started, Simms passed for 2,284 yards and 15 touchdowns, tossed only four interceptions, completed 59.2 percent of his passes, and posted a career-best 92.7 quarterback rating.

Memorable Moments/Greatest Performances

Simms had one of the biggest days of his career in the 1984 season opener, passing for 409 yards and four touchdowns during a 28–27 home win over the Philadelphia Eagles. Simms, who completed 23 of 30 passes on the day, hooked up with Zeke Mowatt, Byron Williams, and Bobby Johnson twice on four scoring plays that covered 24, 65, 35, and 16 yards, respectively.

Simms had another huge game one year later, this time against Dallas, passing for 432 yards and three touchdowns during a heartbreaking 30–29 loss to the Cowboys on October 6, 1985. His touchdown passes included a 51-yard strike to Lionel Manuel and a 70-yarder to George Adams. Simms established a new Giants record the following week, passing for 513 yards during a 35–30 loss to the Cincinnati Bengals.

However, Simms turned in his most memorable performances during the Giants' championship campaign of 1986, making arguably the biggest play of his career against the Vikings on November 16 of that year. With the Giants trailing Minnesota by a score of 20–19 with less than one minute left in the game, Simms found himself faced with a fourth down and 17 yards to go situation. Displaying great coolness under pressure, he subsequently fired a 22-yard strike to Bobby Johnson along the right sideline to keep New York's hopes alive. Simms then led the Giants into field goal position, enabling Raul Allegre to kick the game-winning three-pointer with only seconds left on the clock. Simms later commented, "It's my favorite game in my career, because it's everything I wanted to be as a player. I wanted to be tough, making big throws, immune to pressure, not worried about outcomes."[14]

The very next week, Simms completed a similar clutch pass against Denver, coming up big in a third-and-21 situation by firing a 46-yard strike to Phil McConkey over the middle. Allegre kicked a 34-yard field goal moments later, giving the Giants another last-second victory, this one by a score of 19–16. Simms also had a huge game against the 49ers in San Francisco on December 1, completing 27 of 38 passes for 388 yards and two touchdowns, leading the Giants to a come-from-behind 21–17 victory in a game they once trailed by a score of 17–0.

Nevertheless, there can be no doubting that Simms saved his finest performance for Super Bowl XXI. By completing 22 of 25 passes (with two of his three incompletions being drops by receivers), Simms set new Super Bowl records for consecutive completions (10), passing accuracy (88 percent), and passer rating (150.9). He finished the day with 268 yards passing and three touchdown tosses. When asked about his extraordinary performance, Simms responded, "As a quarterback, I don't ever feel the pressure. Big games . . . every game is the same, and every situation feels the same. You just do what you've been taught to do, almost like a robot. You just go out there and do it because you've done it hundreds of times in practice."[15]

NOTABLE ACHIEVEMENTS

- Passed for more than 3,000 yards six times, including one season with more than 4,000 yards (4,044 in 1984).
- First Giants quarterback to pass for more than 4,000 yards in a season.
- Surpassed 20 touchdown passes four times.
- Completed more than 60 percent of passes twice (1992, 1993).
- Posted quarterback rating of at least 90.0 twice (1987, 1990).
- Ranks second in Giants history in passing yardage, completions, and touchdown passes.
- Two-time NFC Offensive Player of the Week.
- Two-time Pro Bowl selection (1985, 1993).
- 1985 Pro Bowl MVP.
- 1986 Newspaper Enterprise Association First-Team All-Pro selection.
- 1986 Newspaper Enterprise Association NFL MVP.
- Two-time NFC champion (1986, 1990).
- Two-time Super Bowl champion (XXI, XXV).
- Super Bowl XXI MVP.

11

SAM HUFF

The Giants fielded one of the NFL's premier defenses during their glory years of the 1950s and early 1960s. Andy Robustelli, Rosey Grier, Dick Modzelewski, and Jim Katcavage combined to give the Giants as formidable a front four as any in the league, while Emlen Tunnell, Jimmy Patton, and Dick Lynch all starred in the secondary at one time or another. However, the man who tied everything together was Sam Huff, who represented the heart and soul of the Giants' defense in many ways. Mean and nasty, Huff proved to be as physical as any defender in the league, raising his teammates' level of intensity with his aggressive style of play. At the same time, the middle linebacker served as New York's quarterback on defense, calling all the signals on that side of the ball. Huff's exceptional play and outstanding on-field leadership helped the Giants compile an overall record of 73–25–4 from 1956 to 1963, during which time they made six appearances in the NFL Championship Game. Meanwhile, Huff earned four Pro Bowl nominations and five All-Pro selections over that eight-year stretch. Yet, had it not been for the foresight displayed by two of the Giants' offensive coaches in Huff's rookie season, the Hall of Fame linebacker likely never would have appeared in a single NFL game.

Born in Edna Gas, West Virginia, on October 4, 1934, Robert Lee Huff spent his early years in organized football playing on both the offensive and defensive lines at Farmington High School. After earning all-state honors in 1952, Huff received a football scholarship to the University of West Virginia, where he earned All-America honors as an offensive and defensive lineman. The Giants subsequently selected him in the third round of the 1956 NFL Draft with the 30th overall pick.

Although Huff impressed New York's coaching staff with his athletic ability after he joined the team for his first training camp, head coach Jim Lee Howell had a difficult time figuring out where to play him. Furthermore, Howell and offensive assistant Vince Lombardi alienated Huff and fellow rookie Don Chandler with their constant yelling and screaming.

Sam Huff anchored the Giants defense for eight seasons from his middle linebacker position.
Courtesy of SportsMemorabilia.com

Feeling discouraged and homesick, Huff and Chandler left training camp one evening and decided to head home. Fortunately for both men, assistant coaches Lombardi and Ed Kolman intercepted them at the airport and talked them out of leaving.

Considered to be a bit too small to play defensive tackle, Huff subsequently moved to the linebacker spot, where he found a home. Discussing how he got his start there, Huff revealed, "At first, the Giants didn't have any plans to play me as a linebacker. The position I wound up in had never been played because the 4–3 wasn't a standard defense up to that time. It was only an idea at first—football coaches were thinking about it. Tom Landry [Giants defensive coordinator] really started it, and we kind of grew together."[1]

The fact that Huff even got an opportunity to start at middle linebacker for the Giants was actually a matter of happenstance. He played the position for the first time in an exhibition game against the Cardinals after starting linebacker Ray Beck injured his ankle. Huff noted years later,

"Tom Landry put me in there, just as a stand-in. The position just seemed to blend in with whatever talents I had, and I loved playing it."[2]

Huff added, "I think I had the right personality [to play middle linebacker]. I think one of the first things you look for in a linebacker is personality, and I guess I had it . . . a fiercely competitive attitude. Wellington Mara once said I was the kind of guy who'd kick somebody in the head in order to win."[3]

Huff also possessed several other qualities that enabled him to excel at the position. At 6'1" and 235 pounds, he had the size and strength to take on opposing blockers and bring down most of the league's bigger running backs. Huff also had the quickness and agility to drop into pass coverage and stay with the vast majority of the league's swifter backs. Meanwhile, his unique ability to diagnose opponents' plays made him a disruptive force, and his superb peripheral vision allowed him to see the entire field.

Huff also had the good fortune to play behind arguably the NFL's most talented defensive line, to which he gave most of the credit for the tremendous success he experienced in New York when he said, "The defense was set up so the defensive linemen actually kept the blockers off of me. The easiest thing to do was to make tackles because those guys wouldn't let anybody hit me."[4]

The outstanding play of the linemen in front of him, combined with Huff's own natural gifts, enabled him to earn two First-Team All-Pro nominations and three Second-Team selections between 1956 and 1963, during which time the Giants advanced to the NFL Championship Game six times. Meanwhile, Huff helped glamorize the new position of middle linebacker, gaining much of his notoriety from his head-to-head confrontations with the league's top three running backs—Jim Brown of Cleveland, Rick Casares of Chicago, and Jim Taylor of Green Bay.

Speaking of his adversary, Brown said, "Sam was basically the quarterback of that defense, and he had the flair to understand that he was in New York. So he became an instant celebrity by attaching himself to my legs quite often."[5]

In 1959, Huff's growing popularity enabled him to become the first NFL player to be featured on the cover of *Time* magazine. The following year, CBS aired a documentary narrated by celebrated anchorman Walter Cronkite that was entitled *The Violent World of Sam Huff*.

However, an extraordinary era in New York football ended after the Giants lost to Chicago in the NFL Championship Game of 1963. Feeling that he needed to make changes to his roster, head coach Allie Sherman traded away five defensive starters, including Huff, whom he dealt to

Huff helped glamorize the position of middle linebacker in the NFL.
Courtesy of Albersheims.com

Washington for running back Dick James, defensive end Andy Stynchula, and a draft pick. Expressing his anger and sense of betrayal over the deal, Huff subsequently proclaimed, "As long as I live, I will never forgive Allie Sherman for trading me."[6]

Although Huff eventually learned to view the trade from a more logical perspective, he continued to harbor feelings of resentment toward Sherman, stating years later, "It was a terrible period in my life. I was really hurt. I felt terrible about leaving the players. They were my friends, my family—I had grown to love those guys. . . . The only thing that you have to go on as an athlete is your ability to play and win. And we always won. I don't think you can ask more of a player. We won the championship in '56, we went to sudden death in '58. The world champion Chicago Bears who we played in the '63 final—their offense never crossed the 50-yard line in the whole damn game . . . and then to trade off the defensive team . . . that's what hurts, when you do your best, you win, and yet these things happen. That hurt."[7]

Expressing his opinion as to why Sherman elected to trade half of his starting defensive unit, Huff said, "Allie Sherman was an offensive-oriented coach, and he didn't like us because we were Tom Landry's team that he put together defensively."[8]

Although Huff initially balked at the idea of joining the Redskins, he ended up spending five productive years in Washington, earning two First-Team All-Conference nominations and the last of his five Pro Bowl selections. He even exacted a measure of revenge against Sherman, galvanizing his teammates to rout the Giants by a final score of 72–41 on November 27, 1966, in what remains the highest-scoring game in NFL history.

After retiring at the end of the 1967 season, Huff returned for one more year when Vince Lombardi took over as head coach in Washington in 1969. Huff assumed the role of player-coach in his final year in the league, before retiring for good at season's end. He subsequently spent one season coaching Washington's linebacker, before joining the Giants' radio broadcast team as a color commentator. After three years in New York, Huff returned to Washington, where he assumed a similar position. He continued to serve in that capacity until 2012, when doctors discovered he had Alzheimer's disease.

GIANT CAREER HIGHLIGHTS

Best Season

Huff's outstanding play as a rookie in 1956 helped the Giants win the NFL title. Two years later, he earned First-Team All-Pro honors for the first of two straight times by helping the Giants advance to the NFL Championship Game, where they eventually lost to the Baltimore Colts in Sudden Death overtime. However, Huff reached the apex of his career in 1959, when he earned recognition as the NFL's Outstanding Lineman (linebackers at that time were still considered to be linemen). In addition to intercepting one pass, Huff recovered four fumbles, returning one of those for a touchdown. His exceptional play over the course of the regular season led the Giants to a 10–2 record that earned them their third championship game appearance in four years.

Memorable Moments/Greatest Performances

Huff made a number of big plays in his eight years with the Giants, including returning one of his 18 interceptions for a touchdown, returning two of his 11 fumble recoveries for scores, and blocking two punts in 1962. He also led a goal-line stand early in the second half of the 1958 Championship Game that prevented the Colts from increasing their 14–3 lead after they started first-and-goal from the Giants' three-yard line.

Nevertheless, Huff likely will always be remembered most for his confrontations with the great Jim Brown. In order to gain a berth in the 1958 title game against Baltimore, the Giants first had to meet Cleveland in a playoff contest to determine the Eastern Division champion. The Giants defeated the Browns by a score of 10–0, with Huff and company limiting Brown to only eight yards rushing, on seven attempts.

In another extraordinary effort, Huff and his teammates held Brown to just two yards rushing in the second half of a 37–21 win over Cleveland late in 1961. Huff also led a Giant defense that limited Brown to only 40 yards on nine rushes during a 33–6 win over the Browns in week 7 of the 1963 season.

NOTABLE ACHIEVEMENTS

- Named NFL's Outstanding Lineman in 1959.
- Most Valuable Player of 1961 Pro Bowl.
- Four-time Pro Bowl selection.
- Two-time First-Team All-Pro selection.
- Three-time Second-Team All-Pro selection.
- NFL 1950s All-Decade Team.
- Number 76 on the *Sporting News* 1999 list of 100 Greatest Players in NFL History.
- Number 93 on the NFL Network's 2010 list of Top 100 Players of All Time.
- Six-time NFL Eastern Division champion.
- 1956 NFL champion.
- Elected to Pro Football Hall of Fame in 1982.

12

— BRAD VAN PELT —

There likely will be some people who find Brad Van Pelt's lofty 12th-place finish in these rankings to be somewhat surprising. After all, the Giants posted a winning record just once in Van Pelt's 11 seasons with them, compiling an overall mark during that time of only 49–108–2. However, in spite of the Giants' failures as a team, Van Pelt played exceptionally well for them throughout the period, excelling at outside linebacker against both the run and the pass. An opposing tight end's worst nightmare, the 6'5", 235-pound Van Pelt possessed the size, speed, and agility to blanket the NFL's best pass receivers at the position. Meanwhile, in spite of his lanky frame, he also had the strength and quickness to bring down opposing ball carriers near the line of scrimmage. Teaming up with Harry Carson, Brian Kelley, and, later, Lawrence Taylor, Van Pelt became a celebrated member of New York's Crunch Bunch, a fierce group of linebackers that gained general recognition as one of the best linebacking combos in NFL history. Van Pelt's contributions to the unit ended up earning him five Pro Bowl nominations and acknowledgment from the Giants as their player of the decade for the 1970s.

Born in Owosso, Michigan, on April 5, 1951, Bradley Alan Van Pelt proved to be an exceptional all-around athlete during his teenage years, starring in baseball, basketball, and on both offense and defense in football at Owosso High School. After earning all-state honors at quarterback and first-team all-league honors in basketball and baseball at Owosso, Van Pelt found himself being courted by the Detroit Tigers and California Angels when he graduated in 1969. However, choosing to further his education by attending Michigan State University, the 18-year-old Van Pelt declined both offers.

Playing for legendary Spartans coach Duffy Daugherty, Van Pelt earned All-America honors as a safety his last two years at Michigan State. In his senior year, he also became the first defensive player to win the Maxwell Award, presented annually to the nation's best player.

Despite playing for some terrible teams, Brad Van Pelt earned five trips to the Pro Bowl.
Courtesy of PristineAuction.com

Ordinarily, Van Pelt's exceptional college play would have made him an early first-round selection in the 1973 NFL draft. However, with the St. Louis Cardinals already having drafted him as a pitcher, concerns remained as to whether Van Pelt would instead choose a career in baseball. As a result, the All-America safety lasted into the second round, where the Giants selected him with the 40th overall pick. Team owner Wellington Mara subsequently visited Van Pelt's family in Owosso and convinced him to sign with the Giants rather than the Cardinals.

Although Van Pelt had good foot speed, the Giants believed that his size made him better suited to play linebacker in the NFL. Therefore, after he arrived at his first training camp, they shifted him to the left outside linebacker spot, where he typically lined up against the opposing team's tight end. Van Pelt struggled somewhat with the various nuances of his new position his first year in the league, failing to earn a starting job until late in the season. However, he developed into one of the team's top players the following year, establishing himself as a mainstay at the position by intercepting two passes and recovering two fumbles.

Possessing an unusual combination of athleticism and physicality, Van Pelt gradually evolved into one of the NFL's best linebackers in subsequent seasons, earning five consecutive Pro Bowl selections from 1976 to 1980. Excelling as both a pass-defender and a run-stopper, Van Pelt combined with Harry Carson during that period to give the Giants the NFC's top linebacking tandem. Meanwhile, fellow linebacker Brian Kelley, defensive end George Martin, and nose tackle John Mendenhall helped the duo restore New York's defense to prominence in the league, even though the Giants' failures on the offensive side of the ball relegated them to a losing record each season.

Van Pelt ended up spending 11 years in New York, playing for five different head coaches during that time. Although the Giants made the playoffs in 1981 by posting a record of 9–7 under coach Ray Perkins, they also compiled marks of 2–11–1, 2–12, 3–11, and 3–12–1 in other years under coaches Alex Webster, Bill Arnsparger, John McVay, and Bill Parcells, respectively. Yet, through it all, Van Pelt continued to play exceptionally well, intercepting 18 passes as a member of the Giants, while also annually ranking among the team leaders in tackles. And, even though he usually dropped into pass coverage in passing situations, Van Pelt also recorded 19.5 sacks as a Giant.

The drafting of Carl Banks in 1984 essentially marked the end of Van Pelt's time in New York, prompting the Giants to trade the 33-year-old veteran to the Vikings for running back Tony Galbreath. Failing to make an impression in Minnesota, Van Pelt subsequently moved to Oakland, where he spent the next two years playing for the Raiders, before ending his career with the Cleveland Browns in 1986. Over the course of his last three seasons, Van Pelt intercepted two more passes and recorded five more sacks, giving him 20 picks and an "unofficial" total of 24.5 sacks for his career, thereby making him a member of the fairly exclusive 20/20 club. Meanwhile, in a bit of irony, the Giants won the NFL Championship in 1986, Van Pelt's final year in the league.

Always feeling the tug of home, Van Pelt went back to Michigan State following his playing career and earned a degree in kinesiology, the branch of physiology that deals with human movement. He also remained extremely close to his former Crunch Bunch buddies, Harry Carson, Brian

Kelley, and Lawrence Taylor, frequently talking to them on the phone, playing golf with them, and attending memorabilia signing events with them. Van Pelt was quoted back in 2004 as saying, "I feel as comfortable with them [Carson, Kelley, and Taylor] as I do with my brothers. Obviously, your brothers are your brothers. But these three are probably the closest thing to them. Brian and I played 11 years together. I played nine with Harry. Lawrence being the guy he is, it didn't take long for him to fit right in and become one of the guys. I can't really explain why, but they're the only three I stay close with."[1]

Sadly, Van Pelt's longtime friendship with his three former teammates came to an end on February 17, 2009, when his fiancée of many years discovered him slumped in a chair at their home in Harrison, Michigan, dead from an apparent heart attack. Brad Van Pelt was only 57 years of age at the time of his passing.

Shocked by the news of his close friend's passing, Brian Kelley stated:

> It was total devastation. I've known Brad since '73—36 years. I've known him longer than my wife and my kids. Football was 11 years of our life. We had 25 other years when we were together, did things together, and still are doing them together—us and LT and Harry Carson. It's sort of like losing a limb because the four of us are so close. To lose one of us is tough. It's even tough to believe it happened. . . . I'm just going to miss him, miss seeing him at Giants games, miss him calling me about stupid stuff.[2]

Kelley added, "He didn't deserve this. He was just a good person, such a great guy who would give you the shirt off his back. He didn't own a lot of things. . . . He wasn't material. My wife nailed it when she said he had the Peter Pan Syndrome. He just never wanted to grow up."[3]

Kelley, who called Lawrence Taylor to inform him of the sad news, stated that all LT found himself able to say was, "No, no, no."[4]

Upon hearing of Van Pelt's passing, Giants owner John Mara, who called the former linebacker one of the greatest players in team history, said, "If you look at those years, our teams were as bad as could possibly be. We really had some awful teams in the 1970s. He was the one guy who was consistently a good player. It's a shame he left us before our climb back to respectability. I always felt bad he couldn't share in that success."[5]

Meanwhile, Harry Carson expressed his sadness over losing his close friend by saying, "He was a classic teammate who was always there for you. The thing I will remember more than anything else was his friendship and

Van Pelt's outstanding all-around play earned him recognition as the Giants' Player of the Decade for the 1970s.
Courtesy of SportsMemorabilia.com

the times we spent together after football. Those are the things I'll treasure more than anything else."[6]

Speaking of the years they spent together on the football field, Carson stated, "We had success as a group. As a team, we did not have it. But we took great pride in the way that we played the game together."[7]

Once again addressing his loss, Carson said, "I know how he feels about me, and I think he knows how I feel about him, so all is good."[8]

GIANT CAREER HIGHLIGHTS

Best Season

Van Pelt was named First-Team All-Conference by a major news wire service in three different seasons—1976, 1977, and 1979. However, he earned his only "official" First-Team selection by the Associated Press in the first of those years, when he intercepted two passes and recovered two fumbles. Since the Giants posted a record of only 3–11 in 1976 (they finished 5–9 in 1977 and 6–10 in 1979), Van Pelt likely had the least amount of talent surrounding him that year. That being the case, we'll go with 1976, even though any of his Pro Bowl years actually would have made a good choice.

Memorable Moments/Greatest Performances

Van Pelt recorded his first career interception during a 13–10 loss to the Washington Redskins in the 1974 season opener. He registered the first two-interception game of his career more than two years later, picking off a pair of Greg Landry passes during a 24–10 victory over the Detroit Lions on December 5, 1976, that gave the Giants just their third win of the year, against 10 losses. Van Pelt duplicated his earlier effort against Dallas on November 9, 1980, intercepting two Danny White passes during a 38–35 Giants win over the heavily favored Cowboys. Van Pelt also turned in a key interception against the Redskins on October 22, 1978, picking off a Joe Theismann pass and returning it 20 yards during a 17–6 win over Washington that improved the Giants' record to 5–3.

However, Van Pelt's two most notable plays, at least from a personal perspective, occurred during the 1979 campaign. The first of those took place during a 24–14 loss to the Saints, when he hooked up with punter Dave Jennings on a 20-yard pass play following a fake punt. The reception proved to be the only one of Van Pelt's career. He also made a career-long 42-yard return off a recovered fumble at one point during the season.

NOTABLE ACHIEVEMENTS

- Member of 20/20 club (20 interceptions and 24½ sacks).
- Five-time Pro Bowl selection (1976–1980).
- Three-time First-Team All-Conference selection.
- Two-time Second-Team All-Conference selection.
- 1970s Player of Decade for Giants.

13

LEONARD MARSHALL

Excelling against both the run and the pass, Leonard Marshall established himself during his 10 years in a Giants uniform as one of the NFL's finest all-around defensive linemen. After coming to the Giants out of LSU in 1983, Marshall went on to accumulate a total of 79½ sacks over the next 10 seasons, placing him third on the team's "official" all-time sack list. The 6'3", 285-pound defensive end also played the run extremely well, amassing 660 tackles as a member of the Giants. The combination of Marshall and Lawrence Taylor gave the Giants a formidable right side to their defensive front, helping them advance to the playoffs five times in the 10 years the two men played together. New York also won two NFL championships during that time, with Marshall earning Pro Bowl and All-Pro honors two times each. Marshall accomplished all he did as a member of the Giants despite leading some members of the organization to believe that he had a very good chance of eating his way out of the NFL when he first entered the league in 1983.

Born in Franklin, Louisiana, on October 22, 1961, Leonard Allen Marshall decided to pursue a career in football even though his father told him relatively early in life that he considered it to be a stupid game that would prevent him from doing more productive things. Failing to heed his father's advice, Marshall went on to star at defensive end for Louisiana State University, where he also obtained a degree in business management. While at LSU, Marshall helped the Tigers defeat Alabama in their 1982 matchup, prompting legendary Alabama head coach Bear Bryant to subsequently express his regret during a postgame press conference that he failed to recruit the defensive end for his own team.

After one more year at LSU, Marshall became a member of the Giants when they selected him in the second round of the 1983 NFL Draft, with the 37th overall pick. Marshall entered the NFL with a bit of an attitude, stating years later, "I came into camp as a rookie thinking no one was tougher than I was. I figured I was going to come in and kick some tails."[1]

Leonard Marshall's total of 79½ career sacks places him third in team
annals.
Courtesy of SportsMemorabilia.com

However, Marshall instead found himself drawing derision from New
York's coaching staff when he appeared at his first training camp weighing
a bulky 305 pounds. Giants head coach Bill Parcells commented, "We're
going to have to weigh him at the truck station on the turnpike."[2] Meanwhile, a club executive remarked, "We put Leonard on the Cambridge Diet
and he ate half of Cambridge."[3]

The criticism resonated with Marshall, who quickly changed his ways.
Instead of frequenting fast-food restaurants, as he previously did, the rookie
started eating broiled chicken and fish, reducing his body fat from 17.5 to
14.8 percent in the process. He also lost more than 20 pounds, turning
himself into a solid 6'3", 282-pounder. Giants strength and conditioning
coach Johnny Parker later said, "He [Marshall] was one of the hardest-
working guys we had."[4]

Despite working himself into top shape, Marshall made only a minimal impact his first year in the league, recording just 39 tackles and ½ sack. However, he developed into the Giants' top defensive lineman in his second season, making 60 tackles and sacking opposing quarterbacks 6½ times. Marshall improved upon those numbers in 1985, registering a career-high 99 tackles and finishing third in the NFL with 15½ sacks, en route to earning Pro Bowl and Second-Team All-Pro honors for the first of two consecutive times. His outstanding performance prompted the league's players to vote him NFL Defensive Lineman of the Year.

Looking back at the vast improvement he displayed over the course of his first three seasons, Marshall later said, "Pass rushing was like calculus to me when I first got here. It was a phase of the game I had to learn. In 1985, I feel like I got my degree."[5]

Marshall continued to perform at an extremely high level in 1986, making 63 tackles and recording 12 sacks, despite being double-teamed on almost every play. Giants left tackle Brad Benson, who earned a considerable amount of praise for shutting out Washington's Dexter Manley in a critical late-season matchup, said following the contest, "After going against Lenny in practice, Manley was easy."[6]

Although Marshall failed to make the Pro Bowl in any of the next three seasons, he remained one of the NFL's best all-around defensive linemen, compiling a total of 25½ sacks from 1987 to 1989. In the last of those years, he also recorded 81 tackles and the second safety of his career. A lengthy preseason holdout caused Marshall to report late to the Giants in 1990, hampering his performance for much of the year. Yet, he still managed to register 50 tackles and 4½ sacks in helping the Giants advance to the NFC Championship Game, where they faced the two-time defending Super Bowl champion San Francisco 49ers. Marshall made the most famous sack of his career in that contest, forcing Joe Montana to leave the game in the fourth quarter by hitting him from behind so hard that the Hall of Fame quarterback suffered a bruised sternum, a bruised stomach, cracked ribs, and a broken hand.

Marshall remained with the Giants two more years, performing particularly well for them in 1991, when he recorded 80 tackles and 11 sacks. However, he clashed with new head coach Ray Handley during that time, getting into a well-publicized shouting match with him during halftime of a game against the Dallas Cowboys early in 1992. Choosing to test the free-agent market at the end of that 1992 campaign, Marshall subsequently spent the next season with the Jets before moving on to Washington, where he closed out his playing career in 1994. With his heart still in New York,

Marshall earned NFL Defensive Lineman of the Year honors in 1985 by recording 15½ sacks and 99 tackles.
Courtesy of SportsMemorabilia.com

Marshall signed a ceremonial contract with the Giants in 1996 that enabled him to retire as a member of the team. Upon signing the contract, Marshall stated, "I wanted to retire as a Giant because it's where my career began. They were people who believed in my talents and helped mold me into the man I am today, and I wanted to thank them for that."[7]

Marshall ended his career with 83½ regular season sacks, and another 12 in the postseason. His total of 79½ sacks as a member of the Giants places him third on the team's "official" all-time sack list (he ranks fifth on their "unofficial" list). Marshall averaged nearly 10 sacks and 72 tackles per season from 1985 to 1992.

Following his playing career, Marshall spent time working as a business entrepreneur and a radio personality before becoming a professor of sports management and an executive-in-residence at Seton Hall University. He also runs an annual instructional camp for youth football players in south Florida.

Unfortunately, Marshall was diagnosed with chronic traumatic encephalopathy (CTE) in 2013, a degenerative brain disease afflicting many retired football players that has been linked to repeated head trauma. Marshall says that he began to notice symptoms such as memory loss, severe headaches, and mood swings as early as 2006. However, he also states that his quality of life has improved dramatically since February 2016, when he began using cannabidiol, a chemical extract of the cannabis plant, to treat his symptoms.

GIANT CAREER HIGHLIGHTS

Best Season

Marshall made huge contributions to the Giants over the course of the 1986 championship campaign, recording 12 sacks and 63 tackles, intercepting a pass, forcing three fumbles, and recovering three others. He also had outstanding years in 1989 and 1991, registering 9½ sacks and 81 tackles in the first of those campaigns, and compiling 11 sacks and 80 tackles in the second. Nevertheless, there is little doubt that Marshall played his best ball in 1985, establishing career highs with 15½ sacks and 99 tackles, en route to earning NFL Defensive Lineman of the Year honors.

Memorable Moments/Greatest Performances

Marshall really came into his own during the latter stages of the 1984 campaign, performing particularly well in the Giants' 16–13 win over the Los Angeles Rams in the wild-card playoff round. The second-year defensive end recorded several key tackles during the contest, including four solo stops in the Los Angeles backfield.

Continuing to build on the momentum he created late in 1984, Marshall turned in a dominant performance in the 1985 season opener, helping the Giants defeat the Philadelphia Eagles 21–0 by recording 3½ sacks. He again dominated Philadelphia's offensive line three weeks later, registering another three sacks during a 16–10 overtime victory by the Giants.

Marshall also played extremely well in each of New York's first two Super Bowl appearances. He recorded two sacks and recovered a fumble during the Giants' 39–20 victory over Denver in Super Bowl XXI. Four years later, Marshall registered a sack of Buffalo quarterback Jim Kelly during New York's 20–19 win over the Bills in Super Bowl XXV.

Still, it is Marshall's sack of Joe Montana in the 1990 NFC Championship Game for which he is best remembered. With the Giants trailing San Francisco by a score of 13–9 early in the fourth quarter, Marshall hit Montana from behind, jarring the ball loose, and knocking the 49er quarterback out of the contest. The Giants subsequently scored on a field goal before advancing to the Super Bowl on a last-second three-pointer by placekicker Matt Bahr. Marshall's hit on Montana, which caused the quarterback multiple injuries and effectively ended his time in San Francisco, was ranked in 2007 as the third most "devastating hit" in NFL history by Fox Sports Net. Marshall concluded the contest with four tackles, two sacks, and two forced fumbles, earning in the process NFL Defensive Player of the Week honors. Looking back years later on his blindside hit of Montana that ushered in the Steve Young era in San Francisco, Marshall said, "It was one of those situations where I was not trying to make a play to injure or hurt him. I was trying to make a football play to help my team win, and it just happened. It was his calling and my destiny to make a football play. It definitely had an impact on his situation in a negative way, and you hate to see things happen to a guy like that."[8]

NOTABLE ACHIEVEMENTS

- Finished in double-digits in sacks three times, compiling as many as 15 once (15½ in 1985).
- Surpassed 80 tackles three times.
- Finished third in NFL with 15½ sacks in 1985.
- Ranks third all-time on Giants' "official" list with 79½ quarterback sacks.
- Two-time Pro Bowl selection.
- 1985 First-Team All-NFC selection.
- 1986 Second-Team All-NFC selection.
- Two-time Second-Team All-Pro selection (1985, 1986).
- 1985 NFL Defensive Lineman of the Year.
- Two-time NFC champion (1986, 1990).
- Two-time Super Bowl champion (XXI, XXV).

14

CARL BANKS

Despite being overshadowed by Lawrence Taylor his entire time in New York, Carl Banks established himself as one of the greatest linebackers in Giants history. A key contributor to five playoff teams and two NFL championship squads, Banks manned the left outside linebacker spot for the Giants for nine seasons, proving to be the perfect complement to Taylor on the other side of New York's defense. An exceptional run-defender and strong pass-rusher, Banks led the Giants in tackles three times, while also amassing a total of 36 quarterback sacks while playing for Big Blue. Although he appeared in only one Pro Bowl and made First-Team All-Pro just once, Banks played at such a high level that he eventually earned a spot on the NFL 1980s All-Decade Team. Yet, early in his career, it appeared that Banks might never fulfill his enormous potential.

Born in Flint, Michigan, on August 29, 1962, Carl Banks spent his teenage years idolizing two of the NFL's premier outside linebackers—Brad Van Pelt of the Giants and Jack Ham of the Pittsburgh Steelers. Banks, in fact, ended up following Van Pelt to Michigan State, earning All-America honors with the Spartans, before being selected by the Giants with the third overall pick of the 1984 NFL Draft. Although the linebacker position proved to be one of the few strengths for a Giants team that finished the 1983 campaign with a dismal 3–12–1 record, head coach Bill Parcells considered Banks to be too good to pass up after he watched him perform at the Senior Bowl. Commenting on the impression Banks made on him the first time he saw him play, Parcells stated, "I spent six or seven minutes looking at him and never looked at him again. What's the use, unless you wanted to drool? Some things are obvious to you."[1]

Although Banks arrived at his first Giants training camp amid a considerable amount of fanfare, many people wondered exactly how the team intended to use him. Banks recalled several years later, "Everybody was saying, 'Sure, he's a good player, but where's he going to play?' It was kind

Carl Banks proved to be the perfect complement to Lawrence Taylor on the left side of the Giants' defense.
Courtesy of MearsonlineAuctions.com

of hard to hear. You're a first-round draft pick, but people keep talking you down. But I knew I'd fit in."[2]

It actually took Banks a considerable amount of time to become a full-time starter on the Giants defense. Primarily a run-stuffer in college, he ended up splitting time with Byron Hunt at the left outside linebacker position his first two seasons, usually giving way to the latter in passing situations. However, after making only nine starts the previous two years, Banks laid claim to the starting job in 1986, after which he went on to lead the team with 120 tackles. He also recorded 6½ sacks, prompting Lawrence Taylor to say, "I'm so proud of him. Every time you see him play, you say, 'Someone's got to be kidding that this guy didn't make All-Pro.'"[3]

Taylor added, "We feel Carl is an All-Pro, or should be. Some of the other guys get the recognition, but nobody plays the run better than Banks."[4]

Meanwhile, left defensive end George Martin said of the 6'4", 235-pound Banks, "I think he's added balance to our defense. Whereas, before, we had a lot of dominant ballplayers predominantly on our right side, Carl has balanced that out, and it's made us a more effective defense overall."[5]

The presence of Banks on the opposite side of Taylor and right defensive end Leonard Marshall did indeed give the Giants tremendous balance along their defensive front. Teaming up with Taylor, Harry Carson, and Gary Reasons, Banks also gave New York the best linebacking crew in the NFL, forming what came to be known as the Big Blue Wrecking Crew.

As well as Banks played over the course of the 1986 regular season, he improved upon his performance once the playoffs started, accumulating a total of 30 tackles in the Giants' three postseason victories. He began his exceptional run by making seven tackles and dominating San Francisco tight end Russ Francis at the point of attack during New York's 49–3 first-round playoff win over the 49ers. Following the contest, Banks downplayed his performance, stating, "I've had more tackles in a game. I guess I made a few big plays that made me stand out. I led a pretty good defense in tackles. Not making the Pro Bowl doesn't take away from anything I've accomplished."[6]

Banks followed that up with equally impressive efforts against Washington in the NFC Championship Game and Denver in the Super Bowl, leading the Giants in tackles in both of those contests as well.

After being denied a spot in the Pro Bowl the previous year, Banks made it impossible for the voters to ignore him a second time when he registered 101 tackles and a career-high nine sacks in only 12 games during the strike-shortened 1987 campaign. In addition to being named to the Pro Bowl, Banks earned First-Team All-Pro honors.

A lengthy preseason holdout caused Banks to miss all of training camp the following year, adversely affecting his performance in 1988. After signing a $3.6 million, four-year contract one week prior to the start of the regular season, Banks reported to the Giants out of shape and subsequently suffered a bruised knee, a bruised shoulder, and a sprained wrist that further hampered his play throughout the campaign. Failing to live up to the high expectations he set for himself, Banks finished the year with only 62 tackles and 1½ sacks.

Looking back at his poor performance, Banks later stated, "It was hell last year. I was struggling. I'd look at things on film and I just couldn't believe I was playing that way. But there were several factors involved, and I got everything ironed out."[7]

Rebounding in 1989, Banks recorded four quarterback sacks, one interception, and a team-leading 89 tackles. After watching film of Banks at one point during the season prior to his team's meeting with the Giants, Oakland Raiders head coach Art Shell noted, "He's so strong at the point of attack. We go over their personnel as a coaching staff, and, by the time

Banks led the Giants in tackles three times.
Courtesy of MearsonlineAuctions.com

[assistant coach] Terry Robiskie got done talking about their outside line-backers, I said, 'You mean we can't run the ball at all? We might as well go home.'"[8]

Banks also became more of a team leader over the course of the 1989 campaign, after his teammates voted him and Lawrence Taylor defensive co-captains following the offseason retirement of Harry Carson. In speaking of his newfound responsibility, Banks stated, "Normally, I'm not an outspoken type of guy because I try to lead by example. Upon being named captain, I didn't feel like I had to change anything because the guys chose me captain for the man that I am."[9]

A broken wrist limited Banks to only nine games and 50 tackles in 1990. Nevertheless, he proved to be a key contributor down the stretch as the Giants defeated Chicago and San Francisco in the playoffs, before upsetting Buffalo in Super Bowl XXV.

Banks spent two more years with the Giants before signing a three-year contract with the rival Washington Redskins at the conclusion of the 1992 campaign. Even though Banks made 102 tackles for the Redskins in 1993, they released him at the end of the year. He subsequently joined the Browns, spending his final two seasons in Cleveland before retiring at the end of 1995. Banks ended his 12-year career with more than 800 tackles, 39½ sacks, three interceptions, and six fumble recoveries. He also scored two touchdowns. In addition to recording 36 sacks in his nine seasons with the Giants, he made nearly 650 tackles.

Following his retirement, Banks served briefly as the director of player development for the New York Jets before beginning a successful career as a radio personality. One of the voices of Sirius NFL Radio and WFAN, Banks also began serving as an analyst for Giants radio broadcasts in 2007. A successful businessman as well, Banks is now president of his own clothing line, G-III Sports by Carl Banks.

Although Banks spent the final three years of his career playing for other teams, he still considers himself to be very much a member of the Giants family, stating, "'Once a Giant always a Giant' means that you played for one of the best organizations, the best ownership, and it means that you embody a sense of pride in putting on a New York Giants uniform."[10]

GIANT CAREER HIGHLIGHTS

Best Season

Banks played exceptionally well for the Giants in 1986, particularly during the latter stages of the campaign. In addition to leading the team with 120 tackles, he recorded 6½ quarterback sacks. He also made 13 of his 120 tackles behind the line of scrimmage. Continuing to get better as the year wore on, Banks subsequently amassed a team-leading 30 tackles in New York's three postseason victories.

Yet, in spite of Banks's outstanding performance over the course of the 1986 championship campaign, it could be argued that he played even better the following year. Appearing in only 12 games during the strike-shortened 1987 season, Banks registered a team-leading 101 tackles and a career-high nine sacks, en route to earning his only Pro Bowl selection. He also earned unanimous First-Team All-Pro honors.

Memorable Moments/Greatest Performances

Banks made his first NFL start a memorable one, recording 10 tackles, two sacks, and a fumble recovery during a 19–7 win over the Atlanta Falcons on October 14, 1984.

The two touchdowns Banks scored during his career would also have to rank among his most memorable moments. He scored the first of those on October 23, 1988, once again helping the Giants defeat the Falcons by returning an interception 15 yards for the only defensive touchdown of his career. He recorded his only offensive TD one year later, hooking up with backup quarterback Jeff Hostetler on a 22-yard scoring pass that came off a fake field goal attempt during a 21–19 loss to Philadelphia on October 8, 1989.

However, Giants fans will always remember Banks most fondly for his extraordinary play throughout the 1986 postseason. Excelling first against San Francisco during New York's 49–3 first-round massacre of the 49ers, Banks made seven tackles and pressured Joe Montana into a second-quarter interception that led to a Joe Morris touchdown. Banks followed that up by making nine tackles against Washington in the NFC Championship Game. Assuming the injured Lawrence Taylor's pass-rushing duties during that contest, he also put constant pressure on quarterback Jay Schroeder, helping the Giants post a 17–0 victory over the Redskins. Banks then punctuated his exceptional postseason by making a team-leading 14 tackles, four of those for losses, against Denver in the Super Bowl. Looking back at his performance in Super Bowl XXI, Banks said:

> When we won, the memory was just how close I realized I was to becoming Super Bowl MVP. Phil Simms was almost perfect that game, with just three incompletions. If I had to say what was the best game I ever played, it was that game. I might have made the

first seven or eight tackles of the game, including a big goal-line stand. [Banks stopped Broncos running back Sammy Winder for a loss during a key goal-line stand in the first half.] That's the game I'll always remember. It played out almost to the tee of the way I dreamed it.[11]

NOTABLE ACHIEVEMENTS

- Surpassed 100 tackles twice (1986, 1987).
- Recorded nine sacks in 1987.
- Led Giants in tackles three times.
- Ranks tenth all-time on Giants' "official" list with 36 quarterback sacks.
- 1987 Week 13 NFC Defensive Player of the Week.
- 1987 Pro Bowl selection.
- 1987 First-Team All-Pro selection.
- 1987 First-Team All-NFC selection.
- NFL 1980s All-Decade Team.
- Two-time NFC champion (1986, 1990).
- Two-time Super Bowl champion (XXI, XXV).

15

— TIKI BARBER —

Based purely on playing ability and contributions made to the Giants on the football field, Tiki Barber deserves a higher place in these rankings—at the very least, a spot somewhere in the top 10. After all, Barber holds virtually every Giants career and single-season rushing record. One of the most dynamic offensive players in the franchise's rich history, Barber also excelled as a pass receiver, ranking among the team's all-time leaders in receptions and reception yardage. Barber even did an outstanding job of returning punts early in his career, before he eventually found a home in the Giants' starting backfield. However, Barber also proved to be a disruptive force during his time in New York, publicly criticizing his team's coaching staff on more than one occasion and agitating many of his teammates with his narcissistic nature, selfish attitude, and penchant for self-promotion. Furthermore, in spite of the gaudy numbers Barber posted year after year, the manner in which he questioned Eli Manning's leadership ability stunted the latter's development into an elite quarterback, perhaps explaining why the Giants won the NFL Championship the year after Barber announced his retirement. That being the case, I considered it inappropriate to place Barber any higher than 15th on this list, behind several other players he likely would have finished ahead of otherwise.

Born in Roanoke, Virginia, on April 7, 1975, Atiim Kiambu Hakeem-Ah "Tiki" Barber starred at the University of Virginia before being selected by the Giants in the second round of the 1997 NFL Draft with the 36th overall pick. Viewed initially by the Giants as a "change of pace" back who seemed likely to make his greatest impact on third-down passing situations, Barber spent much of his first three seasons returning punts and kickoffs, carrying the ball a total of only 250 times, for just 935 yards. However, he proved to be quite effective coming out of the backfield, making 142 receptions, for more than 1,250 yards and six touchdowns.

With the retirement of Rodney Hampton and the subsequent failure of Ron Dayne to live up to his Heisman Trophy billing, Barber established

Tiki Barber amassed more yards on the ground than anyone else in franchise history.
Courtesy of Rick Sparacino

himself as the Giants' primary running threat in 2000, helping them cap-ture the NFC title by rushing for 1,006 yards and eight touchdowns, while also making 70 receptions, for another 719 yards and one touchdown. Yet Barber also fumbled the ball nine times, a trend that continued in each of the next three seasons as well, until Tom Coughlin assumed head coaching duties in 2004 and cured Barber of his fumbling woes by teaching him how to better protect the ball. Injuries forced Barber to miss two games in 2001, limiting him to 865 yards rushing. Nevertheless, he managed to make a career-high 72 pass receptions for another 577 yards, giving him well over 1,000 yards from scrimmage for the second of seven consecutive times.

Barber developed into one of the NFL's elite running backs in 2002, beginning an extraordinarily successful five-year run that saw him gain more yards from scrimmage than any other player in the league. Barber rushed for 1,387 yards, caught 69 passes, scored 11 touchdowns, and estab-lished a new Giants record by amassing 1,984 yards from scrimmage in 2002. He followed that up by rushing for 1,216 yards, making another 69 receptions, and accumulating 1,677 yards from scrimmage in 2003. Still, the best had yet to come.

The arrival of Tom Coughlin in 2004 helped Barber correct the one glaring weakness in his game. In spite of his impressive rushing and receiving totals, Barber exasperated Giants fans at times with his propensity for fumbling the ball—something he did a total of 35 times between 2000 and 2003. However, Coughlin rectified that situation by teaching Barber to hold the ball vertically instead of horizontally, reducing the running back's total number of fumbles to only nine over the course of the next three seasons. Meanwhile, Barber also began to focus more on strength training in 2004, spending more time in the weight room than in previous seasons. As a result, the speedy and elusive Barber, who previously depended mostly on his quickness, cutback ability, and superior running vision, became a more powerful runner, better suited to break tackles and more adept at delivering punishment to defenders who stood in his path. The Giants also put together a more formidable offensive line under Coughlin, enabling Barber to flourish as never before.

Barber reached the zenith of his career in his final three years in New York, surpassing 1,500 yards rushing and 2,000 yards from scrimmage each season. He established a new Giants record by rushing for 1,518 yards in 2004. Barber also scored 15 touchdowns that year and broke his own team record that he had set two years earlier by amassing a league-leading 2,096 yards from scrimmage. In addition to scoring another 11 touchdowns the following year, Barber rushed for a career-high 1,860 yards and again led the NFL in yards from scrimmage, this time with a total of 2,390. His extraordinary performance earned him Pro Bowl honors for the second of three straight times, the only First-Team All-Pro nomination of his career, and a fourth-place finish in the league MVP voting. After announcing his intention to retire at the conclusion of the 2006 campaign early in the year, Barber went out in style, rushing for 1,662 yards, amassing 2,127 yards from scrimmage, and scoring five touchdowns. Barber ended his career with 10,449 yards rushing and 15,632 yards from scrimmage—both Giants records. He also ranks among the team's all-time leaders with 68 touchdowns, 586 receptions, and 5,183 receiving yards.

Yet, in spite of his many individual accomplishments, Barber left New York a somewhat unpopular figure, especially with his teammates, due to the controversial nature of several comments he made during his career. Barber incurred the wrath of a number of Giants players for the first time in 2002, when he criticized Michael Strahan for holding out for more money following the latter's record-setting performance the previous season. Calling Strahan greedy, Barber suggested that his teammate should have accepted the Giants' initial offer since it would have helped the team get under the salary cap. Barber told the *New York Post* at the time:

Barber twice led the NFL in total yards from scrimmage.
Courtesy of SportsMemorabilia.com

That is absolutely ridiculous, to turn that down. He's already the highest-paid defensive player in the league. He's already making more than most quarterbacks. . . . You got to realize no single player, I don't care how good you are, how many sacks you had, or how many yards you've rushed for, is bigger than the team, period. Michael is not thinking about the team; he's thinking about himself.[1]

Keith Hamilton, one of Strahan's defensive line-mates, subsequently expressed his dissatisfaction with Barber's comments by stating:

Barber hasn't been here long enough, or done enough, to say anything. For him to shoot his mouth off, acting like he's Mr. New York, yeah, I'm ticked off. Strahan is the single-season sack record-holder. He's the AP Defensive Player of the Year. He's one of the best—if not *the* best—defensive ends in the game. And you tell me this guy is being greedy? That's a bunch of crap. I've heard enough. Who is Tiki Barber to shoot his mouth off? What has he done? He talks like he's acting in the best interest of the team. Tell him to give his $7 million [signing bonus] back. Since he's so charitable, why doesn't he volunteer his $7 million? He says all the politically correct things. Ask him if he's giving up some of his money.[2]

Barber also chose to bite the hand that fed him when he publicly criticized Tom Coughlin's coaching style on two separate occasions. Following a shutout loss at home to the Carolina Panthers in the first round of the 2005 playoffs, Barber commented that he felt the Giants had been outcoached by Carolina head coach John Fox, the Giants' former defensive coordinator. Although Barber later apologized, saying that he only meant to suggest that he considered his team's performance to be "unacceptable," everyone understood the true meaning of his words. Barber also criticized the coaching staff's play-calling for abandoning the running game too soon following a 2006 loss to the Jacksonville Jaguars. He finally elected to let his true feelings toward Coughlin surface just prior to his final NFL game, when he told ESPN that the Giants head coach tended to treat him in a condescending manner.

Barber continued to berate Coughlin following his retirement, attributing his decision to leave the game while still at his peak to the Giants head coach's unrelenting style in practice. Barber suggested, "Coughlin pushed me in the direction of television. I don't know if you realize this, but we were in full pads for 17 weeks, and, with the amount of injuries that we had, it just takes a toll on you. You physically don't want to be out there, when your body feels the way you do, in full pads."[3]

However, Barber made his biggest mistake when he angered Giants fans by mocking quarterback Eli Manning's leadership skills during an interview he did prior to the start of the 2007 campaign. Quoted as saying that Manning's motivational pregame speeches sounded "almost comical," Barber subsequently became persona non grata to the Giants and their fans. Meanwhile, Manning dismissed Barber's critique as irrelevant, also questioning his former teammate's leadership skills by telling the *New York Daily News*, "I'm not going to lose any sleep about what Tiki has to say. I guess I could have questioned his leadership skills last year with calling out the coach and having articles about him retiring in the middle of the season, and how he's lost his heart to play. As a quarterback, you're reading that your running back has lost the heart to play the game, and it's about the 10th week. I can see that a little bit at times."[4] Manning, though, made his strongest statement on the field, leading the Giants to the NFL Championship just one year after Barber left the team.

Shortly after he officially announced his retirement, Barber was formally introduced as a correspondent for NBC's *The Today Show* and an analyst for *Football Night in America/Sunday Night Football.* He continued to function in those dual capacities until the *Today Show* relieved him of his duties in 2010. Barber subsequently filed the necessary paperwork to come out of retirement, but no NFL team expressed interest in acquiring his services. He has since assumed the responsibility of cohosting a morning show for CBS Sports Radio with Dana Jacobson and Brian Tierney.

CAREER HIGHLIGHTS

Best Season

Barber rushed for more than 1,500 yards in 2004, led the NFL with nearly 2,100 yards from scrimmage, and scored a career-high 15 touchdowns. He performed equally well two years later, when he rushed for 1,662 yards, amassed 2,127 yards from scrimmage, and scored five touchdowns in his final season. Yet, as well as Barber played those two years, there is little doubt that he had his best season in 2005. In addition to scoring 11 touchdowns, he established career highs with 1,860 yards rushing and 2,390 yards from scrimmage. Barber finished second in the NFL to Shaun Alexander in rushing, and he topped the circuit in all-purpose yards, with his total of 2,390 yards representing the second-highest figure compiled in NFL history at the time (Marshall Faulk amassed 2,429 yards for the Rams in 1999). Meanwhile, Barber's 960 yards from scrimmage in the month of December established a new league record (since broken by Chris Johnson in November 2009). Barber's magnificent performance earned him a fourth-place finish in the league MVP voting.

Memorable Moments/Greatest Performances

Barber turned in a number of epic performances over the course of his career, with the vast majority of those coming in his final few years in the league. He helped the Giants clinch a playoff berth on the final day of the 2002 regular season by rushing for 203 yards and making eight receptions for another 73 yards during a 10–7 overtime victory over the Philadelphia Eagles.

Barber amazingly surpassed the 200-yard mark on three separate occasions in 2005, doing so for the first time on October 30, just two days after the Giants attended the funeral of their longtime owner, Wellington Mara. Leading his team to a 36–0 massacre of the Washington Redskins in a game the Giants entered with a great deal of emotion, Barber rushed for 206 yards and one touchdown. He again rushed for more than 200 yards on December 17 against Kansas City, carrying the ball 29 times for 220 yards and two touchdowns during a 27–17 win over the Chiefs. Barber's touchdown runs went for 41 and 20 yards. He also broke free for a 55-yard gain on another play. Barber punctuated his exceptional year by helping the Giants clinch the NFC East title with a 30–21 win over the Oakland Raiders in the regular season finale. Barber rushed for 203 yards on the day, with his 95-yard scamper in the first quarter establishing a new Giants record for the longest TD run in franchise history.

Barber ironically again rushed for more than 200 yards in the 2006 regular season finale. Making the last regular season game of his career a memorable one, Barber carried the ball 23 times for 234 yards and three touchdowns during a 34–28 Giants win over Washington that enabled them to sneak into the playoffs as a wild card. Barber's TD runs covered 15, 55, and 50 yards, with his 234 yards establishing a new single-game rushing record for the franchise. Unfortunately, Philadelphia eliminated the Giants from the playoffs the following week, bringing Barber's career to an unhappy end. He finished his last game with 26 carries for 137 yards.

NOTABLE ACHIEVEMENTS

- Rushed for more than 1,000 yards six times (2000, 2002–2006).
- Caught more than 50 passes eight times, surpassing 70 receptions twice (2000, 2001).
- Accumulated more than 500 receiving yards six times, topping 700 yards once (719 in 2000).
- Scored more than 10 touchdowns three times (2002, 2004, 2005).
- Averaged more than 5.0 yards per carry three times (2001, 2005, 2006).
- Second Giants player to rush for more than 1,000 yards five straight times.
- Surpassed 2,000 yards from scrimmage three times (2004–2006).
- Led NFL in yards from scrimmage twice (2004, 2005).
- Led NFL with 2,390 all-purpose yards in 2005.
- Finished second in NFL in: rushing yards once, all-purpose yards once, and punt return yards once.

- Third NFL player to accumulate 10,000 career rushing yards and 5,000 career receiving yards.
- Holds Giants career records for most rushing yards (10,449), most total yards (17,359), most yards from scrimmage (15,632), most rushing attempts (2,217), and highest rushing average (4.7 yards per carry).
- Holds Giants single-season records for most rushing yards (1,860 in 2005), most total yards (2,390 in 2005), most 100-yard games (9 in 2004), most 200-yard games (3 in 2005), and most rushing attempts (357 in 2005).
- Holds Giants single-game records for most rushing yards (234 vs. Washington on December 30, 2006) and most yards from scrimmage (276 vs. Philadelphia on December 28, 2002).
- Holds Giants records for most 1,000-yard seasons (6) and longest touchdown run (95 yards vs. Oakland on December 31, 2005).
- Ranks among Giants all-time leaders in receptions (2nd), reception yardage (3rd), rushing touchdowns (2nd), and total touchdowns scored (2nd).
- Six-time NFC Offensive Player of the Week.
- Three-time Pro Bowl selection (2004–2006).
- Three-time All-NFC selection (2002, 2004, 2005).
- 2005 First-Team All-Pro selection.
- Pro Football Reference Second-Team All-2000s Team.
- 2000 NFC champion.

16

— AMANI TOOMER —

Although he never appeared in the Pro Bowl or earned All-Pro honors, Amani Toomer clearly established himself as the greatest wide receiver ever to play for the Giants over the course of his 13 seasons in New York. The holder of virtually every career-receiving record for the Giants, Toomer caught more passes (668) for more yards (9,497) and more touchdowns (54) than any other player in franchise history. The only Giants receiver to surpass 1,000 receiving yards as many as five times, Toomer also topped 70 receptions on four separate occasions. Toomer's consistently outstanding play helped the Giants advance to the playoffs seven times, enabling them to win four division titles, two NFC Championships, and one Super Bowl.

Born in Berkeley, California, on September 8, 1974, Amani Toomer earned All-America honors while playing football at De La Salle High School in Concord, California. Considered to be one of the top high school wide receivers in the nation, Toomer received an athletic scholarship to attend the University of Michigan, where, as a junior in 1994, he became just the third player in school history to accumulate as many as 1,000 receiving yards in a season. After earning All-Big Ten Second Team honors as a senior by making 44 receptions for 758 yards and seven touchdowns, Toomer became a member of the exceptional wide receiver draft class of 1996. With other standout pass-catchers such as Keyshawn Johnson, Terry Glenn, Eddie Kennison, Marvin Harrison, and Eric Moulds all being selected in the first round of the 1996 NFL Draft, Toomer ended up being the seventh receiver taken when the Giants selected him in the second round, with the 34th overall pick.

Toomer spent most of his first three seasons in New York returning punts, although he gradually saw more and more action at wide receiver. Excelling as a return man, he returned two punts for touchdowns as a rookie, leading the NFL with an average of 16.6 yards per punt return. However, Toomer injured his anterior cruciate ligament during a week 7

Amani Toomer (seen here celebrating the Giants' victory over New England in Super Bowl XLII) holds franchise records for most career receptions (668), receiving yards (9,497), and touchdown receptions (54).
Courtesy of Erica Wines

loss to the Washington Redskins, forcing him to spend the remainder of the year on injured reserve. Returning to the Giants the following year, Toomer scored another touchdown on a punt return. He also recorded his first receiving touchdown, scoring from 56 yards out against the Arizona Cardinals. Although not yet a regular member of the Giants' starting offensive unit by 1998, Toomer made significant contributions to the team as a receiver, hauling in 27 passes, for 360 yards and five touchdowns.

A full-time starter by 1999, Toomer combined with Ike Hilliard to become the first Giants tandem to post over 2,100 receiving yards in a season. While Hilliard excelled on routes of the short and intermediate variety, Toomer generally worked his way a little deeper into the opponents' defensive secondary, using his good speed and 6'3", 210-pound frame to his advantage. Toomer set a new team record in 1999 by making 79 receptions. He also scored six touchdowns and amassed 1,183 receiving yards—the second-highest total in Giants history to that point. Toomer followed that up with similarly productive seasons in 2000 and 2001, accumulating more than 70 receptions and 1,000 receiving yards each year, and totaling 13 touchdowns over the course of those two seasons. By making 72 receptions in 2001, Toomer became the first Giants player to catch as many as 70 passes in three straight years.

The 2002 campaign proved to be a record-setting year for Toomer, who established new team marks by making 82 receptions for 1,343 yards. He also scored a career-high eight touchdowns. Toomer made 63 receptions for 1,057 yards and five touchdowns the following year, passing Frank Gifford in the process as the team's all-time leader in pass-receiving yardage (Toomer finished the season with 6,366 total yards).

Toomer experienced a precipitous drop-off in offensive production in 2004, making only 51 receptions, for 747 yards and no touchdowns. However, even though he became more of a possession receiver after Plaxico Burress joined the Giants the following year, Toomer still managed to make 60 receptions, for 684 yards and seven touchdowns. Toomer started off 2006 well, making 32 receptions for 360 yards and three touchdowns in the first eight games. However, his season came to an abrupt end when he suffered a partially torn ACL during a 14–10 win over the Houston Texans on November 5.

Despite lacking the outstanding speed he had earlier in his career, the 33-year-old Toomer returned to the Giants in 2007 to make 59 receptions, for 760 yards and three touchdowns. He also provided veteran leadership to a team that stunned the football world by defeating the heavily favored New England Patriots in the Super Bowl. While serving as mentor to

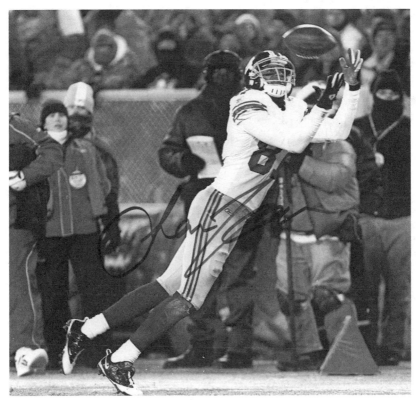

Toomer surpassed 1,000 receiving yards in five straight seasons.
Courtesy of PristineAuction.com

rookie wide receiver Steve Smith, Toomer established a new team record by making his 49th touchdown reception. Toomer spent one more year in New York, making 48 receptions for 580 yards and four touchdowns in 2008, before being released by the Giants at season's end. Although he subsequently signed a one-year contract with Kansas City, Toomer never appeared in a single game for the Chiefs, announcing his retirement when the team released him on September 1. Toomer ended his career with 668 receptions, for 9,497 yards and 54 touchdowns. He scored another three touchdowns on punt returns, and one more on the ground.

Following his playing career, Toomer turned to broadcasting, serving since 2011 as a member of MSG Varsity's team that covers *Friday Night Football*. He also joined NBC Sports Radio in 2012, serving since that time as a cohost with Dan Schwartzman on the nighttime talk show *Going Deep with Amani & Dan*. Not one to shy away from controversy, Toomer has ruffled a few feathers with some of his comments on that program, calling former teammate Jeremy Shockey a "bad teammate and a worse person,"[1] and criticizing Baltimore Ravens icon Ray Lewis for what he considered to be his hypocritical behavior. However, Toomer created the greatest stir with the comments he made only months after former teammate Eli Manning led the Giants to their second Super Bowl win over the New England Patriots in four years. Speaking on Sirius XM Radio, Toomer called Dallas QB Tony Romo "probably the best quarterback in the NFC East."[2]

Toomer added, "If I wanted a guy that is going to throw less interceptions and be more productive . . . higher completion percentage, I'm going to go with Tony Romo."[3]

Choosing to take the high road, Manning subsequently laughed off Toomer's remarks, saying on New York radio station WFAN, "I saw Toomer not too long ago. I just walked up to him and said, 'You know what, I thought Ike Hilliard was a better Giants receiver than you were. Willie Ponder was probably a better receiver than you were.'"[4]

Manning added, "You've got to laugh about it instead of getting upset. There's no point. . . . Amani's a good pal of mine, and still is. So you've got to laugh about it."[5]

GIANT CAREER HIGHLIGHTS

Best Season

Toomer had a big year for the Giants in 1999, when he made 79 receptions, for 1,183 yards and six touchdowns. However, he surpassed all those figures in 2002, when he established career-high marks with 82 receptions, 1,343 receiving yards, and eight touchdowns. Toomer placed third in the league in receiving yards, and he also finished ninth in receiving touchdowns.

Memorable Moments/Greatest Performances

Toomer set a Giants record in his very first NFL game by returning a punt 87 yards for a touchdown during a 23–20 overtime loss to the Buffalo Bills in the 1996 season opener. Toomer's 87-yard punt turn remains the longest in team history. He returned two more punts for touchdowns during his career, accomplishing the feat again as a rookie on October 13, 1996, when he ran 65 yards to give the Giants their only touchdown in a 19–10 loss to Philadelphia. Toomer recorded his final touchdown on a punt return one year later, doing so on October 19, 1997, when he scampered 53 yards for a score during a 26–20 overtime victory over the Detroit Lions.

Toomer made the first of his many memorable pass receptions on December 13, 1998. With the 5–8 Giants hosting the 13–0 Broncos, New York remained surprisingly close to Denver in the game's final minute, trailing by only three points, with the score standing at 16–13. With the Giants in possession of the ball at the Denver 37, Kent Graham lofted a long pass into the corner of the end zone that Toomer gathered in with only 48 seconds remaining on the clock. The scoring play gave the Giants a 20–16 victory that put an end to Denver's hopes for an undefeated season.

Toomer turned in one of the greatest performances of his career on December 5, 1999, when he made six receptions for 181 yards and three touchdowns during a 41–28 victory over the Jets. Toomer's scoring plays covered 61, 9, and 80 yards, as he and Kerry Collins combined throughout the day to torch the Jets' defensive secondary.

Toomer turned in another epic performance against Indianapolis on December 22, 2002, setting a Giants record for a 60-minute game by amassing a total of 204 receiving yards during a 44–27 win over the Colts. His 10 receptions included touchdown catches that covered 82, 21, and 27 yards.

Toomer played a huge role in several of New York's 11 victories in 2005, scoring a last-second touchdown that gave the Giants a come-from-behind 24–23 win over Denver, and gathering in a late 18-yard touchdown pass from Eli Manning that sent their game against Seattle into overtime.

Prior to missing the second half of the 2006 campaign, Toomer turned in a heroic effort against Philadelphia in week 2, helping the Giants overcome a 24–7 fourth-quarter deficit by making a career-high 12 receptions, for 137 yards and two touchdowns. The Giants ended up winning the contest 30–24 in overtime, with an exhausted Toomer having to be carried off the field by trainers after Plaxico Burress scored the winning touchdown.

Toomer also played extremely well during the latter stages of New York's 2007 championship campaign, scoring two touchdowns, including a 52-yard catch-and-run, during the Giants' 21–17 win over Dallas in the division championship game. He also had an excellent Super Bowl, helping the Giants defeat the previously unbeaten Patriots by making a key 38-yard fourth-quarter reception and concluding the game with six receptions for 84 yards.

NOTABLE ACHIEVEMENTS

- Caught more than 70 passes four times, surpassing 80 receptions once (82 in 2002).
- Surpassed 1,000 receiving yards five straight times (1999–2003).
- Averaged more than 15 yards per reception four times.
- Scored eight touchdowns twice (2000, 2002).
- Returned three punts for touchdowns.
- Led NFL with 16.6-yard punt return average in 1996.
- Finished third in NFL with 1,343 receiving yards in 2002.
- Giants all-time career leader in receptions (668), receiving yardage (9,497), and touchdown receptions (54).
- Ranks among Giants all-time leaders in touchdowns (5th) and points scored (10th).
- 1997 Week 8 NFC Special Teams Player of the Week.
- 2003 Week 9 NFC Offensive Player of the Week.
- Two-time NFC champion (2000, 2007).
- Super Bowl XLII champion.

MARK BAVARO

A degenerative knee condition forced Mark Bavaro to leave New York after only six seasons, preventing him from earning a higher place in these rankings. Nevertheless, Bavaro clearly established himself as the greatest tight end in team history during that time, developing into a cult figure to Giants fans, who greatly admired his humility, inner strength, and outstanding athletic ability. An exceptional pass receiver and blocker, the former Notre Dame All-American had no peers at the tight end position in the NFL before injuries began to take their toll on him. In just his second year in the league, Bavaro became the only tight end in Giants history to amass 1,000 receiving yards in a season, en route to earning the first of two consecutive First-Team All-Pro selections. He also gained general recognition throughout the NFL as the league's finest blocker at his position. Meanwhile, his physical and mental toughness earned him the respect and admiration of his teammates and opponents alike, prompting Carl Banks to say on one occasion, "He was the guy who was sort of the standard-bearer for the attitude of the team."[1]

Born in East Boston, Massachusetts, on April 28, 1963, Mark Anthony Bavaro excelled in both football and track and field while growing up in Danvers, 27 miles north of Boston. After earning high school All-America football honors while playing for Danvers High, Bavaro found himself being heavily recruited by several major colleges before finally choosing to play for the University of Notre Dame. Bavaro saw very little action his first two years with the Fighting Irish, but he earned a starting role as a junior and really came into his own the following year, making 32 receptions for 395 yards while also developing a reputation for playing through injuries.

Subsequently selected by the Giants in the fourth round of the 1985 NFL Draft with the 100th overall pick, Bavaro entered his first professional training camp being viewed primarily as a run-blocking tight end. Giants tight end coach Mike Pope revealed that Bavaro demonstrated almost immediately that he had the ability to fill that role, relating an incident

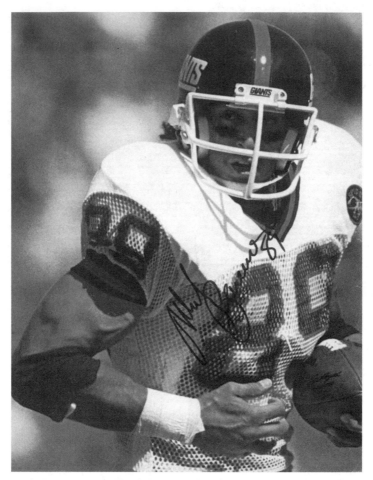

Mark Bavaro symbolized the mental and physical toughness of
the 1986 NFL champion Giants.
Courtesy of MearsOnlineAuctions.com

that took place in the first few days of camp. With Bavaro engaged with a
linebacker in a one-on-one drill, Pope said, "There was a tremendous collision, like when a tackle and defensive end meet. He knocked the guy five,
six yards off the line of scrimmage."[2]

However, Bavaro also ended up surprising everyone with his pass-
receiving skills after he assumed the starting role from Zeke Mowatt when
the latter suffered a season-ending knee injury prior to the start of the
regular season. Bavaro concluded his rookie campaign with 37 receptions,
for 511 yards and four touchdowns. Meanwhile, his exceptional blocking
helped Joe Morris emerge as one of the league's top rushers.

Bavaro blossomed into a star in his second NFL season, making 66 receptions, for 1,001 yards and four touchdowns, in helping the Giants post the league's best record over the course of the regular season. He continued to excel in the postseason, catching another eight passes, for 134 yards and two touchdowns, as the Giants won the Super Bowl.

While Bavaro drew raves for his pass-catching ability, he garnered even more praise for his extraordinary all-around play. Chicago Bears head coach Mike Ditka, a Hall of Fame tight end himself during his playing days, stated, "He [Bavaro] plays the position the way it was meant to be played. Playing tight end is not just catching 70 or 80 passes, but playing in the trenches and always being in the play. And that's what he does. He's the only true tight end in football. He blocks. He catches. He punishes."[3]

After watching Bavaro help the Giants defeat Washington in a critical late-season matchup, former Raiders coach John Madden gushed, "I thought I coached the best blocking tight end [Dave Casper], but now I'm not sure."[4] Madden went on to call Bavaro's performance against the Redskins "the greatest job of any tight end I've ever seen."[5]

Establishing himself as the prototypical tight end of his time, the 6'4", 245-pound Bavaro excelled in every phase of the game. Giants guard Billy Ard said of his teammate, "He is brutal. It takes three guys to bring him down."[6]

Head coach Bill Parcells expressed his admiration for his tight end by saying, "That's one tough, talented football player. I'll tell you one thing— I'm glad he's on our team."[7]

Giants offensive coordinator Ron Erhardt stated, "He's physically tough. If there's a little weakness that we point out to him, the next day he's out working on it. He's just the kind of guy that, if you had to go into the trenches tomorrow, that's the kind of guy you'd like to be in the trenches with."[8]

Indeed, Bavaro's toughness became the stuff of legend to his teammates, who nicknamed him "Rambo" early in his rookie season due to his intense playing style, quiet personality, and physical resemblance to Sylvester Stallone. Yet, displaying the humility and strong moral fiber for which he became so well known, Bavaro asked his teammates not to refer to him in that manner since he told them, "It's disrespectful to Vietnam veterans. Rambo exploited the Vietnam veterans. I have a lot of respect for the men who went there. A lot of my family went there."[9]

In addition to establishing himself as one of the Giants' best players over the course of the 1986 championship campaign, Bavaro came to symbolize the mental and physical toughness of the team in many ways. He made a strong impression on his teammates at one point during the season by playing five games with a fractured jaw that the club listed on the injury report as a "chipped tooth." He also started two games with a cracked big toe that the team described as "sprained." Such efforts prompted Harry Carson to say, "When you start rating guys on toughness, put Mark Bavaro at the top of the list."[10]

Although the Giants failed to return to the playoffs in 1987, Bavaro had another big year, making 55 receptions, for 867 yards and eight touchdowns during the strike-shortened campaign. He followed that up by making 53 catches, for 672 yards and four touchdowns in 1988, before knee problems limited him to only seven games and 22 receptions in 1989. Playing through pain throughout much of the 1990 season, Bavaro recorded just 33 receptions, five of which went for touchdowns. However, he contributed mightily to the Giants' 20–19 victory over Buffalo in Super Bowl XXV by making two key third-down receptions that kept scoring drives alive. He also did an excellent job of blocking for Ottis Anderson, who ended up rushing for 102 yards and one touchdown.

With the condition of Bavaro's knees having worsened, the Giants initially cut him in July 1991, before electing instead to sign him to a one-year deal and place him on the physically unable to perform list. Bavaro sat out the year, spending the 1991 campaign serving as the tight end coach at Saint Dominic Savio High School in East Boston, Massachusetts.

Despite being advised to retire several times by the doctor who worked on his knee, Bavaro chose to return to the NFL in 1992, signing a one-year contract to play for the Cleveland Browns and former Giants assistant coach Bill Belichick. After one year in Cleveland, Bavaro moved on to Philadelphia, where he spent his final two seasons before retiring at the conclusion of the 1994 campaign. He ended his career with 351 receptions, for 4,733 yards and 39 touchdowns. While playing for the Giants, he caught 266 passes, for 3,722 yards and 28 touchdowns.

Following his retirement, Bavaro lived with his wife in Naples, Florida, for three years, before the couple decided to move back up north to Boxford, Massachusetts, near Bavaro's hometown of Danvers. He pursued a career as a sales trader for an equity block-trading firm, trading large blocks of stocks for institutions and hedge funds. In 2007, Bavaro was appointed vice president of DesignCentrix, a premier Chicago exhibit house. He has also done work as a pro-life activist.

Looking back at the time he spent in New York, Bavaro says, "I was only here six years; it wasn't like I played here for 15 or 20 years. But those were six special years for the franchise, and, because of that, I'll always, always feel like a Giant."[11]

A degenerative knee condition brought Bavaro's days in New York to a premature end.
Courtesy of PowersAutographs.com

GIANT CAREER HIGHLIGHTS

Best Season

Bavaro had an outstanding year for the Giants in 1987, earning his second straight First-Team All-Pro selection by making 55 receptions, for 867 yards and a career-high eight touchdowns. He also averaged 15.8 yards per reception—the highest mark he posted in any single season. Nevertheless, I decided to go with Bavaro's 1986 campaign since he established career highs with 66 receptions and 1,001 receiving yards. Furthermore, the Giants won the Super Bowl, and Bavaro's exceptional blocking helped Joe Morris set a new team record by rushing for 1,516 yards.

Memorable Moments/Greatest Performances

Bavaro had the biggest statistical day of his career on October 13, 1985, when he set a new Giants record by making 12 receptions during a 35–30 loss to the Cincinnati Bengals. Bavaro's 176 receiving yards also represented a career-high mark for him. He made his biggest catch of the year in the Giants' 17–3 divisional playoff win over the San Francisco 49ers, hauling in with one hand an 18-yard touchdown pass from Phil Simms.

Bavaro turned in perhaps his most memorable performance on September 28, 1986, helping the Giants overcome an early 17–0 deficit to the New Orleans Saints by making seven receptions, for 110 yards and one touchdown, during a 20–17 New York victory. Bavaro accomplished all he did despite having two teeth knocked out and his jaw x-rayed during the early stages of the contest.

Yet the play for which Bavaro is best remembered occurred during another come-from-behind win, this one against the 49ers in a game played in San Francisco on Monday night, December 1, 1986. With the Giants trailing by a score of 17–0 early in the second half, Bavaro caught a short 10-yard pass over the middle and proceeded to drag Ronnie Lott and several other 49ers another 21 yards, bouncing off seven different defenders in the process, before finally being brought down. Bavaro's effort totally changed the momentum of the contest, providing much of the impetus for the Giants to mount a second-half comeback that resulted in a 21–17 victory. Bill Parcells later said, "That play totally ignited us."[12] Meanwhile, Joe Morris stated, "That play epitomized how tough Mark was, and how we wanted to be as a team."[13]

NOTABLE ACHIEVEMENTS

- Surpassed 1,000 receiving yards once (1,001 in 1986).
- Caught more than 50 passes three times, topping 60 receptions once (66 in 1986).
- Finished third in NFL with eight touchdown receptions in 1987.
- Two-time Pro Bowl selection (1986, 1987).
- Two-time First-Team All-Pro selection (1986, 1987).
- Two-time First-Team All-NFC selection (1986, 1987).
- Two-time NFC champion (1986, 1990).
- Two-time Super Bowl champion (XXI, XXV).

18

FRAN TARKENTON

After capturing three straight Eastern Conference titles from 1961 to 1963, the Giants won a total of only 10 games the next three seasons, concluding the 1966 campaign with an embarrassing record of 1–12–1. Desperately seeking to improve their fortunes, team ownership made a bold move prior to the start of the 1967 season, trading its first- and second-round picks in each of the next two drafts to the Minnesota Vikings for quarterback Fran Tarkenton. The six-year veteran, who earned the starting job in Minnesota early in his rookie season, had previously acquired the nicknames "The Mad Scrambler" and "Frantic Fran" due to his tendency to avoid the opposing team's pass rush by running all over the field. Doing so caused him to frequently butt heads with Vikings head coach Norm Van Brocklin, who disdained the idea of a mobile quarterback, stating on numerous occasions that no NFL team had the ability to win with one. Although Tarkenton led the Giants to a winning record just once over the course of the next five seasons, he brought a level of respectability to his new team, helping them compile an overall mark of 33–37 during that time. "Frantic Fran" also generated a great deal of excitement in New York, using his creativity and resourcefulness to give the Giants one of the NFL's more unpredictable offenses.

Born in Richmond, Virginia, on February 3, 1940, Francis Asbury Tarkenton attended Athens High School in Athens, Georgia, after which he enrolled at the University of Georgia. Starting at quarterback for his college team, Tarkenton led the Bulldogs to the 1959 Southeastern Conference championship. The expansion Minnesota Vikings subsequently selected him in the third round of the 1961 NFL draft, with the 29th overall pick.

Although only 21 years old when he first entered the NFL, Tarkenton made an immediate impact in Minnesota, leading the Vikings to a 37–13 upset win over the Chicago Bears in their first league game by coming off the bench to pass for 250 yards, throw four touchdown passes, and run for another score. He remains the only player in league history to pass for four touchdowns in his NFL debut.

Unfortunately, the Vikings won only two more games in their inaugural season, with Tarkenton experiencing the usual growing pains of any rookie quarterback after taking over as the team's starter early in the year. And, even though Tarkenton performed relatively well over the course of his next five seasons in Minnesota, the Vikings posted a winning record just once, prompting most people around the league to view the quarterback as something of an oddity. Tarkenton noted years later, "When I began my NFL career in 1961, I was a freak. The reason was simple: I played quarterback and I ran. There were no designed runs in our playbook, but I would scramble out of the pocket when a play broke down—nowadays, that likely would be called 'extending the play.' When I ran forward for yardage, it was never the design of the play, but just something that happened when nothing else worked. . . . It was not a skill set that was embraced. Plenty of people mocked it, and the rest wrote it off."[1]

One of the people who wrote it off was Tarkenton's head coach in Minnesota, Norm Van Brocklin, who earlier starred at quarterback for the Rams and Eagles en route to earning a place in the Pro Football Hall of Fame. Van Brocklin made his distaste for running quarterbacks well known to Tarkenton, who often found himself clashing with his head coach. Growing increasingly unhappy with his situation in Minnesota, Tarkenton asked to be traded to another team—a request Vikings management granted by dealing him to the struggling Giants.

Joining a team in New York that finished with the league's worst record the previous year, Tarkenton performed wonders, leading the Giants to a record of 7–7 in each of his first two seasons with them. Despite being physically overmatched by their opponents on many occasions, the Giants remained competitive, due primarily to Tarkenton's ingenuity and sense of originality. Particularly proud of the contributions he made to the 1967 Giants team that scored 106 more points than the previous year's squad, Tarkenton suggested years later:

> That team in New York, that first year that I was there, we finished 7–7. That was the finest accomplishment of any of my 18 years in professional football. It was a rag-a-muffin team that played hard and played together, had heart and had soul. Allie [Sherman] did a great job with that team and, for us to be 7–7, was like being 14–0 for any other team. It was the best year any team I ever played

Fran Tarkenton brought a level of respectability to the Giants during his five-year stay in New York.
Courtesy of RMYAuctions.com

on ever had. We spread the field, we put men in motion, we had nobody in the backfield, and the reason we had to do this is that we didn't have a big offensive line. So, we had to use the short passing game to be our running game. The "West Coast Offense" as we know it today was absolutely started in New York, and they let me be a part of that architecture, and we had more fun with it.[2]

Tarkenton threw for 3,088 yards and 29 touchdowns in 1967, placing among the league leaders in both categories en route to earning the third Pro Bowl selection of his career. He appeared in the next three Pro Bowls as well, performing particularly well in 1970, when he nearly led the Giants into the playoffs with a record of 9–5. During that time, Tarkenton worked his magic to get as much as possible out of the extremely limited talent that surrounded him. Although New York's offense also included speedy wide-out Homer Jones, versatile running back Ron Johnson, and reliable tight end Bob Tucker at different times, it also featured one of the league's smallest and least imposing offensive lines, forcing the six-foot, 190-pound Tarkenton to spend a considerable amount of time running for his life. He also needed to use every bit of his creativity to come up with ways to employ the services of the other less-talented skill position players that typically littered the Giants' roster.

However, even Tarkenton found himself unable to improve the Giants' situation in 1971, when the team finished a disappointing 4–10. Believing that he had no chance of winning in New York, Tarkenton expressed to management his desire to go elsewhere, prompting the team to send him back to Minnesota for two veterans, a rookie, and two high draft picks.

Tarkenton spent his final seven seasons with the Vikings, leading them to six NFC Central Division titles and three Super Bowl appearances. During that time, he led all NFL quarterbacks in pass completions three times, completion percentage twice, and touchdown passes and passing yardage one time each. He appeared in three more Pro Bowls, earned one First-Team All-Pro selection and one Second-Team nomination, and was named the NFL's Most Valuable Player and Offensive Player of the Year in 1975, when he led the Vikings to a superb 12–2 record.

After passing for a career-high 3,468 yards in 1978, Tarkenton elected to retire at the end of the year. He ended his career as the NFL's all-time leader in pass completions (3,686), passing yardage (47,003), and touchdown passes (342). He also rushed for 3,674 yards, a figure that places him fourth all-time among NFL quarterbacks, behind only Randall Cunningham, Steve Young, and Michael Vick. Tarkenton's numbers in his five years with the Giants include 1,051 pass completions, 13,905 passing yards, 103 touchdown passes, and 1,126 rushing yards. He ranks among the team's all-time leaders in each of the first three categories.

Nevertheless, Tarkenton's inability to win a championship and poor performance in the three Super Bowls in which he appeared prevent many people from viewing him as one of the greatest quarterbacks in NFL history. The Pro Football Hall of Fame didn't necessarily agree, though, inducting Tarkenton into its ranks in 1986, in just his third year of eligibility. The *Sporting News* also included him among its elite, ranking him number 59 on its list of the 100 Greatest Football Players.

Following his retirement, Tarkenton appeared on the television show *That's Incredible!* and also worked part time on *Monday Night Football*. He later established himself as a pioneer in the computer software industry,

Tarkenton earned Pro Bowl honors in four of his five seasons with the Giants.
Courtesy of RMYAuctions.com

founding a program generator company he called Tarkenton Software. After touring the country promoting CASE (computer-aided software engineering) with Albert F. Case Jr. of Nastec Corporation, Tarkenton eventually merged his software firm with James Martin's KnowledgeWare. He served as president there until he sold the company to Sterling Software in 1994.

GIANT CAREER HIGHLIGHTS

Best Season

It could be argued that Tarkenton had his two best years for the Giants in 1967 and 1970. In the first of those campaigns, he passed for more than 3,000 yards (3,088) for the only time as a member of the team. He also threw a career-high 29 touchdown passes, posted a completion percentage of 54.1, and rushed for 306 yards and two touchdowns. Furthermore, as we saw earlier, Tarkenton considers his direction of the team to a 7–7 record that season to be the greatest accomplishment of his career.

On the other hand, Tarkenton compiled similarly impressive numbers three years later, when he led the Giants to a 9–5 record that almost earned them a spot in the playoffs. Although he passed for fewer yards (2,777) and threw fewer touchdown passes (19) than he did in 1967, he also posted a higher completion percentage (56.3) and threw fewer interceptions (12, as opposed to the 19 he tossed in 1967). Tarkenton also earned All-Pro honors for the only time as a member of the Giants, being awarded a spot on the Second Team.

However, even though the Giants concluded the 1969 campaign with a record of only 6–8, the feeling here is that Tarkenton played his best ball for them that year. In addition to nearly equaling the marks he posted in 1967 by passing for 2,918 yards and compiling a completion percentage of 53.8, he led all NFL quarterbacks with a passer rating of 87.2 that surpassed the figures he compiled the other two seasons (85.9 in 1967 and 82.2 in 1970). It is true that Tarkenton's 23 touchdown passes fell six short of the mark he posted two years earlier. But he also threw only eight interceptions, less than half the total he threw in 1967. Furthermore, in Homer Jones, Tarkenton had an elite wide receiver to whom he could throw in 1967. Meanwhile, in 1970, Ron Johnson gave the Giants the running game they previously lacked, while tight end Bob Tucker served as an outstanding target for Tarkenton in the passing game. But Jones proved to be much less of a factor in 1969, and Johnson and Tucker didn't arrive until the following season. Therefore, Tarkenton did not have much of a supporting cast that year. That being the case, he had his best all-around season for the Giants in 1969.

Memorable Moments/Greatest Performances

Tarkenton played a number of exceptional games for the Giants, with several of those coming in his first season in New York. Although the Giants lost to the Vikings by a score of 27–24 in Tarkenton's first appearance against his former team on November 5, 1967, the New York quarterback performed extremely well, completing 12 of 23 passes, for 270 yards and three touchdowns. He also ran for 56 yards. Three weeks later, Tarkenton led the Giants to a 44–7 mauling of the Philadelphia Eagles by completing 20 passes, for 261 yards and another three touchdowns. Tarkenton concluded the campaign in style, completing 16 of 28 passes, for 275 yards and four touchdowns during a 37–14 win over the St. Louis Cardinals that enabled the Giants to finish the season with a record of 7–7.

Tarkenton continued his outstanding play in 1968, turning in his two best efforts on September 29 and December 8. On the first of those dates, he helped the Giants improve their record to 3–0 by throwing for 264 yards and two touchdowns during a 48–21 pasting of the Washington Redskins. Tarkenton's touchdown passes both went to Homer Jones, covering distances of 82 and 56 yards. Although the Giants lost to the St. Louis Cardinals 28–21 on December 8, Tarkenton had one of his biggest passing days as a member of the team, throwing for 325 yards and tossing touchdown passes of 73 and 68 yards—the first to Homer Jones and the second to Joe Morrison.

Tarkenton gained a measure of revenge against his old team in the first game of the 1969 campaign, leading the Giants to a come-from-behind 24–23 win over the Vikings by tossing two fourth-quarter touchdown passes to Don Herrmann. Tarkenton finished the day 19 for 34, for 224 yards and three touchdowns. Meanwhile, the 24 points surrendered by Minnesota's defense ended up being the highest total the unit allowed all season. Later in the year, Tarkenton helped put an end to New York's seven-game losing streak by passing for 252 yards and four touchdowns during a 49–6 victory over the Cardinals.

Tarkenton played arguably his best game for the Giants the following year, leading New York to a 35–17 win over the Cardinals on October 25, 1970, by completing 15 of 18 passes, for 280 yards and five touchdowns. The victory evened the Giants' record at 3–3, moving them to within one game of first place in the Eastern Division. Three weeks later, Tarkenton led the Giants to their sixth consecutive victory—a memorable 35–33 comeback win over the Washington Redskins. With the Giants trailing Washington 33–14 at the start of the fourth quarter, Tarkenton led his team to three scoring drives in the final period, with the biggest play being a 57-yard TD connection with fullback Tucker Frederickson. The win remains one of the greatest come-from-behind efforts in franchise history.

NOTABLE ACHIEVEMENTS

- Passed for more than 3,000 yards once (3,088 in 1967).
- Threw more than 20 touchdown passes three times (1967, 1968, 1969).
- Rushed for more than 300 yards twice (1967, 1968).
- Led NFL quarterbacks in passer rating once (87.2 in 1969).
- Finished second among NFL quarterbacks in passes completed three times, passing yardage twice, touchdown passes twice, and passer rating once.
- Ranks among Giants all-time leaders in pass completions (5th), passing yardage (5th), and touchdown passes (4th).
- Four-time Pro Bowl selection (1967–1970).
- 1970 Second-Team All-Pro selection.
- Number 59 on the *Sporting News* 1999 list of 100 Greatest Players in NFL History.
- Number 91 on the NFL Network's 2010 list of Top 100 Players of All Time.
- Elected to Pro Football Hall of Fame in 1986.

Y. A. TITTLE

M ost people around the NFL believed that Y. A. Tittle had very little left when the Giants acquired him from the San Francisco 49ers prior to the start of the 1961 season. A 13-year veteran at that juncture, the 34-year-old quarterback spent most of the previous season sitting on the bench after being displaced by the much younger John Brodie as the starter in San Francisco. However, Tittle ended up proving everyone wrong, reestablishing himself as one of the NFL's top signal-callers by leading New York to three consecutive Eastern Division titles. Along the way, he set numerous team and league records, earning NFL MVP honors in some form or fashion in each of those three seasons.

Born in Marshall, Texas, on October 24, 1926, Yelberton Abraham Tittle attended Louisiana State University, where he made a name for himself as a junior by being named MVP of the legendary 1947 Cotton Bowl, which, played during an ice storm, ended in a scoreless tie between LSU and Arkansas. Although the Detroit Lions subsequently selected him in the first round of the 1948 NFL Draft with the sixth overall pick, Tittle instead elected to begin his professional playing career with the Baltimore Colts of the All-America Football Conference. He spent his first two seasons in the AAFC before he began competing against NFL players for the first time when the Colts joined the more established league in 1950. However, after that particular Colts franchise folded at the conclusion of the 1950 campaign, Tittle became a member of the San Francisco 49ers.

Tittle spent the next 10 years in San Francisco, experiencing many highs and lows during his time there. After serving primarily as Frankie Albert's backup his first season with the 49ers, Tittle established himself as the team's starting quarterback in 1952. He played well over the course of the next nine seasons, earning Pro Bowl honors four times, while typically ranking among the league's top passers. Gradually acquiring the nickname "Colonel Slick" for his clever ball-handling and sharp play-calling skills, Tittle developed a reputation for being the league's best long passer. Yet, at

Y. A. Tittle led the Giants to three consecutive championship game appearances.
Courtesy of RMYAuctions.com

the same time, he exhibited outstanding "touch" on his shorter passes. Tittle had his best year for the 49ers in 1957, when he led all NFL quarterbacks in pass completions (176) and pass completion percentage (63.1). He also finished second in passing yardage (2,157) and passer rating (80.0), en route to earning First-Team All-Pro honors and recognition from the UPI as the NFL's Most Valuable Player.

Yet, in spite of Tittle's solid play, the 49ers failed to make the playoffs in any of those years, leaving the quarterback feeling somewhat unfulfilled.

His situation worsened in 1960, when he lost his starting job to 25-year-old John Brodie.

With his days as a starter in San Francisco apparently over, Tittle found new life when the 49ers traded him to the Giants for guard Lou Cordileone at the conclusion of the 1960 campaign. After initially considering retiring rather than switching teams at such an advanced age, Tittle decided to take a more positive approach to his situation, stating years later, "Throwing a football was the best thing I could do in life, and I had done it since I was in the sixth grade. So I took my old shoulder pads that I'd used for 16 years and went to New York feeling like a rookie trying to make the team for the first time."[1]

With the popular Charlie Conerly having spent virtually all of the previous 13 seasons serving as the Giants' primary signal-caller, many of Tittle's new teammates greeted him with a certain amount of resentment when he first arrived in New York. However, he soon won them over with his exceptional passing ability and outstanding leadership skills.

Pat Summerall, who played for the Giants from 1958 to 1961, later noted, "We didn't have anybody, nor had we had anybody, who came close to throwing the ball as well as he [Tittle] did. I mean, the ball, you could hear it whistling when he let it go."[2]

Before long, Tittle became the toast of New York, earning Pro Bowl honors his first year with the Giants by leading them to the Eastern Division title with a record of 10–3–1. The team's outstanding performance prompted the Newspaper Enterprise Association to name Tittle MVP of the National Football League.

Tittle followed that up with an even better year in 1962, earning the first of two straight First-Team All-Pro selections and recognition by the UPI as the league's Most Valuable Player. En route to leading the Giants to a fabulous 12–2 record, the 35-year-old quarterback established new career highs with 200 pass completions, 3,224 passing yards, and 33 touchdown passes, which broke the league record of 32 previously shared by Johnny Unitas (1959) and Sonny Jurgenson (1961). Included in Tittle's record-setting season was an amazing effort he turned in against the Washington Redskins on October 28 in which he tied an NFL record by throwing seven touchdown passes.

Tittle had another great year in 1963, passing for 3,145 yards and breaking the record he had set one year earlier by throwing 36 touchdown passes. In so doing, he became the first player in NFL history to toss 30 or more TD passes in consecutive seasons. Tittle's exceptional performance led the Giants to a record of 11–3, helping them earn their third straight

Tittle holds franchise records for most TD passes in a season (36) and in a game (7).
Courtesy of RMYAuctions.com

division title, and prompting both the Associated Press and the Newspaper Enterprise Association to name the quarterback league MVP.

Unfortunately for Tittle and the Giants, the 1963 campaign also ended in disappointing fashion, with the Bears defeating them in the NFL Championship Game by a score of 14–10. During the contest, Tittle suffered a painful leg injury that caused him to throw five interceptions to Chicago defenders.

The 1963 title game against the Bears represented Tittle's last opportunity to win the NFL Championship that had eluded him throughout his career. Age, injuries, and a poor supporting cast adversely affected the 38-year-old quarterback's performance the following year, enabling the Giants to compile a record of just 2–10–2. After throwing 86 touchdown passes and 46 interceptions the three previous seasons, Tittle completed only 10 touchdown passes and threw 22 interceptions in 1964. He announced his retirement at the end of the year, leaving the game with more passing yards (33,070) and touchdown passes (242) than any other quarterback in NFL history. His numbers with the Giants include 10,439 yards passing and 96 TD passes.

Following his retirement, Tittle, who worked as an insurance salesman in the off-season during his playing days, founded his own company, which he called Y. A. Tittle Insurance & Financial Services. The Pro Football Hall of Fame inducted him into its ranks in 1971, even though he never won an NFL Championship. The voters recognized the many qualities that made him a winner, even if the same could not always be said about the teams he directed. After spending his final years suffering from dementia that adversely affected his memory and limited his conversation to a handful of topics, Tittle died of natural causes on October 8, 2017, some two weeks shy of his 91st birthday.

GIANT CAREER HIGHLIGHTS

Best Season

Tittle had an exceptional year in 1962, leading the Giants to a 12–2 record by passing for a career-high 3,224 yards and establishing a new NFL record by throwing 33 touchdown passes. However, he performed even better the following year, leading his team to a record of 11–3 by passing for 3,145 yards and surpassing the mark he had set one year earlier by tossing 36 TD passes. Tittle led the NFL with a 60.2 completion percentage and a 104.8 passer rating in 1963, surpassing by a fairly wide margin the figures of 53.3 percent and 89.5 he had posted the previous season. Meanwhile, the Giants, who finished second in the league with 398 points scored in 1962, finished well ahead of everyone else the following season, tallying a total of 448 points.

Memorable Moments/Greatest Performances

Tittle turned in a number of memorable performances over the course of the 1962 and 1963 campaigns, putting his name in the record books on numerous occasions. He played his greatest game on October 28, 1962, leading the Giants to a 49–34 win over the Washington Redskins by throwing seven touchdown passes. Tittle's TD passes included a 63-yarder to Frank Gifford, tosses of 2 and 22 yards to Joe Morrison, a 32-yard completion to Del Shofner, and three tosses to Joe Walton, one for 26 yards and the other two for 5 yards apiece. While Tittle's seven touchdown passes tied an NFL record that still stands, his 505 yards passing enabled him to join George Blanda as the only quarterbacks to reach the 500-yard mark up to that point. Frank Gifford later told him, "That was the greatest passing performance I've ever seen."[3]

Reflecting back on the events of the day, Tittle maintained that he had no desire to remain in the game long enough to throw for seven touchdowns, stating years later, "I wasn't even sure I could play that week. I had injured my arm in the previous game. But it worked out OK."[4]

Coerced by his teammates into reentering the game after completing his sixth TD pass, Tittle recalled that teammate Gifford subsequently told him, "If you don't call a pass, we're walking off the field."[5]

Just two weeks later, Tittle once again throttled the opposing team's defense, throwing six touchdown passes during a 41–10 win over Dallas.

Tittle's fabulous 1963 campaign also included a number of extraordinary efforts. After tossing four touchdown passes during a 37–21 win over the Cowboys in week 6, the aging quarterback completed another four TD passes two weeks later in leading the Giants to a 38–21 victory over the Cardinals. Tittle was at it again in week 10, throwing another four touchdown passes during a 48–14 win over his former team, the San Francisco 49ers. He finished the year in style, completing three TD passes during a 33–17 win over Pittsburgh that clinched New York's third straight Eastern Conference title. Tittle's three TD passes in the season's final week established a new NFL record, also making him the first quarterback to surpass 30 touchdown passes in consecutive seasons.

Yet, ironically, the most indelible image that most people have of Tittle is one that shows him in perhaps his darkest moment. Knocked to the ground by defensive lineman John Baker during a September 20, 1964, loss to the Pittsburgh Steelers, a dazed Tittle is shown in a photograph taken by Morris Berman of the *Pittsburgh Post-Gazette* bloodied and kneeling in the end zone after just having thrown an interception that a Pittsburgh defender returned for a touchdown. Tittle, who was in his final NFL season, suffered a concussion and a cracked sternum on the play. Regarded as one of the most iconic images in the history of American sports and journalism, the photo came to represent the plight of Tittle and the Giants at that time. Although the quarterback played out the rest of the season, he retired at the end of the year after leading New York to a disappointing 2–10–2 record.

Tittle stated years later, "That was the end of the road. It was the end of my dream. It was over."[6]

NOTABLE ACHIEVEMENTS

- Passed for more than 3,000 yards twice (1962, 1963).
- Passed for more than 30 touchdowns twice (1962, 1963).
- Led NFL quarterbacks in touchdown passes twice, pass completion percentage once, and passer rating once.
- Holds share of NFL single-game record with seven touchdown passes (October 28, 1962).
- Passed for more than 500 yards in one game (October 28, 1962).
- Established new NFL record (since broken) in 1963 by throwing 36 touchdown passes.
- First NFL quarterback to surpass 30 touchdown passes in consecutive seasons (1962, 1963).
- Holds Giants single-season record for touchdown passes (36 in 1963).
- Ranks fifth all-time on Giants in career touchdown passes (96).
- Three-time Pro Bowl selection (1961–1963).
- Two-time First-Team All-Pro selection (1962, 1963).
- Two-time Newspaper Enterprise Association (NEA) NFL MVP (1961, 1963).
- 1962 UPI NFL MVP.
- 1963 AP NFL MVP.
- Three-time NFL Eastern Division champion.
- Elected to Pro Football Hall of Fame in 1971.

20

JIMMY PATTON

Jimmy Patton—the one constant in a Giants secondary that saw many other players come and go during his career—likely would be better remembered today had his ascension into stardom not come on the heels of the incredible success Emlen Tunnell experienced in his years in New York. Joining the Giants in 1955, Patton gradually developed into arguably the NFL's top safety by 1958, Tunnel's last year with the team. Having played alongside Tunnell his first four years in the league, Patton invariably suffered in any comparisons made between the two men. Nevertheless, he ended up making quite a name for himself as well, earning Pro Bowl and First-Team All-Pro honors five times each, en route to finishing his career second only to Tunnel on the Giants' all-time list in interceptions (52) and interception return yardage (712). Also an outstanding punt and kickoff returner, Patton accumulated a total of 735 yards on 28 kickoff returns early in his career, before he began concentrating almost exclusively on shutting down opposing receivers. In fact, as a rookie in 1955, Patton became the first NFL player ever to return both a kickoff and a punt for a touchdown in the same game.

Born in Greenville, Mississippi, on September 29, 1933, James Russell Patton Jr. attended the University of Mississippi, where he starred on both offense and defense. Playing running back and safety, Patton helped lead the Rebels to the 1954 SEC Championship, earning in the process a place in the Mississippi Sports Hall of Fame and a spot on the Ole Miss Team of the Century from 1892 to 1992.

Subsequently selected by the Giants in the eighth round of the 1955 NFL Draft with the 92nd overall pick, Patton joined a New York secondary that included future NFL head coach Dick Nolan and future Hall of Famers Emlen Tunnell and Tom Landry. Seeing limited duty as a rookie, Patton struggled somewhat his first year in the league, being abused by opposing wide receivers and running backs, who often ran over him. Nevertheless, he acquitted himself quite well on special teams, registering a 69-yard

Jimmy Patton ranks second in franchise history in
interceptions and interception-return yards.
Courtesy of NearMintCards.com

touchdown on a punt return, while also returning a kickoff 98 yards for a
touchdown.

After earning a starting spot in his second season, Patton developed
into one of the league's better safeties by his third year in the league,
intercepting three passes, one of which he returned 50 yards for the first
defensive touchdown of his career. It wasn't until 1958, though, that Patton established himself as a true star. In perhaps his finest season, Patton
led the NFL with 11 interceptions, en route to earning the first of his five
consecutive Pro Bowl selections. He also earned First-Team All-Pro honors
for the first of five straight times.

Patton intercepted at least five passes in each of the next five seasons as well, recording as many as eight thefts in 1961, when he registered the last touchdown of his career by returning one of those 51 yards for a score. Displaying a nose for the football throughout his career, he also made 15 fumble recoveries. Meanwhile, Patton's 9.9 speed in the 100-yard dash and college background as a running back made him a threat every time he got his hands on the ball. Accumulating a total of 712 return yards on his 52 interceptions, he averaged almost 14 yards per return over the course of his career.

Patton used his speed, instincts, and outstanding peripheral vision to establish himself as one of the NFL's best ball hawks. He also played the run well, doing an excellent job of studying his opponents' tendencies so that he could bring them down in the open field. On one occasion, Patton exhibited the intellectual approach he took to his craft when he discussed the techniques he employed against opposing ball carriers:

> When a fullback like Jimmy Brown of the Cleveland Browns breaks loose up the middle, I don't watch his head. He can fake me with his head. I watch his belt buckle, and I keep my eye on it, just the way a batter watches a baseball. He can't wiggle that belt buckle. I get down low enough to get below his shoulder and try to hit him head on. It's easy enough to get to Brown's belly. Holding on to him is another matter. A fullback like Brown can spin you right over, but I can usually manage to hold on to something.
>
> A breakaway runner like Bobby Mitchell of the Browns or Hugh McElhenny of the San Francisco 49ers really gives me fits. You've got to beat their blockers, and then you've got to watch out for their fakes. Mitchell has literally faked me off my feet. It's too risky to tackle them low. I hit them high and wrestle them down. It's not the way you're taught in college, and it's not pretty—but it's effective.[1]

Playing behind such other defensive standouts as Andy Robustelli, Jim Katcavage, and Sam Huff also enabled Patton to excel for much of his career. However, when New York's defense fell apart at the conclusion of the 1963 campaign, Patton experienced a decrease in productivity, intercepting a total of only four passes from 1964 to 1966. Announcing his retirement at the end of the 1966 season, Patton ended his career with 52 interceptions and a total of four touchdowns. The Giants appeared in six title games and captured one NFL championship in his 12 years with them.

Jimmy Patton (seen here closing in on Dallas wide receiver Frank Clarke) earned Pro Bowl and All-Pro honors five times each while playing for the Giants.
Courtesy of RMYAuctions.com

Unfortunately, Patton's life after football proved to be all too brief. Driving to Virginia to see his dying sister, Patton lost his life in a one-car accident near Villa Rica, Georgia, on December 22, 1972. He was only 39 years old at the time of his passing.

CAREER HIGHLIGHTS

Best Season

Patton earned Pro Bowl and First-Team All-Pro honors for the first of five straight times in 1958, when he had the finest season of his career. In addition to leading the NFL with 11 interceptions, Patton finished second in the league with 183 interception return yards. His 11 picks represent a single-season franchise record.

Memorable Moments/Greatest Performances

On October 30, 1955, Patton became the first player in NFL history to return both a punt and a kickoff for a touchdown in the same game, accomplishing the feat during a 35–7 win over the Washington Redskins. After scoring on a 98-yard kickoff return in the first quarter, rookie Patton concluded the day's scoring with a 69-yard punt return in the fourth quarter.

Patton scored the first defensive touchdown of his career two years later, on October 20, 1957, when he returned an interception 50 yards for a touchdown during a 35–0 mauling of the Pittsburgh Steelers. He scored his final touchdown against the Washington Redskins on November 5, 1961, returning an interception 51 yards for a score during a lopsided 53–0 New York victory.

Patton may well have played his greatest game, though, against the Chicago Bears on December 2, 1962, when he intercepted three passes during a 26–24 Giants victory that enabled them to clinch their second consecutive Eastern Conference title.

NOTABLE ACHIEVEMENTS

- Led NFL with 11 interceptions in 1958.
- Finished second in NFL with 183 interception-return yards in 1958.
- Led NFL with two non-offensive touchdowns in 1955.
- Holds Giants record for most interceptions in a season (11 in 1958).
- Ranks second all-time on Giants with 52 career interceptions and 712 interception return yards.
- First NFL player ever to return both kickoff and punt for TD in same game (October 30, 1955).
- Five-time Pro Bowl selection.
- Five-time First-Team All-Pro selection.
- Six-time NFL Eastern Division champion.
- 1956 NFL champion.

RODNEY HAMPTON

odney Hampton did not accomplish nearly as much in the NFL as Emmitt Smith, whom the Dallas Cowboys selected seven picks ahead of him in the 1990 NFL Draft. Hampton doesn't hold league records for most rushing yards and most touchdowns scored on the ground. He didn't appear in eight Pro Bowls and earn First-Team All-Pro honors four times. Nevertheless, Hampton, whom the Giants selected with the 24th overall pick of the 1990 draft, fashioned a career in the NFL that far exceeded those turned in by the other three running backs chosen before him, establishing himself in the process as one of the finest all-around backs in team history. New York's career leader in rushing upon his retirement in 1997 (he has since slipped to second), Hampton is one of only two Giants running backs to rush for more than 1,000 yards in a season five straight times. He is also the only Giants runner to rush for as many as 10 touchdowns in a season on three separate occasions. Hampton's outstanding running helped the Giants make the playoffs in three of his eight years in New York, with the team winning the Super Bowl in his rookie campaign of 1990. And, while Hampton cannot lay claim to Smith's long list of individual honors, he did quite well for himself, appearing in consecutive Pro Bowls in 1992 and 1993.

Born in Houston, Texas, on April 3, 1969, Rodney Craig Hampton starred at the University of Georgia before choosing to enter the NFL Draft with one year of collegiate eligibility still remaining. On draft day, Hampton sat and waited patiently as four of the nation's other top running backs heard their names called before his in the first round. After the Jets committed one of their worst draft blunders by selecting Blair Thomas with the second overall pick, the Cowboys (17), Packers (19), and Falcons (20) chose Emmitt Smith, Darrell Thompson, and Steve Broussard, respectively. The Giants subsequently made Hampton that year's 24th overall pick, beginning in the process a long and successful association.

Rodney Hampton retired in 1997 as the Giants' all-time leading rusher.
Courtesy of SportsMemorabilia.com

Viewed primarily as a "between-the-tackles" runner coming out of college, the 5'11", 225-pound Hampton was not generally considered to have great breakaway speed. However, he possessed nimble feet and surprising quickness for a man of his proportions, making him a serious threat once he got into the open field. More than anything, though, Hampton proved to be a perfect match for the Giants' smash-mouth style of play, bowling over would-be tacklers near the line of scrimmage and keeping the chains moving while simultaneously wearing down opposing defenses over the course of 60 minutes.

Although Hampton gained 455 yards on the ground and caught 32 passes for another 274 yards his first year in the league, he spent much of his rookie campaign serving primarily as Ottis Anderson's backup. However, with the 33-year-old Anderson nearing the end of his career, the Giants clearly viewed Hampton as their halfback of the future, even after he broke his leg attempting to recover a Jeff Hostetler fumble in a playoff victory over the Chicago Bears during the team's successful run to the NFL Championship.

Fully recovered by the start of the 1991 season, Hampton displaced Anderson as the Giants' primary running threat, carrying the ball 256 times, for 1,059 yards and 10 touchdowns. He also made 43 receptions for 283 yards. Hampton followed that up by earning Pro Bowl honors in each of the next two seasons. Playing for a Giants team that finished just 6–10 under second year head coach Ray Handley in 1992, Hampton rushed for 1,141 yards and 14 touchdowns, placing near the top of the NFL rankings in both categories. Following the dismissal of Handley at season's end, Hampton helped the Giants return to the playoffs under new head coach Dan Reeves the ensuing year by rushing for 1,077 yards and five touchdowns.

Although the Giants failed to gain a postseason berth in 1994, finishing the campaign with a record of 9–7, Hampton had another solid year, rushing for 1,075 yards and six touchdowns. However, dissatisfied somewhat with his 3.3 rushing average (the lowest of his career), the Giants began to search for his replacement, selecting Michigan running back Tyrone Wheatley with the 17th overall pick of the 1995 draft, and also signing fellow Georgia Bulldog and 1982 Heisman Trophy winner Herschel Walker as a free agent. Determined to keep his starting job, Hampton returned to top form in 1995, rushing for 1,182 yards and 10 touchdowns for a Giants team that finished just 5–11.

Having surpassed the 1,000-yard mark in rushing for the fifth consecutive time in 1995, Hampton drew a considerable amount of interest from other teams when he became a free agent at the end of the year. The San Francisco 49ers, in particular, expressed interest in acquiring the 26-year-old running back's services, offering him a blockbuster six-year, $16.45 million contract. However, even though the Giants apparently had Wheatley waiting in the wings, they elected to match the offer, re-signing Hampton to a deal that included a $3.6 million signing bonus.

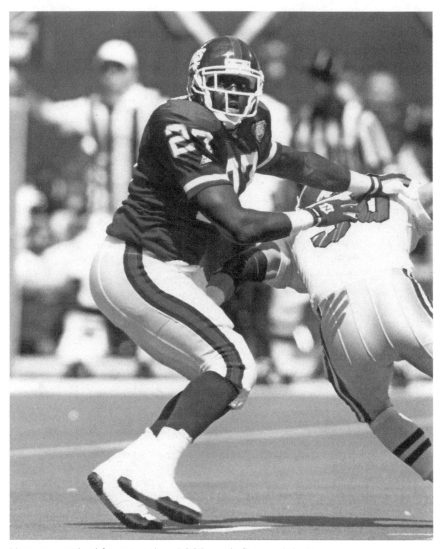

Hampton rushed for more than 1,000 yards five straight times as a member of the Giants.
Courtesy of PristineAuction.co

Unfortunately, the pounding Hampton took over the course of his first six seasons began to take its toll on him in 1996, limiting him to only 827 yards and one touchdown. Furthermore, having added another 15 or 20 pounds to his already sturdy frame, Hampton appeared to be a step or two slower, no longer possessing the quickness to break away from tacklers at the line of scrimmage. As a result, Wheatley began to assume a larger role in the team's running game, limiting to some degree the number of touches Hampton received. Hampton's already disappointing campaign ended in dismal fashion in the season's next-to-last game when he had to leave an embarrassing home loss to the 2–12 New Orleans Saints with what the *New York Times* described in its postgame report as a "bruised right knee."

As it turned out, Hampton's injury proved to be far more serious, forcing him to undergo arthroscopic surgery to remove loose cartilage team doctors believed was causing the problem. Slow to recover from the surgery, Hampton ended up losing his starting job to a rotation of significantly younger backs that included Wheatley and second-round draft pick Tiki Barber. Unable to return to the field until the Giants hosted Washington on December 13, Hampton appeared in only two games in 1997, rushing for just 81 yards on 23 carries. The Giants subsequently elected to release him at the end of the year, after signing free-agent running back Gary Brown to a much less expensive one-year deal. Upon announcing Hampton's release to the assembled media, Giants general manager Ernie Accorsi stated, "Words come up short when you try to explain what Rodney has meant to the entire organization. He has conducted himself with great pride and dignity."[1]

Meanwhile, Hampton remained determined to land a job somewhere in the NFL, proclaiming, "I'm playing next year, just not with the Giants. I guess it's kind of sad because I spent a lot of years in New York. I'll miss the Giants, but it's time to move on."[2]

Although the Arizona Cardinals and Dallas Cowboys both looked into the possibility of acquiring Hampton as a potential backup, neither team made him an official contract offer, prompting the 29-year-old veteran to announce his retirement. Hampton ended his career as the Giants' all-time leader in rushing yards (6,897) and rushing touchdowns (49). He also caught 174 passes, for 1,309 yards and two touchdowns. He ran for more than 100 yards in a game 17 times while playing for the Giants.

Following his retirement, Hampton started a program known as "Hamp's Camp," which not only serves as a free football camp to young people but also teaches them self-esteem and strives to give them a sense of responsibility and self-discipline. Hampton began his program as a means of giving back to youngsters and offering them the same opportunity he had as a child. Commenting on the coaches who helped shape his athletic career and character during his formative years, Hampton said, "They taught me three things—belief in myself, work hard, and be disciplined."[3]

CAREER HIGHLIGHTS

Best Season

Although Hampton had big years for the Giants in 1991 and 1995, rushing for a career-high 1,182 yards in the second of those campaigns, he had his best all-around season in 1992. Playing for a team that won only six games during the regular season, Hampton rushed for 1,141 yards and a career-best 14 touchdowns, ranking in the league's top three in both touchdowns and rushing touchdowns. He also made 28 receptions for another 215 yards, amassing in the process a career-high 1,356 yards from scrimmage. Furthermore, Hampton posted the highest rushing average of his career (4.4), en route to earning the first of his two consecutive Pro Bowl selections.

Memorable Moments/Greatest Performances

Hampton began his NFL career in style, racing 89 yards for a touchdown in a preseason game against Buffalo the very first time he carried the ball as a pro.

Hampton had one of his best all-around games on October 11, 1992, carrying the ball 21 times for 167 yards, in leading the Giants to a 31–21 win over the Cardinals. Hampton's runs included a 63-yard touchdown scamper—the longest of his career. He also made a 31-yard reception, giving him a total of 198 yards on the afternoon.

Hampton also turned in a fabulous performance against the Vikings on January 9, 1994, leading the Giants to a 17–10 victory over Minnesota in the first round of the postseason tournament. Hampton rushed for 161 yards and two touchdowns on the day, with the game's most memorable play being his third-quarter TD run of 51 yards that saw him break four tackles and straight-arm two defenders before finally crossing the goal line. He also made six receptions for another 24 yards.

Hampton had another huge game against the New Orleans Saints on September 24, 1995, rushing for 149 yards and tying Ron Johnson's single-game team record by scoring four touchdowns during a 45–29 Giants win.

Ironically, Hampton turned in one of his finest performances in a losing effort to Dallas. With the 5–9 Giants playing the 10–4 Cowboys in the next-to-last week of the 1995 regular season, Hampton carried the ball 34 times for 187 yards in a 21–20 loss to the eventual Super Bowl champions.

Yet Hampton remembers most fondly a game in which he carried the ball 11 times for only 43 yards. Returning to action on December 13, 1997, after having missed the first 14 games of the campaign following arthroscopic surgery to repair his injured knee, Hampton helped the Giants run out the clock during a 30–10 win over the Washington Redskins that enabled them to clinch the NFC East title. Looking back at the feelings he experienced that day when the fans at Giants Stadium greeted him with a rousing ovation, Hampton said years later, "For all the 100-yard rushing games I had, it's the Washington game that I'll reflect back to. I appreciated the fans' ovation."[4]

NOTABLE ACHIEVEMENTS

- Rushed for more than 1,000 yards five times (1991–1995).
- Scored at least 10 touchdowns three times (1991, 1992, 1995).
- First Giants player to rush for more than 1,000 yards five straight times.
- Surpassed 40 receptions once (43 in 1991).
- Finished third in NFL with 14 touchdowns in 1992.
- Finished fourth in NFL with 1,059 rushing yards and 1,546 all-purpose yards in 1991.
- Retired as Giants all-time leader in rushing yardage (6,897) and rushing touchdowns (49).
- Ranks among Giants all-time leaders in rushing yardage (2nd), rushing touchdowns (3rd), and total touchdowns scored (8th).
- Shares Giants record with four touchdowns in one game (September 24, 1995).
- 1991 Week 6 NFC Offensive Player of the Week.
- Two-time Pro Bowl selection (1992, 1993).
- 1990 NFC champion.
- Super Bowl XXV champion.

JESSIE ARMSTEAD

The heart and soul of the Giants' defense for the better part of a decade, Jessie Armstead overcame a serious knee injury in college and early questions about his size, or lack thereof, to eventually become one of the finest outside linebackers in team history. An extremely intense and emotional player, Armstead served as one of New York's team leaders from 1996 to 2001, during which time he led all Giant defenders in tackles on five separate occasions. Using his outstanding quickness to excel against both the pass and the run, Armstead appeared in five consecutive Pro Bowls while playing for the Giants. He also earned All-NFL honors three times. Yet, had it not been for a decision he made while still only 17 years of age, Armstead likely never would have been fortunate enough to play a single game in the NFL.

Born in Dallas, Texas, on October 26, 1970, Jessie Willard Armstead attended David W. Carter High School in Dallas, where he played for an extremely talented team that featured four other future NFL players: Clifton Abraham, Joe Burch, Le'Shai Maston, and Darius Smith. Considered to be the most talented young football player in the state of Texas, Armstead earned All-America honors three straight times while at Carter High, becoming the first high school player to accomplish that feat.

Nevertheless, Armstead developed a somewhat dubious reputation in high school after being arrested for shoplifting two pairs of tights and a T-shirt. Seeing the hurt in his mother's eyes when she learned of his transgression, Armstead promised never to wound her in such a manner again after serving his punishment by spending 10 hours in juvenile detention. Approached one year later by fellow Division I recruits Derric Evans and Gary Edwards to join them in a series of robberies of video stores and fast-food restaurants, the 17-year-old Armstead refused, choosing the promising career in football that he knew awaited him over a possible life of pain and imprisonment. While Evans and Edwards ended up being sentenced in

Jessie Armstead led the Giants in tackles five straight times.
Courtesy of PristineAuction.com

September 1989 to 20 years and 16 years, respectively, in prison, Armstead went on to star at the University of Miami.

Years later, Armstead called his decision not to join his two high school teammates "the turning point in my life,"[1] also stating, "I think about it all the time. I could have gone with them. I went with them everywhere else. I made a choice."[2]

Armstead added, "There was no temptation. I knew I was a million-dollar chip waiting to be cashed. I told them that wasn't for me. They looked at me like I was selling them out. But you have to make your own choice. Your friends will tell you that it's cool to go along, but that isn't cool."[3]

Armstead subsequently enrolled at Miami, where he starred on the university's national championship teams of 1989 and 1991 despite needing reconstructive knee surgery as a sophomore to repair a torn anterior cruciate ligament. After working extremely hard to return to the lineup as a junior, Armstead eventually regained his 4.5-second speed in the 40-yard dash. Meanwhile, he added 15 pounds of muscle onto his frame, making him a much more solid 6'1", 225-pounder. Yet many scouts still considered him to be a bit too small to succeed at the professional level heading into the 1993 NFL Draft. And when they factored into the equation the severity of his earlier injury, Armstead's stock ended up plummeting, with the linebacker lasting into the eighth round, until the Giants finally selected him with the 207th overall pick. Annoyed somewhat by the obvious snub, Armstead responded to all those who questioned his size by saying, "After it's all over, I want to be able to take my hat off to those people and say, 'I knew I could do it.' People like that don't know Jessie Armstead. You can't measure a person's heart."[4]

Although he occasionally saw action with the regular defensive unit, Armstead spent most of his first three years in New York performing on special teams. During that time, though, he built himself up further, increasing his weight to 237 pounds while still retaining his outstanding running speed. Ready to assume a more prominent role by 1996, Armstead moved into the starting lineup and made a team-leading 114 tackles (83 of them solo), en route to earning a spot on *Sports Illustrated*'s All-Pro Team.

Armstead led the Giants in tackles in each of the next four seasons as well, performing particularly well in 1997, when he broke Lawrence Taylor's "official" team record by making 132 tackles (101 of them solo). He also recorded 3½ sacks and two interceptions, returning one of those 57 yards for a touchdown. Armstead's exceptional campaign earned him First-Team All-Pro honors. He made First-Team All-NFC the following year, when he surpassed 100 tackles for the third straight time, intercepted another two passes, and recorded five sacks. Armstead made 124 tackles (97 solo) and registered a career-high nine sacks in 1999, en route to earning First-Team All-NFC and Second-Team All-Pro honors. He made Second-Team All-Pro again the following year, when he helped the Giants capture the NFC title by making five sacks and surpassing 100 tackles for the fifth consecutive time. Armstead started all 16 games for the Giants in each of those five seasons.

Armstead earned five Pro Bowl selections and three All-Pro nominations while playing for the Giants.
Courtesy of SportsMemorabilia.com

Despite lacking great size and strength, Armstead's outstanding speed enabled him to establish himself as one of the NFL's premier outside linebackers during the latter half of the 1990s. His great quickness made him particularly effective against the pass, allowing him to keep up with opposing running backs. Armstead also played the run extremely well, using his agility to slip blocks and arrive at the hole the same time as opposing runners.

Although Armstead's production slipped somewhat in 2001, he still managed to have a solid year, taking part in 88 tackles. However, salary cap considerations prompted the Giants to release the 31-year-old veteran at season's end. Armstead subsequently signed a three-year, $4.5-million deal with the Washington Redskins, fulfilling the first two years of that contract before announcing his retirement at the conclusion of the 2003 campaign. Armstead ended his career with nearly 1,000 tackles (752 of them solo), 40 sacks, and 12 interceptions. He recorded 779 tackles (597 solo), 30½ sacks, and all 12 interceptions as a member of the Giants.

Armstead compiled an impressive stat-line while playing for the Giants, but it was his enthusiasm and passion for the game as much as anything that helped make him such an integral contributor to any success the team experienced during his time in New York. Armstead and the Giants displayed their mutual appreciation for each other on June 13, 2007, when the former linebacker signed a one-day contract with the team so that he might officially retire as a New York Giant. Upon inking the deal, Armstead stated, "This is the perfect opportunity. You see certain guys get to do this, like Emmitt Smith did with Dallas. You always think of Emmitt as a Cowboy. I wanted to do that with the Giants. . . . It's real special to know it wasn't a one-way street either."[5]

One year later, the Giants hired Armstead to be a "special assistant/ consultant." Serving in that capacity ever since, Armstead is involved with special projects, defensive assignments, player development, and free agent recruiting.

GIANT CAREER HIGHLIGHTS

Best Season

Armstead had a big year in 1999, when he had a hand in 124 tackles and recorded a career-high nine sacks en route to earning First-Team All-Conference and Second-Team All-Pro honors. However, he had performed slightly better two years earlier, establishing a new "official" team record by making 132 tackles. Armstead also registered 3½ quarterback sacks, intercepted two passes, and scored a defensive touchdown in 1997, earning unanimous First-Team All-Pro honors in the process.

Memorable Moments/Greatest Performances

Armstead returned two interceptions for touchdowns during his career, making his first pick-6 a memorable one. With the Giants and Arizona Cardinals tied at 21 heading into overtime on October 8, 1995, Armstead intercepted a Dave Krieg pass and returned it 58 yards for the winning score in a 27–21 Giants victory. He scored the second touchdown of his career a little over two years later, returning an interception 57 yards for a TD during a 31–21 Giants victory over the Eagles on December 7, 1997. Armstead intercepted another pass during the contest and helped record a sack of Philadelphia quarterback Bobby Hoying, en route to earning NFC

Defensive Player of the Week honors. Armstead had another huge game against the Eagles on October 3, 1999, recording two sacks during a 16–15 Giants win.

NOTABLE ACHIEVEMENTS

- Surpassed 100 tackles five times (1996–2000).
- Topped 100 solo tackles once (101 in 1997).
- Led Giants in tackles five times (1996–2000).
- Recorded nine sacks in 1999.
- Tied for 11th all-time on Giants' "official" list with 30½ quarterback sacks.
- 1993 Week 11 NFC Special Teams Player of the Week.
- 1997 Week 15 NFC Defensive Player of the Week.
- Five-time Pro Bowl selection (1997–2001).
- 1997 First-Team All-Pro selection.
- Two-time Second-Team All-Pro selection (1999, 2000).
- Three-time First-Team All-NFC selection (1997, 1998, 1999).
- 2000 NFC champion.

CARL "SPIDER" LOCKHART

arl "Spider" Lockhart had the misfortune of joining the Giants in 1965, shortly after they entered into the darkest period in franchise history. He spent the next 11 years in New York, retiring at the conclusion of the 1975 campaign having played for teams that posted a winning record just twice. The Giants had very little talent in most of those years, particularly on the defensive side of the ball, where Lockhart proved to be one of the few bright spots. Although the 6'2", 175-pound defensive back hardly intimidated opposing receivers with his wiry frame, he played with abandon, making the impact of a much larger man by throwing his body all over the field. An outstanding ball-hawk, Lockhart ended his career with 41 interceptions, placing him third on the team's all-time list. Lockhart's talent, physical style of play, and intensity made him the heart and soul of the Giants' defense during his time with them, earning him respect throughout the league in spite of the overall lack of success experienced by his team.

Born in Dallas, Texas, on April 6, 1943, Carl Ford Lockhart played his college ball at North Texas before being selected by the Giants in the 13th round of the 1965 NFL Draft with the 169th overall pick. A long shot to make the Giants' roster when he arrived at his first training camp, Lockhart soon found himself drawing praise from the team's secondary coach, Hall of Fame safety Emlen Tunnell, who nicknamed him "Spider" for the way he weaved a defensive web around opposing receivers.

Earning the starting left cornerback job as a rookie, Lockhart played well his first year in the league, intercepting four passes and returning them for a total of 117 yards. However, after finishing 7–7 in 1965, the Giants plummeted to the depths of the National Football League the following season, compiling a record of just 1–12–1 and allowing their opposition a league record (for a 14-game schedule) 501 points over the course of the campaign. Nevertheless, the defensive unit's horrendous performance did not prevent Lockhart, who intercepted six passes, from being named to the Pro Bowl for the first time.

Carl "Spider" Lockhart ranks third in Giants history with 41 career interceptions.
Courtesy of RMYAuctions.com

Moved from cornerback to free safety in 1967, Lockhart continued to play well for a Giants team that improved its record to 7–7. In addition to intercepting five passes, he recovered a league-leading four fumbles. Lockhart earned Pro Bowl honors for the second time the following season, when he intercepted eight passes, which he returned for a total of 130 yards and two touchdowns. His outstanding play also earned him First-Team All-Conference honors from the *Sporting News*.

Despite being a member of the NFL wars for only four years by 1968, Lockhart had already established himself as one of the Giants' team leaders, and the backbone of their defense. The team's coaches and players knew that they had in Lockhart someone on whom they could depend.

Andy Robustelli, who got to know Lockhart even though he left the Giants one year before the latter arrived in New York, said, "He [Lockhart] always was a guy who could rally people around the flag. The ballplayers knew it, and the coaches knew it. A coach could pull him over to the side and say, 'Get them going,' and he would. He was a leader in his own way."[1]

And speaking of Lockhart's aggressive style of play, Robustelli added, "He really had no reason playing football with that body. But he was scrappy and he got it done. He had a big heart. They say if you have a big heart you can do anything."[2]

Meanwhile, Frank Gifford, who also remained extremely close to the team after his playing career ended, stated, "It was amazing what he could do with that little body. He reminded me of Don Burroughs, who played for the Rams and Philadelphia. Burroughs was called 'The Blade.' He played a lot like Spider and was All Pro about 10–12 years before. He could really hit. The thing that surprised me about Spider is that he wasn't very fast. But he had great perception. And he was a hell of a hitter; a whacker."[3]

Tucker Frederickson, who came to the Giants the same time as Lockhart, said of his close friend and longtime teammate, "I don't think he crunched people. But he wasn't afraid to stick them. He had a huge heart, and he played with it. He was 175, 180 at the most, but he played like he was 210."[4]

Although Lockhart never made it back to the Pro Bowl, he continued to anchor the Giants' secondary the next several years, intercepting another 18 passes between 1969 and 1975. He had another outstanding year in 1970, intercepting four passes and providing veteran leadership to a young defense that helped the Giants improve their record to 9–5. Lockhart's contributions to the team earned him First-Team All-Conference honors. The Pro Football Writers also named him to their All-NFL Second Team.

However, Lockhart's performance began to slip somewhat by 1975, and when the Giants concluded the campaign with a record of only 5–9, the 32-year-old veteran chose to announce his retirement. In addition to ending his career with a total of 41 interceptions that places him third on the Giants' all-time list, he shares the team record with three picks in one game. Lockhart served as New York's defensive captain his final eight years in the league.

Following his retirement, Lockhart continued to live in the northern New Jersey area, residing in the town of Teaneck. He became a stockbroker, working with Prudential-Bache. However, his life took a sudden turn in 1981, when he learned he had lymphoma, a cancer of the lymph nodes. Lockhart lived with the illness another five years, before finally losing his

Lockhart played for only two winning teams in his 11 seasons with the Giants.
Courtesy of RMYAuctions.com

battle with it on July 9, 1986, when he died in his sleep at Hackensack Medical Center. He was only 43 years of age at the time of his passing. In his honor, the Giants wore a "Spider patch" on their uniforms throughout their NFL championship-winning season of 1986.

Tucker Frederickson, who remained close with Lockhart long after the two men left the game, expressed his sadness when learning of his friend's passing: "Spider and I came in together. We were both scared to death. We were good friends from day one. We had a lot of fun together. I'm really shook up. He was a good friend. It's tough to lose a good friend."[5]

Lockhart's widow later won a $15.7 million malpractice suit against St. Vincent's Hospital in which she claimed that the facility had misdiagnosed her husband's illness in 1979 as swollen lymph nodes when he originally told a doctor there that he feared he had cancer. Another diagnosis two years later confirmed Lockhart's initial suspicions.

CAREER HIGHLIGHTS

Best Season

Lockhart earned the only First-Team All-Conference selection of his career in 1970, when his four interceptions and outstanding all-around play helped the Giants post a 9–5 record that represented their best mark in his 11 years with them. Nevertheless, Lockhart clearly had his best season in 1968, when he earned Pro Bowl honors for the second time by establishing career highs with eight interceptions, 130 interception return yards, and two touchdown interceptions.

Memorable Moments/Greatest Performances

Ironically, Lockhart turned in perhaps the greatest performance of his career during a 49–40 loss to the Cleveland Browns on December 4, 1966. Although the Giant defense surrendered 326 yards and three touchdowns through the air to the Browns that day, Lockhart tied a team record by intercepting Cleveland quarterback Frank Ryan three times.

Lockhart tied another team record two years later, when he returned an interception for a touchdown in two straight weeks. He registered his first defensive touchdown during a 34–25 victory over Philadelphia on September 22, 1968, returning an errant John Huarte pass 72 yards for a score. The following week, Lockhart returned a Sonny Jurgensen aerial 47 yards for a touchdown during a 48–21 win over Washington.

NOTABLE ACHIEVEMENTS

- Led NFL with two touchdown interceptions and two non-offensive touchdowns in 1968.
- Finished third in NFL with eight interceptions in 1968.

- Led NFL with four fumble recoveries in 1967.
- Holds share of Giants' record with three interceptions in one game (December 4, 1966).
- Holds share of Giants' record with touchdown interceptions in consecutive weeks (September 22, 1968; September 29, 1968).
- Ranks third all-time on Giants with 41 career interceptions.
- Two-time Pro Bowl selection (1966, 1968).
- 1970 First-Team All-Conference selection.

24

MARK HAYNES

Largely forgotten by Giants fans due—at least, in part—to the fact that he spent only five full seasons in New York, Mark Haynes remains arguably the most underappreciated player ever to man the position of cornerback for the New York Giants. Haynes also failed to receive the credit he deserved during his playing days because he failed to cooperate with the press at times. Nevertheless, the fact remains that Haynes played exceptionally well during his relatively brief time in New York, earning three Pro Bowl selections, two First-Team All-Pro nominations, and two Second-Team selections. A true "shut-down" corner, Haynes used his speed, quickness, and excellent instincts to blanket opposing wide receivers. Meanwhile, he made outstanding use of his powerful 5'11", 198-pound frame to help shut down the opposition's running game by taking on blockers at the point of attack. Only disagreements with Giants management prevented Haynes from establishing the sort of legacy in New York that ultimately would have earned him a place in the team's Ring of Honor.

Born in Kansas City, Kansas, on November 6, 1958, Mark Haynes spent his first three years at the University of Colorado playing safety, before moving to left cornerback as a senior. Subsequently selected by the Giants in the first round of the 1980 NFL Draft with the 8th overall pick, Haynes struggled in his first NFL season, experiencing so many difficulties early in the year after being shifted to right cornerback that rookie free agent Mike Dennis claimed the starting job from him three games into the campaign. However, Haynes showed marked improvement after the Giants moved him to his more familiar position of left cornerback when the regular starter there, Terry Jackson, injured himself at midseason. In fact, Haynes played so well that Jackson moved to the right side when he returned to the team later in the year.

Yet, even though Haynes played better ball during the season's second half, he continued to experience philosophical differences with Don Pollard, the Giants' defensive backfield coach, who wanted the rookie cornerback to

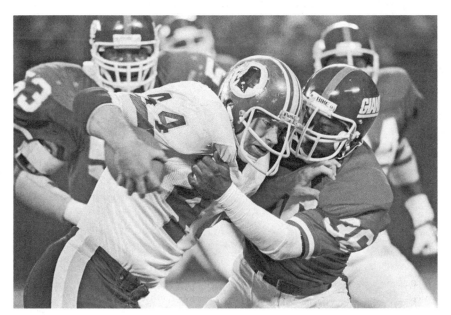

Mark Haynes (seen here taking on John Riggins) earned four consecutive All-Pro selections while playing for the Giants.
Courtesy of SportsMemorabilia.com

change his techniques and do everything the way he suggested. Haynes later expressed his dissatisfaction with Pollard by saying, "The guy tried to make clones out of everybody."[1]

It wasn't until the Giants relieved Pollard of his duties at the end of the year that Haynes really began to come into his own. By the time the second-year corner reported to camp prior to the start of the 1981 campaign, the Giants had revamped their coaching staff, replacing Pollard with Fred Glick and making Bill Parcells their new defensive coordinator. Parcells and Glick gave Haynes much more freedom than did Pollard, allowing him the opportunity to use any technique he wished to employ, as long as it fell within the framework of the defense. Glick said, "I told him to do it his way. I said, 'If you're wrong, we'll correct you.' That's the way I've always coached. He's got his own techniques to do everything. He lines up differently. He likes to bump and run, and he does it when others don't because they're afraid they won't catch up to their man. He can catch up. I think he's the best cornerback in the league."[2]

By the end of Haynes's second season, he was indeed among the very best cornerbacks in the NFL. Although his lack of a reputation prevented him from earning Pro Bowl honors, he was named First-Team All-Pro by both *Pro Football Weekly* and the Newspaper Enterprise Association. The Associated Press also accorded him Second-Team All-Pro honors. Meanwhile, Haynes earned First-Team and Second-Team All-NFC honors from *Pro Football Weekly* and the UPI, respectively.

Haynes continued to excel in 1982, earning the first of three straight Pro Bowl selections and unanimous First-Team All-Pro honors. Perhaps the only thing preventing Haynes from gaining general recognition as the finest all-around cornerback in the game was the fact that he intercepted a total of only three passes over the course of his first three seasons. However, Glick explained Haynes's low pick total by saying, "The reason for that is because he plays his man so tight that he's tipping or batting away the ball. He doesn't have time to intercept."[3]

Meanwhile, Beasley Reece, who played behind Haynes in New York's defensive secondary at the free safety position, suggested that the latter rarely made mistakes, claiming that his man beat him only three or four times over the course of the 1981 and 1982 campaigns. At the same time, Reece noted that such a low number was "incredible for a cornerback."[4]

Haynes established a new career high by intercepting three passes in 1983, en route to earning Second-Team All-Pro honors. He reached the high point of his career the following year, earning unanimous First-Team All-Pro honors by recording seven interceptions, which he returned for 90 yards.

Yet, in spite of his exceptional play, Haynes continued to receive little publicity from the New York media. Even-tempered, quiet, and seemingly unemotional, Haynes often gave outsiders the impression that he cared little about what went on during games and in the locker room. However, those close to Haynes knew that his behavior merely reflected his overall attitude toward life. Choosing on one rare occasion to defend his actions by speaking to a member of the press corps, Haynes stated, "People who know me understand me. They know where I'm coming from. They know I'm no egomaniac. Nothing really excites me or gets me mad. Everybody's got to live his own life as it is. I'm happy. I like myself."[5]

Haynes added, "I don't like to lose. But there's always another game next week, and I have to prepare for that. I don't dwell on losses, but I don't dwell on wins, either."[6]

Unfortunately, the 1984 campaign ended up being Haynes's last season as a full-time starter in New York. Looking for a three-year deal worth just over $2 million, Haynes held out for 93 days prior to the start of the 1985 season, before finally settling for considerably less when the premature birth and subsequent hospitalization of his second daughter presented him with

Haynes proved to be a true shutdown corner during his time in New York.
Public domain (author unknown)

bills he needed to pay. Returning to the Giants after signing a one-year deal worth $400,000, Haynes seemed mostly disinterested much of the time, prompting Mark Bavaro to say, "He never looked like he was giving you an effort. He obviously was unhappy. He wanted to get out."[7]

After losing his starting job and appearing in only five games for the Giants in 1985, Haynes basically forced the Giants to trade him at the end of the year. They finally accepted two second-round draft choices and a sixth-rounder from the Denver Broncos for the disgruntled cornerback, thereby bringing to a close that chapter in Haynes's career. Haynes spent the next four years in Denver, starting for the Broncos in 1987 and 1988, and playing for them in each of the next three Super Bowls. An injured back compromised his performance in 1989, causing him to lose his starting job once again, and prompting him to announce his retirement when the Broncos cut him at the end of the year. Haynes ended his career with 17 interceptions, 13 of which he recorded while playing for the Giants.

GIANT CAREER HIGHLIGHTS

Best Season

Although Haynes played extremely well for the Giants from 1981 to 1983, he had his best year for them in 1984, when he finished fourth in the NFL with a career-high seven interceptions. His outstanding performance earned him unanimous First-Team All-Pro honors for the second time.

Memorable Moments/Greatest Performances

Haynes intercepted two passes in one game for the only time in his career on November 18, 1984, picking off two Neil Lomax passes during a 16–10 Giants victory over the St. Louis Cardinals. However, he made arguably his most memorable play as a member of the Giants on special teams, recovering a fumble in the Philadelphia end zone following a Joe Danelo kickoff during New York's 27–21 upset win over the Eagles in the first round of the 1981 NFC playoffs. Haynes's touchdown gave the Giants a 20–0 first-quarter lead that they nursed the rest of the way.

NOTABLE ACHIEVEMENTS

- Intercepted seven passes in 1984.
- Three-time Pro Bowl selection (1982, 1983, 1984).
- Two-time First-Team All-Pro selection (1982, 1984).
- Two-time Second-Team All-Pro selection (1981, 1983).
- Three-time First-Team All-Conference selection (1981, 1982, 1984).
- Pro Football Reference Second-Team All-1980s Team.

25

ALEX WEBSTER

One of the most popular players in Giants history, Alex Webster used his toughness, desire, and determination to become a star in New York in spite of his somewhat limited natural ability. Blessed with good size but only average speed, Webster willed his way into becoming a significant contributor to Giants teams that appeared in six NFL Championship Games between 1956 and 1963. Speaking of his longtime teammate, Frank Gifford once marveled, "He [Webster] was always amazing to me. He was always in the worst shape of anyone who ever played, probably. He smoked and drank, not to excess, and then he'd come out and play a whole game and run over people. He was one tough dude."[1]

Webster's toughness enabled him to establish himself as the Giants' all-time leader in rushing yards (4,638) and rushing touchdowns (39) at the time of his retirement in 1964. He continues to rank in the top five in both categories. He also earned two Pro Bowl nominations and two Second-Team All-NFL selections during his 10 years in New York. Webster's many accomplishments tend to support the contention made by former All-Pro tackle Al DeRogatis, who originally discovered him while scouting another player in the Canadian Football League. Speaking of the man who eventually became known to his teammates as Big Red, DeRogatis noted, "If you looked at Alex from the standpoint of his natural talent, from the standpoint of speed—the ingredients that we see today in the great athlete—well, that wasn't Alex Webster. But, if you look for a man who was a great fighter, a guy that you wanted on your side when the going really got tough, then you'd want Alex Webster to be with you."[2]

Born in Kearny, New Jersey, on April 19, 1931, Alexander Webster lost his father to cancer at an early age in 1941. Nevertheless, young Alex learned to excel in sports, starring in football at Kearny High en route to earning an athletic scholarship to North Carolina State University. After performing extremely well in college as a single-wing tailback on offense and a safety on defense, Webster was selected by the Washington Redskins

Alex Webster proved to be a key contributor to Giant teams that won six
division titles and one NFL championship.
Courtesy of RMYAuctions.com

in the 11th round of the 1953 NFL Draft with the 123rd overall pick.
However, after trying him out exclusively in the secondary, the Redskins
elected to cut Webster, telling the young man that they considered him to
be too slow to play safety in the NFL.

Undeterred, Webster traveled north to Canada, where he spent the
next two years starring at running back for the Montreal Alouettes. Webster
eventually returned to the United States, though, thanks to Al DeRogatis,
who urged the Giants to sign the NC State product after watching him play
one day. DeRogatis, who was on assignment in Montreal to scout quarterback Sam Etcheverry for the Giants, later recalled, "When I came back, I
told the Giants that Webster was the big man they had been looking for."[3]

Standing 6'3" and weighing 225 pounds, Webster had good size and
strength. He also brought with him to New York his reputation as a bar-
room brawler, taking that attitude with him to the field. Although Webster
lacked outstanding speed, he had an explosive first step out of his stance

that enabled him to hit the hole quickly. He also enjoyed punishing defenders with his slashing style of running.

Fellow Giants running back Frank Gifford said, "He was so strong at 230-plus pounds that it was impossible to arm-tackle him. . . . People either bounced off him or he ran over them. Every time he got the ball, he turned into a grinding machine."[4]

Webster excelled in his first year in New York, leading the Giants in rushing with 634 yards, on only 128 carries. His 5.0-yard rushing average placed him third in the league. Webster also accumulated 269 receiving yards and scored six touchdowns. He followed that up by finishing second on the team in rushing with 694 yards in the championship season of 1956. After another solid year, Webster earned his first Pro Bowl selection in 1958 by scoring six touchdowns and amassing 677 all-purpose yards. However, he proved to be less productive in each of the next two seasons, with injuries hampering his performance considerably in 1960.

The Giants gradually changed their offensive philosophy during Webster's tenure with them. They employed a four-man backfield his first several years in New York, with right halfback Webster joining left halfback Frank Gifford, fullback Mel Triplett, and quarterback Charlie Conerly behind the line of scrimmage. They converted to a two wide-receiver, two running-back offense, though, after acquiring Y. A. Tittle and speedy wide-out Del Shofner prior to the start of the 1961 campaign. With Gifford joining Shofner on the outside, Webster moved to fullback, where he spent the remainder of his career.

Thriving in his new role, Webster had his two most productive seasons in 1961 and 1962. In the first of those campaigns, he rushed for a career-high 928 yards, finishing third in the league in that category. He also caught 26 passes for another 313 yards, en route to earning Pro Bowl honors for the second time in his career. Webster followed that up by amassing 1,220 all-purpose yards in 1962, with 743 of those coming on the ground, and the other 477 coming through the air.

However, those turned out to be Webster's last two effective seasons. With injuries and advancing age catching up to him, he rushed for a total of only 465 yards the next two years, prompting him to announce his retirement at the conclusion of the 1964 campaign. In addition to ending his career as the Giants' all-time leading rusher, Webster ranked second in touchdowns scored, crossing the opponent's goal line a total of 56 times over the course of his career.

Following his retirement, Webster served as an assistant under head coach Allie Sherman for two years before replacing Sherman at the helm

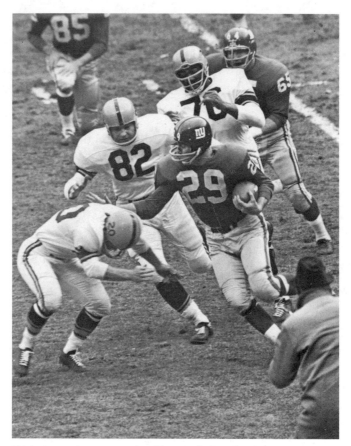

Webster ranks among the Giants' all-time leaders in both rushing yards and rushing touchdowns.
Courtesy of RMYAuctions.com

after the Giants lost all five of their preseason games in 1969. Webster remained in charge for the next five years, leading the Giants to the only two winning records they posted from 1964 to 1980, and being named UPI NFL Coach of the Year in 1970, when his team compiled a surprising mark of 9–5. Nevertheless, he experienced little overall success as New York's head coach, posting a composite record of 29–40–1 during that time.

Looking back at Webster's coaching legacy, Frank Gifford said, "He inherited a team without much talent. He didn't have anyone like himself. And he was really too good of a guy to do it. He was a guy's guy. He was a hell of an assistant coach. But to make some of the decisions he had to make as a head coach would be very tough for Alex."[5]

Turning in his resignation after the Giants finished just 2–11–1 in 1973, Webster elected to pursue a career away from football. For a time, he did promotional work for food and tobacco companies. He later owned a restaurant and bar in Florida, before breathing problems brought on by years of smoking forced him to spend his last several years going in and out of hospitals. Stricken with lung cancer and emphysema, Webster passed away in Port St. Lucie, Florida, at the age of 80 on March 3, 2012. Upon hearing of his passing, Giants co-owner John Mara said, "Alex was one of the all-time great Giants. He contributed so much to our team as a player, assistant coach, and head coach. He was an even better person. We shall miss him dearly."[6]

Years earlier, Al DeRogatis—the man primarily responsible for Webster first coming to New York in 1955—summarized the impact he made on the Giants during his playing days when he said, "To me, the great era of the Giants—they point to other athletes on that team—but, when it was really tough, it was the big redhead from Kearny, N.J. who did it. They always went to Alex Webster. He instinctively had it. He was a winner."[7]

CAREER HIGHLIGHTS

Best Season

Webster earned Second-Team All-NFL honors for one of two times in 1956, when he rushed for 694 yards and scored a career-high 10 touchdowns. He also played extremely well in 1962, when he amassed 1,220 yards from scrimmage (743 yards rushing and 477 yards on pass receptions), scored nine touchdowns, and caught a career-best 47 passes.

Nevertheless, the feeling here is that Webster had his finest season in 1961, when he earned the second of his two Pro Bowl selections by rushing for a career-high 928 yards and making 26 receptions for another 313 yards, leaving him with a career-best total of 1,241 yards from scrimmage. He also scored five touchdowns and finished with a 4.7-yard rushing average that represented the second-highest mark of his career.

Memorable Moments/Greatest Performances

Webster had the first big rushing day of his career in the second game of the 1955 season, carrying the ball 20 times for 139 yards and one touchdown during a 28–17 loss to the Chicago Cardinals. Big Red also recorded the longest run of his career that day, lugging the ball 71 yards before finally being brought down. He had another outstanding game in week 6, leading the Giants to a 35–7 victory over the Washington Redskins by scoring on touchdown runs of 52 and 42 yards.

Webster had a couple of big days the following year as well, scoring three touchdowns against the defending champion Cleveland Browns during a 21–9 Giants win on October 14, 1956. Webster's three scores tied a team record that stood until Ron Johnson crossed the goal line four times against Philadelphia 16 years later.

Although Webster rushed for only 27 yards during New York's 47–7 win over Chicago in the 1956 NFL Championship Game, he contributed mightily to the victory by making a key 50-yard reception in the second quarter, scoring two second-half touchdowns, and amassing 103 all-purpose yards.

Still, the play for which Webster is perhaps best remembered occurred during the Giants' loss to the Baltimore Colts in the 1958 title game. With Baltimore holding a 14–3 lead midway through the third quarter and the Giants in possession of the ball deep in their own territory, quarterback Charlie Conerly hit Kyle Rote with a pass near the New York 35-yard line. Maneuvering his way up field, the Giants receiver broke two tackles before being hit from behind by Colts safety Andy Nelson, who jarred the ball loose from Rote at the Baltimore 35. Webster, who had been trailing the play, scooped up the pigskin at the 25-yard line and nearly carried it into the end zone before being knocked out of bounds at the 1 by a Colts defender. Giants fullback Mel Triplett banged it in for a touchdown on the next play, closing the gap to 14–10 and putting New York right back in the contest.

NOTABLE ACHIEVEMENTS

- Gained more than 1,000 yards from scrimmage twice (1961, 1962).
- Scored 10 touchdowns in 1956.
- Ranks among Giants all-time leaders in rushing yardage (5th), rushing touchdowns (5th), and total touchdowns scored (6th).
- Two-time Pro Bowl selection (1958, 1961).
- Two-time Second-Team All-Pro selection (1955, 1956).
- Six-time NFL Eastern Division champion.
- 1956 NFL champion.

26

JOE MORRIS

Though diminutive in stature, Joe Morris used his huge heart, tremendous quickness, and great physical strength to eventually establish himself as one of the finest running backs ever to carry the ball for the New York Giants. After spending his first 2½ NFL seasons sitting on the Giants' bench, Morris went on to become the first player in team history to rush for more than 1,000 yards in back-to-back seasons. He also became the first Giants runner to surpass the 1,000-yard mark as many as three times, concluding his seven-year stint in New York as the team's all-time leader in rushing yardage and touchdowns scored on the ground. Nevertheless, Morris always felt as if he had something to prove, spending most of his career battling questions about his height, blocking and pass-catching skills, and ability to run on real grass. Such doubts caused the 5'7" Morris to play the game with a huge chip on his shoulder, prompting him to say on one occasion, "I feel like I have to prove myself every game, but that doesn't bother me. It's the same with people always calling me 'Little Joe.' That's always going to be there. Those things don't bother me anymore. I'm a little running back in stature only. I'm a big person in most other aspects of life."[1]

Born in Fort Bragg, North Carolina, on September 15, 1960, Joseph Edward Morris grew up nearly one hour away in Southern Pines, N.C., before moving with his family to Massachusetts as a teenager. After starring in football locally at Ayer High School, Morris attended Syracuse University, where he spent the next four years shattering all of the school's existing rushing records, surpassing in the process such all-time greats as Jim Brown, Ernie Davis, Floyd Little, and Larry Csonka.

However, after being selected by the Giants in the second round of the 1982 NFL Draft with the 45th overall pick, Morris found that his college accomplishments meant little to his new employers. With the Giants picking Michigan running back Butch Woolfolk one round earlier than Morris, the latter saw very little action over the course of the next 2½

Joe Morris finished second in the league with 1,516 yards rushing when the Giants won the NFL championship in 1986.
Courtesy of SportsMemorabilia.com

seasons, serving primarily as Woolfolk's backup and occasionally returning kickoffs. Morris later described that period of time as "almost three years of anguish."[2]

Adding to the young running back's woes was the lack of success he experienced whenever he received an opportunity to play. Described by Giants tackle Brad Benson as a "momentum runner,"[3] Morris played his best when he saw a considerable amount of action, needing at least 15 carries a game to maximize his effectiveness. Failing to use him accordingly, the Giants received little production from their backup halfback, who struggled to gain yardage and fumbled all too often. Morris later noted, "When I was given opportunities early in my career, I would press so hard trying to make great plays because I knew I was only in for so long. So I made mistakes. I couldn't relax. That wasn't me."[4]

The one saving grace for Morris ended up being that Woolfolk fared no better. Having grown weary of the former first-round draft pick's inconsistent play, head coach Bill Parcells finally inserted Morris into the starting unit midway through the 1984 campaign. Morris responded by rushing for 68 yards and three touchdowns during a 37–13 Giants victory over the Washington Redskins. He continued to play well the rest of the year, concluding the campaign as New York's leading rusher, with a total of 510 yards on the ground.

Morris developed into an elite running back the following year, finishing fourth in the NFL with 1,336 rushing yards and leading the league with 21 touchdowns. His 1,336 yards on the ground made him just the second Giants running back to surpass the 1,000-yard mark in a season (Ron Johnson was the first). His touchdown runs included jaunts of 65, 58, 56, and 41 yards. Particularly effective during the second half of the campaign, Morris rushed for 999 yards in the season's final nine games.

After signing a new deal with the Giants hours before the 1986 season opener, Morris carried into the campaign the momentum he had established one year earlier, running for 14 touchdowns and a career-high 1,516 yards, en route to finishing second in the league in rushing. His outstanding season included eight 100-yard games, earning him his second straight Pro Bowl selection and his only First-Team All-Pro nomination. Morris then helped the Giants defeat Denver in the Super Bowl by rushing for 67 yards, catching four passes for another 20 yards, and scoring a touchdown.

Even though the Giants' overpowering defense received much of the credit for their successful run to the Super Bowl, several of their players considered Morris to be the most indispensable member of the team. Fullback Maurice Carthon, who spent most of his time blocking for Morris, said of his backfield mate, "He's the heartbeat of our offense."[5]

Guard Chris Godfrey stated, "We'd be lost without him."[6]

Meanwhile, safety Kenny Hill proclaimed, "Last year, he [Morris] was the Giants' Most Valuable Player for being the best player on this team. I think he's an even more vital cog in our success this year than last year. I don't know if there is another back in this league as essential to their team as he is to ours. He kept us in a lot of games and put us in a position to win several others."[7]

Hill added, "Joe Morris is what you call an impact player. Defenses alter their entire schemes to neutralize him, [just] like offenses change their entire schemes to neutralize Lawrence Taylor."[8]

Although he stood only 5'7" tall, Morris possessed a powerful 195-pound frame that presented a unique challenge to opposing defenders. Denver linebacker Karl Mecklenburg said, "He's a strange combination. He's a small power runner."[9]

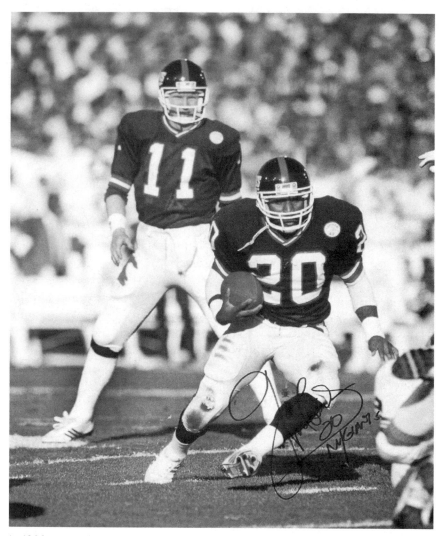

In 1988, Morris became the first Giants running back to surpass 1,000 yards rushing three times.
Courtesy of AmericanMemorabilia.com

Suggesting that his lack of height did not necessarily equate to him being "small," Morris stated, "Defensive players see a runner 5-foot-7, and they expect to encounter 160 pounds. I weigh 35 pounds more than that. I'm not a scat-back guy. I'm a 6-2 guy in a 5-7 body. The only time I notice my size is when I watch game films. I notice how big those other guys are compared to me."[10]

Giants strength and conditioning coach Johnny Parker supported Morris's contention, calling the running back one of the team's strongest players. To emphasize his point, Parker stated, "Not pound-for-pound—just one of the strongest."[11]

Meanwhile, offensive line coach Fred Hoaglin said, "This guy hits the hole faster than anyone I've been around in 20 years."[12]

An injury shortened Morris's 1987 season, limiting him to just 11 games. As a result, he rushed for only 658 yards and three touchdowns. However, he returned the following year to surpass 1,000 yards for the third time in his career, rushing for 1,083 yards and five touchdowns.

The 1988 campaign ended up being Morris's last season in New York. A broken right foot sidelined him for the entire 1989 season. He subsequently failed to beat out Ottis Anderson for the starting job upon his return, also losing out to rookie Rodney Hampton in the battle for the backup spot. Unable to earn a place on the roster, Morris suffered the humiliation of being cut by the Giants, who felt little remorse over having to part ways with their all-time leading rusher. The running back's lengthy holdout prior to the start of the 1986 campaign had created a significant amount of animosity on both sides. Morris further alienated himself from team management the following year when he became one of the more vocal supporters of the players' strike. He also shared a love–hate relationship with head coach Bill Parcells, with the two men eventually reaching a point where they rarely spoke to one another.

After spending the previous two years out of football, Morris signed with the Cleveland Browns prior to the start of the 1991 campaign. He spent his final season in Cleveland serving primarily as a backup before retiring at the end of the year. He ended his career with 5,585 yards rushing, 52 touchdowns, and a rushing average of 4.0 yards per carry. He ran for 5,296 yards and scored 50 touchdowns while playing for the Giants.

Since retiring from football, Morris has worked in real estate and insurance. For a time, he also owned part of the New Jersey Red Dogs of the Arena Football League, sharing that honor with fellow ex-Giants Carl Banks and Harry Carson.

Now almost 60 years old, Morris can look back at comments he made more than a quarter of a century ago knowing that he fulfilled his wishes. Morris said at that time, "I've always got to prove myself. It's a never-ending battle. I just want people to say that Joe Morris does his job, not that he's too small. Maybe one day, when I'm 50 years old and I'm on a street corner, they're going to say, 'You know, that little guy was a pretty good player.'"[13]

GIANT CAREER HIGHLIGHTS

Best Season

Morris had a big year for the Giants in 1985, rushing for 1,336 yards and a league-leading 21 touchdowns, en route to earning Second-Team All-NFC honors and the first of two straight Pro Bowl selections. However, it could be argued that he performed even better the following year, when he finished second in the NFL with a career-high 1,516 yards rushing. Morris also placed fourth in the league with 1,749 yards from scrimmage, 201 more than he amassed the previous season. Although Morris's total of 15 touchdowns in 1986 left him six short of the mark he had compiled one year earlier, he earned unanimous First-Team All-Pro and All-NFC honors. Furthermore, he helped lead the Giants to the Super Bowl. All things considered, Morris had the best season of his career in 1986.

Memorable Moments/Greatest Performances

Morris made his first carry in the NFL a memorable one, scoring from three yards out against Green Bay during a 27–19 loss to the Packers on September 20, 1982. He also turned in an outstanding performance in his first pro start, rushing for 68 yards and three touchdowns, in helping the Giants defeat the Washington Redskins by a score of 37–13 on October 28, 1984. Later in the year, Morris rushed for 100 yards in a contest for the first time, carrying the ball 16 times for 107 yards during a 31–21 loss to the St. Louis Cardinals on December 9.

A true force by 1985, Morris established himself as arguably the league's top breakaway threat during the second half of the campaign, scoring on runs of 65, 58, 56, and 41 yards. After rushing for 132 yards during a 22–20 victory over Tampa Bay on November 3, Morris scored three touchdowns for the second time in his career two weeks later during a heartbreaking 23–21 loss to Washington. Although the Giants lost to the Cleveland Browns by a score of 35–33 on December 1, Morris rushed for 131 yards and another three touchdowns. He followed up that effort by rushing for 129 yards and three touchdowns the very next week against the Houston Oilers, in leading the Giants to a 35–14 win. However, Morris saved his finest performance for the final game of the regular season, helping the Giants clinch a playoff berth by running for 202 yards and three touchdowns during a 28–10 win over the Pittsburgh Steelers. He then helped lead the Giants to a 17–3 victory over San Francisco in the first round of the playoffs by carrying the ball 28 times for 141 yards.

Morris also turned in a number of exceptional performances during the championship campaign of 1986, excelling in particular during one mid-season stretch that saw him gain more than 100 yards in five of six contests. He played perhaps his two best games in back-to-back weeks against two of New York's fiercest rivals. After rushing for 181 yards and two touchdowns during a 27–20 win over Washington on Monday night, October 27, Morris ran for another 181 yards and two touchdowns the very next week during a 17–14 victory over Dallas. He punctuated his great season by rushing for 313 yards in the Giants' three postseason victories, including a 159-yard, two-touchdown performance against the San Francisco 49ers.

NOTABLE ACHIEVEMENTS

- Rushed for more than 1,000 yards three times (1985, 1986, 1988).
- Scored at least 15 touchdowns twice, surpassing 20-mark once (21 in 1985).
- First Giants player to rush for more than 1,000 yards in consecutive seasons (1985, 1986).
- Led NFL with 21 touchdowns in 1985.
- Finished third in NFL with 15 touchdowns in 1986.
- Finished second in NFL with 1,516 yards rushing in 1986.
- Retired as Giants all-time leader in rushing yardage (5,296) and rushing touchdowns (48).
- Ranks among Giants all-time leaders in rushing yardage (3rd), rushing touchdowns (4th), and total touchdowns scored (9th).
- Holds Giants single-season record with 21 touchdowns scored (1985).
- 1986 Week 8 NFC Offensive Player of the Week.
- Two-time Pro Bowl selection (1985, 1986).
- 1986 First-Team All-Pro selection.
- 1986 First-Team All-Conference selection.
- 1985 Second-Team All-Conference selection.
- 1986 NFC champion.
- Super Bowl XXI champion.

27

KYLE ROTE

A serious knee injury early in his professional career prevented Kyle Rote from ever fulfilling the enormous potential he displayed while starring at Southern Methodist University. Nevertheless, showing the same tenacity that enabled him to overcome a series of tragic events that beset him early in life, Rote ended up carving out quite a career for himself in New York, establishing himself at the time of his retirement in 1961 as the Giants' all-time leader in pass receptions (300), receiving yardage (4,797), and touchdown receptions (48). Rote earned four Pro Bowl nominations and two Second-Team All-NFL selections in his 11 years with the Giants, whom he captained to four NFL title game appearances and one world championship. However, equally significant to Rote's on-field contributions is the impact that he made in the lives of the other players around him. Admired and respected by every one of his teammates, Rote reached a level of popularity so great that many of them ended up naming their sons after him. Giants quarterback Y. A. Tittle, who joined the team late in Rote's career, once remarked, "There has probably never been a nicer person to ever play the game. Everyone liked Kyle Rote. Fans liked him, sportswriters liked him, players liked him. He was just a good person and an outstanding football player. There's nothing negative about Kyle Rote. I've never found anyone who dislikes Kyle Rote."[1]

Born in Bellevue, Texas, on October 27, 1927, William Kyle Rote led a star-crossed life that saw him experience both great success and terrible tragedy. At the age of 14, young Kyle lost his mother in a freak automobile accident that also badly injured his father. Kyle's older brother, after returning home briefly from fighting in the Pacific during World War II to attend their mother's funeral, subsequently perished at the battle of Iwo Jima. The younger Rote, a teenager with no mother, no brother, and a crippled father, found solace in athletics, turning to sports as a means of filling the void that existed in his life.

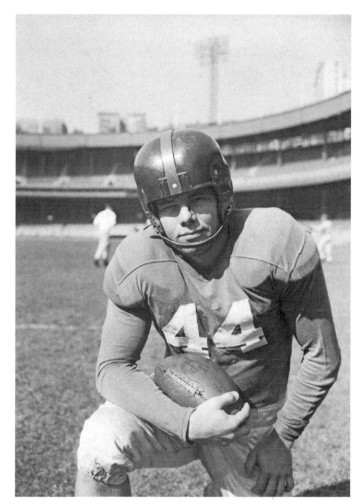

Kyle Rote retired in 1961 with more pass receptions, receiving yards, and touchdown catches than anyone else in franchise history.
Public domain (author unknown)

After starring in football, baseball, basketball, and track at Thomas Jefferson High School in San Antonio, Texas, Rote accepted an athletic scholarship to Southern Methodist University, where he became one of the most celebrated collegiate football players in the country. Playing in the same backfield as fellow All-American Doak Walker, Rote stepped into the limelight in 1949 by turning in a legendary performance against heavily favored Notre Dame. With Walker unable to play due to injury,

SMU entered the contest against the top-ranked Fighting Irish as 27½-point underdogs. However, Rote almost defeated the nation's number-one team singlehandedly, running for 115 yards, throwing for 146 others, and scoring all three of his team's touchdowns in a surprisingly close 27–20 loss. Still considered to be perhaps the greatest game ever turned in by any SMU player, Rote's effort was later voted by the Texas Sportswriters Association as "The Outstanding Individual Performance by a Texas Athlete in the First Half of the 20th Century." In fact, Rote's performance made such a lasting impression on the Fighting Irish that, a quarter of a century later, they made him an "Honorary Member" of their championship team. Rote followed that up by running for 762 yards, passing for 490 others, and scoring 13 touchdowns as a senior in 1950, en route to earning a second-place finish in the Heisman Trophy voting.

Fortunate enough to win the right to make the first selection of the 1951 NFL Draft through a special lottery, the Giants subsequently tabbed Rote, whom they envisioned starring for them in the backfield for many years to come. However, Rote found his performance at the NFL level compromised somewhat by an injury he suffered in training camp as a rookie. Stepping into a hole in the Giants' preseason practice field at Jonesboro, Arkansas, Rote tore a knee ligament—an injury from which he never fully recovered. Forced to play at less than 100 percent the remainder of his career, he never again displayed the outstanding speed he demonstrated during his years at SMU. Yet, after spending his first three years in New York working primarily out of the Giants' backfield, Rote moved to wide receiver, where he developed into one of the top pass-catchers in the league.

Frank Gifford, who joined the Giants one year after Rote came aboard, later noted, "He [Rote] had an incredible career, considering he did it on one leg. Had he not stepped in the hole, he would be in the Hall of Fame, and I probably wouldn't be."[2]

Looking back at that particular time in Giants history, Wellington Mara stated, "The outstanding backs of that era were Alex Webster and Frank Gifford. Before Kyle hurt his knee, he was as powerful a runner as Webster was, and as smooth a runner and as good a receiver as Gifford was."[3]

With his speed diminished, Rote focused on his route-running skills after moving to wide receiver, developing moves as good as almost anyone in the league. Discussing Rote's shiftiness after he moved to the outside, Mara suggested, "He was a great receiver without having that much speed anymore. But he made some great moves on people. We had many pictures of him going one way and the defender going the other way."[4]

Rote had two of his most productive seasons for the Giants in 1954 and 1955, earning Pro Bowl honors for the second and third of four consecutive times. In the first of those campaigns, he caught 29 passes for 551 yards and two touchdowns. The following year, he made 31 receptions for 580 yards and eight touchdowns. Rote made it to the Pro Bowl for the final time in his career in 1956, helping the Giants win the NFL championship by catching 28 passes for 405 yards and four touchdowns. After seeing his performance slip somewhat in each of the next three seasons, Rote returned to top form in 1960, establishing new career highs with 42 receptions and 750 receiving yards. He surpassed both marks the following year, making 53 catches for 805 yards.

In spite of his outstanding productivity, Rote elected to announce his retirement at the conclusion of the 1961 campaign, ending his career with more pass receptions, touchdown receptions, and receiving yardage than any other player in Giants history. He spent the next two years serving as the team's backfield coach before beginning a long and successful career in broadcasting. Having spent the previous several off-seasons working as sports director at a New York radio station, Rote had already put the wheels in motion for a second career after his playing days ended. Moving into the studio, he became one of NBC's most popular sportscasters of the late 1960s and early 1970s.

Sam Huff, who eventually followed a similar path, discussed the influence Rote had on him and others like him: "Every athlete that goes into broadcasting—guys like Pat Summerall and Frank Gifford—owes him a debt of gratitude. He really did the first locker room report show by an athlete. Kyle Rote did that at Yankee Stadium. When I was traded to Washington, I copied what he did, and I still do a locker room show for the Redskins."[5]

Rote's foresight really should not have come as much of a surprise to any of his teammates. Long considered to be one of the most intelligent players in the game, Rote had such an understanding of the sport that the Giants once sent him on the road to scout a game between Chicago and Green Bay while he was still performing for them as an active player.

Y. A. Tittle, who spent just one full season in New York with Rote, said of his former teammate, "Kyle Rote was one of the smartest football men of that era. He had a great offensive mind regarding the passing game, and football in general."[6]

Rote was also an extremely compassionate man, serving as the founder and first elected president of the NFL Players Association, which spent its formative years during the mid-1950s fighting for equal rights for all

Rote played for Giants teams that won four division titles and one NFL championship.
Public domain (author unknown)

players, with the intent of making certain that players of all races received equal treatment when their teams played on the road.

After many years in front of the television camera, Rote retired, choosing to spend his remaining years living privately, out of view of the general public. He passed away on August 15, 2002, in Baltimore, Maryland, from complications resulting from hernia surgery performed on him several days earlier. Rote was 74 at the time of his passing.

Rote's longtime friend Frank Gifford said of his former teammate, "He was an artist, he was a poet, and he was a kind, gentle man who was a great athlete. That's pretty rare."[7]

Perhaps Kyle Rote dabbled in art and poetry as a means of expressing the pain he carried with him from his youth. Never fully able to escape the sadness that engulfed him for the first time as a teenager, Rote also smoked and drank heavily. It may well have been those excesses that contributed to his eventual demise.

Paying tribute to Rote in his book *The Glory Game*, Frank Gifford concluded his work with a poem his close friend had written that bore the title *To My Teammates*:

So many things I've wished I'd said, and wished much more I'd done
Back when we functioned as a team, back when the game was fun.
So many times—I now recall, those humid summer days
When we could barely practice through our list of basic plays.
But then—someone among our group—would walk that extra mile
And lead us to complete the task, to exit with some style.
The mind grows dim as years move on—and details fade away
But essence of that band of boys is with me ev'ry day.
I've often thought that if we've learned some lessons during life,
The best of them at least were learned back then—on fields of strife.
I also feel the bonds we made did bind—solidify—
Those careful, precious memories, until the day we die.[8]

CAREER HIGHLIGHTS

Best Season

Rote had outstanding all-around years in 1952 and 1953. In the first of those campaigns, he rushed for 421 yards and caught 21 passes for another 240 yards. He followed that up by rushing for 213 yards and making 26 receptions for 440 yards and five touchdowns in 1953. Rote also had a fine season in 1955, when he earned one of his two Second-Team All-NFL selections by catching 31 passes for 580 yards and eight touchdowns. However, Rote's final two years in the league proved to be his two most productive. In 1960, he made 42 receptions for 750 yards and a career-high 10 touchdowns. The following season, he established career highs in receptions (53) and pass receiving yardage (805). He also caught seven touchdown passes. Rote's 1960 and 1961 campaigns would both have been good choices, but I eventually settled on the first of those years since he scored more points and posted a higher yards-per-catch average (17.9 to 15.2).

Memorable Moments/Greatest Performances

Rote recorded the longest touchdown reception of his career on November 1, 1953, against the Chicago Cardinals, giving the Giants a 23–20 win over Chicago with a 75-yard TD catch late in the fourth quarter. He made another long TD grab two years later, scoring for the second time in the game by hauling in a 71-yard pass during a 30–23 loss to the Pittsburgh Steelers.

Rote had back-to-back big games in October of 1960, following up a nine-reception, 135-yard, two-TD performance against the St. Louis Cardinals with a seven-reception, 116-yard, one-TD effort against the Pittsburgh Steelers. The Giants' 35–14 and 19–17 wins in those two contests improved their record to 3–0.

Rote turned in another outstanding performance later in the year, giving the Giants an early 14–0 lead over the rival Philadelphia Eagles by making first-quarter TD grabs of 71 and 11 yards. He finished the day with four receptions for 124 yards. However, the Eagles came storming back, defeating the Giants 31–23, to all but clinch the Eastern Conference title.

Rote had the last big day of his career on November 19, 1961, when he made six receptions for 129 yards and two touchdowns during a 45–21 win over Pittsburgh that improved the Giants' record to 8–2.

NOTABLE ACHIEVEMENTS

- Caught more than 50 passes once (53 in 1961).
- Made 10 touchdown receptions in 1960.
- Averaged better than 17 yards per reception four times, including one season with average in excess of 20 yards per catch (20.3 in 1958).
- First Giants receiver to catch 300 passes.
- Finished second in NFL with eight TD receptions in 1955.
- Finished third in NFL with 10 TD receptions in 1960.
- Ranks among Giants all-time leaders in pass receptions (12th), pass receiving yardage (6th), touchdown receptions (2nd), and total touchdowns scored (7th).
- Four-time Pro Bowl selection.
- Two-time Second-Team All-Pro selection.
- Named to Giants 75th Anniversary All-Time Team.
- Four-time NFL Eastern Division champion.
- 1956 NFL champion.

28

TUFFY LEEMANS

The first Giants player to lead the NFL in rushing, Tuffy Leemans proved to be a jack-of-all-trades in his eight years in New York. In addition to excelling as a runner from both the fullback and halfback positions, Leemans completed 25 touchdown passes over the course of his career, returned punts, and did an outstanding job from his spot in the defensive backfield. Leemans's tremendous versatility prompted either or both the NFL and at least one major wire service to award him All-NFL honors each year from 1936 to 1942. It also enabled the Giants to remain perennial contenders during his time with the team, helping them advance to the NFL title game a total of four times. The late Wayne Millner, a Pro Football Hall of Famer who once starred at end for the Washington Redskins, summarized his former foe's all-around skills years later when he suggested, "Tuffy Leemans had it all. He could run, pass, and catch, and he played truly outstanding defense. He was aggressive, dedicated, and gave 100 percent at all times to a game he loved. In my opinion, he ranks among the all-time greats."[1]

The fact that Leemans became a member of the Giants can be credited largely to Wellington Mara, who once said, "If I am remembered for nothing else, I'd like to be remembered for discovering Tuffy Leemans. It's a good thing the Redskins didn't move to Washington until 1937 or we could never have gotten Tuffy."[2]

Born in Superior, Wisconsin, on November 12, 1912, Alphonse Emil Leemans began his collegiate football career at the University of Oregon before following his coach to George Washington University when the latter switched schools at the end of Leemans's freshman campaign. After gradually breaking into the Colonials' starting lineup as a sophomore, Leemans spent the remainder of his three years at George Washington starring in virtually every aspect of the game, establishing himself in the process as a true running-passing-kicking triple threat. Having witnessed a particularly brilliant all-around effort turned in by Leemans against Alabama in 1935,

Tuffy Leemans led the NFL with 830 yards rushing in 1936.
Courtesy of Albersheims.com

a young high school boy named Wellington Mara, who happened to be vacationing in Washington at the time, subsequently recommended to his father Tim that the Giants' owner sign the burgeoning star when he became eligible to turn pro. On the advice of his son, the elder Mara selected Leemans in the second round, with the 18th overall pick, when the NFL held its first college draft in 1936.

The Giants never regretted selecting Leemans, who burst upon the NFL scene in 1936, leading the league with 206 carries and 830 yards rushing. He also threw for 258 yards and three touchdowns, en route to earning

Second-Team All-NFL honors. The following season, Leemans finished fourth in the league with 586 all-purpose yards, accumulating 429 of those on the ground and amassing the other 157 on pass receptions. Fitting in extremely well with coach Steve Owen's crunching A-formation attack, the hard-running 6-foot, 195-pound Leemans proved to be the Giants' "go-to" player in clutch situations.

Cliff Battles, the Washington Redskins' fleet-footed halfback who eventually gained induction into the Pro Football Hall of Fame, later recalled, "When we'd play the Giants and they needed two or three yards, they almost always would call on Tuffy to smash over tackle. But, no matter how prepared we were, Tuffy usually would make it. He had great balance and great competitiveness. I never saw a better player than Leemans!"[3]

Meanwhile, Mel Hein, who anchored New York's offensive line throughout Leemans's tenure with the team, said, "Tuffy was a very hard runner . . . not a lot of great speed, but he had a knack of driving through people, and he was tough."[4]

Leemans continued to perform well for the Giants in subsequent seasons, placing second in the NFL with 463 rushing yards in 1938, before coming in third two years later with a mark of 474. In fact, he finished in the league's top 10 in rushing in each of his first six seasons. He also placed in the top 10 in rushing touchdowns four times, and in all-purpose yards five times. Leemans's accomplishments become even more impressive when it is considered that the Giants employed a two-platoon system on both offense and defense throughout virtually his entire career. Coach Steve Owen put together two supposedly equal units, and then alternated them from quarter to quarter, with each team playing on both offense and defense.

Wishing to honor Leemans for his outstanding all-around contributions to the team over the course of his first six seasons, the Giants named December 7, 1941, "Tuffy Leemans Day" at the Polo Grounds. They presented him with a silver tray, a watch, and $1,500 in defense bonds. However, subsequent news of the Japanese attack on the U.S. naval base at Pearl Harbor ended up spoiling the day's festive mood.

Leemans spent two more years in New York, with injuries forcing him to retire at the conclusion of the 1943 campaign. More of a passing threat than a featured runner after sustaining a brain concussion and permanent left ear damage during a 1942 collision with Chicago's George Wilson, Leemans subsequently also found himself unable to enlist in the military during World War II. Upon his retirement, he ranked among the NFL's all-time leaders in rushing yardage (3,132) and rushing touchdowns (17). Leemans also passed for 2,318 yards and 25 touchdowns. After leaving the game,

Leemans earned All-Pro honors five times while playing for the Giants.
Courtesy of Albersheimsstore.com

Leemans returned to Washington, where he spent several years coaching at Carroll High School and owning a successful bowling business. He passed away on January 19, 1979, in Hillsboro Beach, Florida, at the age of 66.

Leemans's relatively modest career numbers kept him out of the Pro Football Hall of Fame a full 34 years after he played his last NFL game against Washington in 1943. However, he finally gained admittance in 1978, just one year before he passed away. Upon his election, Leemans stated, "I didn't know if I was ever going to make it. It was like I had two yards to go, had used up three downs, and had only one more chance to make it."[5]

CAREER HIGHLIGHTS

Best Season

Although Leemans appeared on the Second Team a number of times, he earned his only First-Team All-Pro selection in 1939, when he finished fourth in the league with 614 all-purpose yards and ranked in the top 10 with 429 yards rushing and five touchdowns. Nevertheless, he had his finest all-around season for the Giants in his rookie campaign of 1936, when, in addition to leading the NFL with 206 rushing attempts and 830 yards rushing, he finished second in the league with 852 all-purpose yards, scored two touchdowns, passed for three others, and recorded a career-high six interceptions.

Memorable Moments/Greatest Performances

Leemans got his career with the Giants off to a memorable start, running for a 46-yard touchdown the first time he ever carried the ball in the NFL. Still, he made arguably the most significant run of his career against the Green Bay Packers in the 1938 NFL Championship Game, rushing for a first period score that ended up providing the winning margin in the Giants' 23–17 victory that brought them their second title in five years.

NOTABLE ACHIEVEMENTS

- Led NFL with 206 carries and 830 yards rushing in 1936.
- Two-time Pro Bowl selection (1938, 1941).
- 1939 First-Team All-Pro selection.
- Four-time Second-Team All-Pro selection.
- NFL 1930s All-Decade Team.
- Four-time NFL Eastern Conference champion.
- 1938 NFL champion.
- Elected to Pro Football Hall of Fame in 1978.

29

KEN STRONG

The numbers Ken Strong compiled in his eight years with the Giants could hardly be described as overwhelming. Playing halfback on offense and defensive back on defense, while also serving as the team's placekicker, Strong rushed for a total of only 853 yards, accumulated just 198 receiving yards, scored only 13 touchdowns, and tallied just 324 total points. Although those represented solid figures for the era during which Strong played, they pale in comparison to the statistics players have typically posted since the age of specialization began right around the time he appeared in his last game. But rating Strong on the basis of his performance in any single phase of the game would do him a grave injustice since it was his ability to help his team win in every conceivable way that made him so valuable. After watching Strong perform on the gridiron for several years, legendary sports writer Grantland Rice wrote in 1939, "Considering the test of both college and pro football, I'd say the battle of the swift and strong was among Ken Strong, Jim Thorpe, and Ernie Nevers, with Bronco Nagurski close up. Strong and Thorpe had greater variety; this gives them the edge. I mean everything that belongs to football—running, blocking, tackling, passing, and every type of kicking."[1]

Born in West Haven, Connecticut, on March 21, 1906, Elmer Kenneth Strong Jr. first established himself as a budding sports star during his four years at West Haven High School. After subsequently entering New York University in 1925, Strong began to build a reputation as one of the nation's most outstanding and versatile athletes. Serving as the placekicker and featured running back on NYU's football team, Strong led the nation in scoring as a senior, tallying a total of 162 points, on 22 touchdowns and 30 extra points. Meanwhile, Strong's exceptional power-hitting earned him general recognition as the best baseball prospect to come out of a New York school since Lou Gehrig graduated from Columbia University a few years earlier.

Strong elected to pursue a career in both sports following his graduation from NYU in 1929, signing a minor league contract with the New

In addition to starring for the Giants on both offense and defense, Ken Strong served as the team's placekicker throughout his career. Courtesy of RMYAuctions.com

York Yankees, while simultaneously inking a deal with the NFL's Staten Island Stapletons. However, the 6'1", 205-pound outfielder's baseball career came to an abrupt end in 1931, when he broke a bone in his wrist after running into an outfield wall, leaving him unable to properly throw a baseball.

Forced to concentrate solely on football, Strong developed into a one-man show in Staten Island, scoring 45 percent of the points the Stapletons tallied in his four years with them. He earned All-Pro honors in three of his four seasons with the club, making it onto the First Team twice and being named to the Second Team once. However, with the Stapletons experiencing little in the way of success on the field and at the box office, they folded at the conclusion of the 1932 campaign, leaving Strong free to sign with the New York Giants.

Strong set an NFL Championship Game record that stood for 30 years when he scored 17 points during the Giants' 30–13 victory over the Chicago Bears in the 1934 title tilt.
Courtesy of RMYAuctions.com

Strong continued his outstanding all-around play in New York, excel-ling as a rusher, placekicker, and defender. He led the NFL in scoring in his first year with his new team, tallying a total of 64 points, on six touch-downs, 13 extra points, and five field goals, en route to earning First-Team All-Pro honors for the final time in his career. Strong followed that up by rushing for a career-high 431 yards for the NFL champion Giants in 1934.

He experienced one of his finest moments against Chicago in the NFL title game that year, leading New York to a 30–13 victory by scoring two touchdowns, converting two extra points, and kicking a 38-yard field goal. Strong's 17 points scored established a new NFL Championship Game record—one that stood for the next 30 years.

The Giants repeated as Eastern Conference champions in 1935, thereby advancing to their third straight NFL Championship Game. Although they ended up losing to Detroit by a final score of 26–7, Strong gave the Giants their only touchdown of the contest, scoring on a 42-yard pass from quarterback Ed Danowski.

A salary dispute with the Giants prior to the start of the ensuing season prompted Strong to jump to the New York Yankees of the rival American Football League. After spending three years with the Yankees, Strong returned to the Giants in 1939, serving them almost exclusively as a kicker after injuring his back early in the season. He elected to retire at the end of the year, but, with many of the NFL's best players serving in the military during World War II, he returned to the Giants for one last fling in 1944. Functioning solely as a placekicker, Strong spent four more years in New York before retiring for good at the conclusion of the 1947 campaign. Strong left the game as the Giants' all-time scoring leader, with 324 points, on 13 touchdowns, 35 field goals, and 141 extra points. Over the course of his NFL career, he earned All-NFL honors a total of five times, making First-Team All-Pro on three separate occasions.

After experiencing a good deal of success in the business world following his retirement, Strong returned to the Giants for one more year in 1962, serving as special kicking coach for his star pupil, Don Chandler. The Giants advanced to the NFL Championship Game that year, doing so for the seventh time in Strong's nine-year association with the club. The Pro Football Hall of Fame opened its doors to Strong in 1967, 12 years before he passed away in New York at the age of 73.

GIANT CAREER HIGHLIGHTS

Best Season

Strong earned First-Team All-Pro honors for the only time as a member of the Giants in 1933, when he led the NFL with 64 points scored, rushed for 272 yards, gained another 146 yards on pass receptions, and scored six touchdowns. However, he averaged only 2.8 yards per carry and amassed just 418 total yards from scrimmage that year. Meanwhile, Strong averaged just over three yards per carry the following year and accumulated a total of 483 yards from scrimmage, 431 of those on the ground and another 52 through the air. Strong also scored six touchdowns for the second straight time in 1934, en route to finishing fourth in the league with 56 points scored. Furthermore, the Giants won the NFL championship in the second campaign, with their fullback/kicker leading them to victory by tallying 17 points. All things considered, Strong had his best year for the Giants in 1934.

Memorable Moments/Greatest Performances

Strong made history on November 26, 1933, when he became the first known NFL player to attempt and score on a fair catch kick, doing so during a win over the visiting Green Bay Packers. The 30-yard kick—the shortest of its kind in NFL history—continues to keep Strong's name in the record books, making him one of only four players ever to make a successful fair catch kick attempt.

Nevertheless, Strong turned in the most memorable performance of his career in the 1934 NFL Championship Game against the Chicago Bears, scoring 17 points, on two touchdowns, two extra points, and a field goal. Strong's 38-yard field goal and touchdown runs of 11 and 42 yards on the Polo Grounds' ice-covered surface helped the Giants defeat the Bears by a score of 30–13, in what eventually became known as the "Sneakers Game."

NOTABLE ACHIEVEMENTS

- Led NFL in points scored, field goals made, extra points made, and field goal percentage once each.
- Ranks 13th all-time on Giants in points scored (324).
- 1933 First-Team All-Pro selection.
- 1934 Second-Team All-Pro selection.
- NFL 1930s All-Decade Team.
- Six-time NFL Eastern Conference champion.
- 1934 NFL champion.
- Elected to Pro Football Hall of Fame in 1967.

30

— CHARLIE CONERLY —

The "other quarterback" in the NFL Championship Game of 1958 commonly referred to as the "Greatest Game Ever Played," Charlie Conerly spent his entire career being overshadowed by other exceptional players. Throughout the 1950s, Conerly took a backseat to more highly publicized quarterbacks such as Otto Graham, Norm Van Brocklin, and the master himself, Johnny Unitas. He also frequently found himself playing second fiddle in New York to some of his more colorful Giants teammates like Frank Gifford, Sam Huff, Emlen Tunnell, and Andy Robustelli. But, by the time "Chuckin' Charlie" left the game in 1961, he ranked among the NFL's all-time career leaders in most statistical categories, including pass completions (1,418), touchdown passes (173), and total passing yards (19,488). He also held the league record for most passes completed in a single game (36, against the Steelers in 1948). While those numbers might seem modest by today's standards, they all represented Giant team records until Phil Simms came along years later and shattered virtually all of them.

Still, statistics tell only so much about Conerly and how much he meant to his Giant teammates. A tremendous leader who demanded the best from himself and others around him, Conerly had the respect and admiration of everyone who lined up alongside him in the offensive huddle. Alex Webster, Conerly's teammate in New York for seven seasons, said of him: "He's the greatest quarterback I've ever seen. I've never met a man so cool under fire. His courage never fails to amaze me."[1]

Born in Clarksdale, Mississippi, on September 19, 1921, Charles Albert Conerly Jr. grew up in poverty, hoping to make a better life for himself through football. After enrolling at the University of Mississippi in 1942, Conerly temporarily put his education and athletic career on hold when U.S. involvement in World War II prompted him to join the military. Serving as a Marine in the South Pacific the next three years, Conerly fought in the battle of Guam before earning his discharge. However, while

Charlie Conerly quarterbacked the Giants to victory in the 1956 NFL
Championship Game.
Courtesy of AlbersheimsStore.com

he was away, the Washington Redskins selected him in the 13th round of
the 1945 NFL Draft with the 127th overall pick.

Choosing instead to return to Mississippi in 1946, the 25-year-old
Conerly led the Rebels to their first Southeastern Conference title one
year later by leading the nation in pass completions. Serving as the team's
tailback and primary passer, Conerly also rushed for nine touchdowns and
passed for 18 others, en route to earning consensus All-America honors and
a fourth-place finish in the Heisman Trophy balloting.

Conerly's advanced age (he was already 27 years old when he graduated) scared off many teams when he became eligible once more for the
NFL Draft. However, he proved to be a steal after the Giants selected him
in the 7th round in 1948. Converting from a single-wing college tailback to
a quarterback in head coach Steve Owen's A-formation, Conerly established
a new team record by throwing 22 touchdown passes as a rookie. He also
rushed for five other scores.

The Giants decided to switch from the A-formation and single- and
double-wing offense to the newly popular T-formation prior to the start of

the 1949 campaign, hiring Allie Sherman as backfield coach to work with Conerly on the timing and execution of the new system. Having grasped all the concepts presented to him by Sherman, Conerly expressed his satisfaction with the new formation, suggesting that the idea of running the ball less frequently and becoming more of a pocket-passer appealed to him very much. Speaking in his strong southern drawl, Conerly stated, "Man, with the T-formation, I can play quarterback until they put me in a rockin' chair."[2]

Conerly's words proved to be quite prophetic since he spent another 13 years in the NFL, continuing to compete until he reached age 40. During that time, he established himself as one of the league's top quarterbacks, even though he failed to gain as much notoriety as some of his contemporaries. Serving as New York's primary starter at quarterback in 13 of his 14 seasons with the team, Conerly led the Giants to an overall record of 58–31–1 as a starter, helping them advance to four NFL title games and win one league championship. He also doubled as the team's punter in a few of those years, averaging 38.9 yards per punt over the course of his career. Conerly earned Pro Bowl honors in 1950 and 1956, leading the Giants to a 10–2 record in the first of those campaigns, and guiding them to the NFL Championship in the second. He performed so well at the age of 38 in 1959 that the Newspaper Enterprise Association named him the NFL's Most Valuable Player.

Although Conerly posted solid numbers in most seasons, he failed to compile the sort of eye-popping statistics one tends to look for in potential Hall of Fame candidates. That being the case, Conerly never quite made it into Canton, even though the men who played alongside him felt that his toughness and exceptional leadership ability clearly earned him a spot.

Frank Gifford, who lobbied intensely through the years for Conerly's induction, provided insight into his former teammate's grit and determination by relating an incident that took place in the quarterback's rookie season. Speaking of Conerly and the effort he put forth to remain in a game after suffering a serious injury, Gifford explained, "He broke his nose really badly—they literally called a timeout, and then they called another one while they stopped the bleeding . . . they stuck stuff up there until it would stop bleeding. You try to get them to do that today, they would be yelling, 'Get my agent!'"[3]

It was that sort of intestinal fortitude that prompted Allie Sherman to once say, "Charlie Conerly is one of the strongest men of character, of inner strength, of any mortal I've ever known. You know, they talk about who would you like to have next to you in a foxhole—that's the man you want. He was just great under pressure. He was tremendous."[4]

Conerly started behind center for the Giants for 13 seasons.
Courtesy of RMYAuctions.com

Meanwhile, in discussing his team's longtime quarterback, Wellington Mara stated, "Charlie is the best player who is not in the Pro Football Hall of Fame. He has better numbers than some quarterbacks who are there."[5]

Having established himself as the Giants' all-time passing leader in most statistical categories by 1961, Conerly announced his retirement at the end of the year. He subsequently returned to his home in Clarksdale, where he owned and operated a chain of shoe stores in the Mississippi Delta region. His ruggedly handsome looks also enabled him to take on the role of the "Marlboro Man" in television commercials following his retirement. Although Conerly spent most of his time down south, he occasionally returned to New York to attend Giants games and appear at the annual dinner of the College Football Hall of Fame, of which he was a member. Conerly lived until the age of 74, passing away from heart failure on February 13, 1996, after undergoing triple-bypass surgery nearly five months earlier. His name and legacy are memorialized by the Conerly Trophy, given annually to the best college football player in the state of Mississippi.

Following Conerly's passing, Frank Gifford spoke of the manner in which the quarterback's quiet leadership helped the Giants capture the NFL championship in 1956. He also discussed the pivotal role Conerly played in helping football grow in popularity in New York during the 1950s, pointing out, "The next year, the Giants had a sellout every game because of what we did in 1956. Charlie was the biggest reason for that."[6]

CAREER HIGHLIGHTS

Best Season

The Giants posted outstanding 10–2 and 8–3–1 records in 1950 and 1956, respectively, enabling Conerly to make the Pro Bowl for the only two times in his career. However, he compiled extremely modest numbers in each of those campaigns. Conerly completed only 42.4 percent of his passes in 1950, for just 1,000 yards and eight touchdowns. He put up somewhat better numbers in 1956, completing just under 52 percent of his passes, for 1,143 yards and 10 touchdowns. Yet Conerly actually had several other more productive seasons, with his rookie campaign of 1948 and his MVP year of 1959 topping the list. In his first year in the league, Conerly completed just over 54 percent of his passes, throwing for a career-high 2,175 yards and 22 touchdowns in the process. He also rushed for 160 yards and five touchdowns. But, through no fault of Conerly, the Giants finished the season just 4–8. On the other hand, they compiled an exceptional mark of 10–2 in 1959, with Conerly leading them to victory in eight of his nine starts. "Chuckin Charlie" threw for less yardage (1,706) and completed fewer touchdown passes (14) than he did in 1948. But he posted the highest completion percentage of his career (58.2) and led all NFL quarterbacks in passer rating for the only time, with a mark of 102.7. Conerly didn't come close to that figure in any other season. All things considered, Conerly had his best season in 1959.

Memorable Moments/Greatest Performances

While the epic performance Johnny Unitas turned in during 1958's NFL Championship Game has become a part of football lore, few people seem to remember that Charlie Conerly also played extremely well in that contest.

The Giants quarterback completed 10 of 14 passes, for 187 yards and one touchdown, in leading his team to two second-half scores that forced the Colts to stage a furious comeback in the closing moments of regulation.

Conerly also turned in a number of exceptional efforts over the course of the following regular season. With the Giants expected to lose their 1959 season opener to the Los Angeles Rams, he completed 21 of 31 passes for 321 yards, in leading his team to a 23–21 upset win. Later in the year, the 38-year-old quarterback returned to the field after missing two straight games with a twisted ankle to throw three touchdown passes during a 30–20 win over the Chicago Cardinals. Just one week later, on November 29, 1959, the Giants chose to honor Conerly for his many contributions to the team over the years by celebrating "Charlie Conerly Day" at Yankee Stadium. In storybook fashion, Conerly threw three touchdown passes during a 45–14 victory over the Washington Redskins that clinched at least a tie for the Eastern Conference championship.

Although Conerly served primarily as Y. A. Tittle's backup in his final NFL season, the 40-year-old quarterback still had a few heroic efforts left in him. Coming off the bench to replace an injured Tittle in game 13 of the 1961 regular season, Conerly threw three touchdown passes to lead the Giants to a 28–24 win over Philadelphia that put his team in first place to stay. Reflecting back on Conerly's contributions to the team over the course of the 1961 campaign, Giants head coach Allie Sherman later said, "I went to Charlie four times that year. He brought us home each time."[7]

NOTABLE ACHIEVEMENTS

- Passed for more than 2,000 yards twice (1948, 1949).
- Passed for more than 20 touchdowns once (22 in 1948).
- Led NFL quarterbacks with 102.7 passer rating in 1959.
- Led NFL quarterbacks in pass-to-interception ratio twice.
- Finished second in NFL in touchdown passes twice and passing yardage once.
- Ranks among Giants all-time leaders in completions (4th), passing yardage (3rd), and touchdown passes (3rd).
- Two-time Pro Bowl selection (1950, 1956).
- 1959 Newspaper Enterprise Association NFL MVP.
- Four-time NFL Eastern Division champion.
- 1956 NFL champion.

31

RAY WIETECHA

The only man to snap the ball to a Giants quarterback from 1954 to 1962, Ray Wietecha proved to be a true iron man over the course of his NFL career, which he spent entirely with the Giants. Appearing in 130 consecutive games (including the playoffs), Wietecha never missed a game in his 10 NFL seasons, establishing himself during that time as one of the league's top centers. Anchoring offensive lines that also featured standouts Jack Stroud, Bill Austin, Darrell Dess, and Hall of Fame tackle Roosevelt Brown, Wietecha earned four Pro Bowl selections, one First-Team All-Pro nomination, and two Second-Team selections. His outstanding blocking and exceptional leadership ability helped the Giants win five Eastern Division titles and one world championship.

Born in East Chicago, Indiana, on November 4, 1928, Raymond Walter Wietecha manned the center position for the first time while playing for his high school team in Gary, Indiana. After briefly attending Michigan State University, Wietecha transferred to Northwestern, where he earned All-Big-10 honors playing center for the Wildcats team that defeated California in the 1949 Rose Bowl. Following his graduation from Northwestern, Wietecha put in three years with the Marine Corps during the Korean War and played minor league baseball in the Washington Senators organization for a short period of time before signing with the Giants, who had selected him in the 12th round of the 1950 NFL Draft with the 150th overall pick.

Although Wietecha did not earn the starting center job until his second year in New York, he appeared in every game for the Giants as a rookie. Taking over as the team's starting center in his sophomore campaign, Wietecha subsequently became the only player to snap the ball to legendary Giant quarterbacks Charlie Conerly and Y. A. Tittle for the next nine years.

The Giants went from also-rans to perennial contenders during Wietecha's time with them, appearing in the NFL Championship Game five times between 1956 and 1962, and winning the title in 1956 by trouncing

Ray Wietecha played every minute of every game on offense for nine straight seasons.
Courtesy of NearMintCards.com

the Bears 47–7, due in no small part to the play of Wietecha and the offensive line. Although Wietecha stood only 6'1" and weighed just 225 pounds, he developed a reputation as a formidable blocker. Equally important were his intelligence and leadership skills. Speaking of those less-tangible qualities, Wietecha said, "I could remember assignments. I told players what to do. I was in charge of that little group up front."[1]

Allie Sherman once supported his center's contention, stating, "Wietecha is the best in the league. Ray Wietecha is my quarterback up front. Ray calls out all the 'bastard' defenses. We face anything other than the standard 4–3, Ray spots it, calls it out, switches our blocking assignments on the line. And block? That man's a bear."[2]

Perhaps more than anything else, though, the thing that separated Wietecha from the other centers in the league was the accuracy he displayed on his long snaps. Snapping the ball without peering back at the kicker so that he could prepare himself more quickly to contend with onrushing defensive linemen, Wietecha drew raves from punters and placekickers around the league.

Pat Summerall once recalled, "In four years of placekicking with the Giants I never saw the laces of the football. Wietecha always snapped the ball with the strings facing front."[3]

An innovator in getting the laces back in proper fashion for the place-kick holder, Wietecha recalled the startled reaction he received one year at the Pro Bowl from one of the NFL's best kickers: "Tommy McDonald was the holder and Lou Groza was the kicker. This was my first year in the Pro

Ray Wietecha (#55) looks for someone to block downfield.
Public domain (author unknown)

Bowl—practice was over and they wanted to kick some. I got over the ball like I always did. The ball is in front of me. I looked between my legs to see where Tommy was—okay, I got him—and I picked my head up and I snapped the ball back. And they went crazy. They said, 'This guy doesn't even look, and the strings always come back perfect. All you have to do is put the ball down and the strings are right there.'"[4]

The outstanding play of Wietecha and the rest of the Giants' offensive line enabled quarterbacks Charlie Conerly and Y. A. Tittle to feel secure in the pocket. It also allowed running backs Frank Gifford and Alex Webster to thrive. Although the names of offensive linemen rarely appear in the newspaper headlines, Wietecha once noted, "When we won, the Giants' offensive line became famous. I became well known."[5]

Wietecha added that he benefited greatly from spending his entire career with the Giants, stating, "I was fortunate, too, in that I only played with one club. I became a leader. I believe I understood football. I could remember assignments . . . if someone wanted to know something, I could tell them. And I took advantage of that."[6]

Hoping to pursue a career in coaching, Wietecha announced his retirement at the conclusion of the 1962 campaign after earning Second-Team All-NFL honors for the second time. He spent the next two years coaching the offensive line of the Los Angeles Rams, before moving on to Green Bay, where he assumed a similar role under Vince Lombardi. After leaving Green Bay, Wietecha spent one year in Buffalo and five back in New York with the Giants, coaching their offensive line from 1972 to 1976. He subsequently served as an assistant coach for the Baltimore Colts and the USFL's Chicago Blitz and Arizona Wranglers before taking on a scouting position with the Packers from 1985 to 1995. After leaving the game, Wietecha retired to Phoenix, Arizona, where he passed away from an aneurysm on December 14, 2002, at the age of 74.

CAREER HIGHLIGHTS

Best Season

Wietecha played at an extremely high level throughout virtually his entire career, earning a nomination to at least one All-NFL team in six of his nine years as a starter. However, he had his best season in 1958, when he earned unanimous First-Team All-Pro honors for the only time.

Memorable Moments/Greatest Performances

New York's 47–7 victory over Chicago in the 1956 NFL Championship Game would have to be considered the highlight of Wietecha's career. The Giants' offensive line dominated the Bears' defensive front over the course of the contest, opening up holes that allowed running backs Mel Triplett, Frank Gifford, and Alex Webster to rush for a total of 126 yards and three touchdowns, while providing ample protection for quarterbacks Charlie Conerly and Don Heinrich, whom Chicago sacked just once. Although Roosevelt Brown copped Lineman of the Game honors, a great deal of credit must also be given to Wietecha, who provided leadership and direction to his line-mates throughout the contest.

NOTABLE ACHIEVEMENTS

- Never missed a game in 10 seasons with Giants, appearing in 130 consecutive contests, including the playoffs.
- Four-time Pro Bowl selection.
- 1958 First-Team All-Pro selection.
- Two-time Second-Team All-Pro selection (1959, 1962).
- Five-time NFL Eastern Division champion.
- 1956 NFL champion.

JIM KATCAVAGE

A member of the Giants' outstanding defensive front four that helped them advance to the NFL Championship Game six times between 1956 and 1963, Jim Katcavage spent 13 years in New York, establishing himself during that time as one of the NFL's premier defensive ends. An outstanding pass-rusher and solid run-defender, Katcavage earned three Pro Bowl selections and two First-Team All-Pro nominations while manning the left defensive end position for the Giants. Working opposite perennial All-Pro Andy Robustelli on the other side of New York's defensive line, Katcavage gave the Giants a fearsome pass rush from both end positions. Although quarterback sacks did not become an official NFL statistic until 1982, Katcavage recorded an "unofficial" total of 96½ sacks over the course of his career, placing him third all-time on the Giants' unofficial list.

Born in Wilkes-Barre, Pennsylvania, on October 28, 1934, James Richard Katcavage played his college ball at the University of Dayton, where he anchored his team's defensive front. After being selected by the Giants in the fourth round of the 1956 NFL Draft with the 45th overall pick, Katcavage spent his first professional season playing both defensive end and tackle, helping the Giants capture their first NFL title in 18 years. After finishing the previous season with a record of only 6–5–1, the Giants posted a mark of 8–3–1 in 1956, holding eight of their 12 opponents to fewer than 20 points, and limiting three teams to single digits. They continued to excel on defense in the NFL Championship Game, holding the Chicago Bears to just seven points during an overwhelming 47–7 victory.

Although Katcavage made only minor contributions to the Giants over the course of their championship campaign, his role expanded in subsequent seasons. Taking over as the team's starting left defensive end in 1957, Katcavage remained in that spot for the next 12 years, giving New York arguably the league's most formidable front four from 1957 to 1963. With tackles Dick Modzelewski and Rosey Grier bottling up opposing offenses from their interior posts and ends Robustelli and Katcavage applying

Jim Katcavage recorded an "unofficial" total of 96½ quarterback sacks in his 13 seasons with the Giants.
Courtesy of EACGallery.com

constant pressure from the outside, the Giants' defensive line played with rare unity and cohesion. Very much like Robustelli on the opposite side, the 6'3", 237-pound Katcavage used his quickness to his advantage, gradually developing into one of the league's top pass-rushers. He earned Pro Bowl and All-Pro honors each year from 1961 to 1963. In addition to accumulating 96½ "unofficial" sacks over the course of his career, Katcavage recovered 19 fumbles, intercepted one pass, and recorded three safeties, tying him for second on the all-time list in the last category.

Extremely tough as well, Katcavage had a high threshold for pain according to Wellington Mara, who said of the former end, "Jim was one of our greatest defensive linemen. He played the defensive end position on

Katcavage teamed up with Andy Robustelli to give the Giants the NFL's best pass-rushing duo.
Courtesy of FootballCardGallery.com

all our great teams in the 1950s and '60s. I remember one game where he broke his collarbone in the first half and finished the game."[1]

Katcavage continued to shine even after the Giants fell from the NFL's elite, earning First-Team All-Conference honors in 1964 and 1966. He remained on the team until 1968, retiring at the end of the season to assume the role of coach for New York's linemen. He remained in that post until 1973, after which he left the game for good. Aside from an occasional public appearance, Katcavage enjoyed a relatively quiet post-football life, retiring to his home in Maple Glen, Pennsylvania, where he passed away on February 22, 1995, after suffering a heart attack. Katcavage was only 60 years old at the time of his passing.

CAREER HIGHLIGHTS

Best Season

Although it is often difficult to gauge the performance of defensive linemen and linebackers who played prior to the 1980s due to the extremely limited availability of statistical data, Katcavage was credited with 25 "unofficial" sacks in 1963. Such an inordinately high number, particularly over the course of a 14-game schedule, would seem to make the 1963 campaign the best of Katcavage's career. Fellow defensive end Andy Robustelli vouched for the accuracy of the total, suggesting that the players and team both tracked the number of sacks quite closely. Commenting years later on the motivation for recording such figures, Robustelli said, "You know why? We were paid $5 for each one."[2] However, Robustelli added that the money went to charity.

Memorable Moments/Greatest Performances

One of Katcavage's more memorable moments took place on October 7, 1962, when he recorded the only interception of his career during a 31–14 win over the St. Louis Cardinals.

Although Katcavage registered three safeties over the course of his career, he experienced perhaps his finest moment in the next-to-last week of the 1963 season, when he recovered a fumble in the end zone during a 44–14 victory over the Washington Redskins, scoring in the process his only career touchdown. Discussing the play after the contest, Katcavage beamed, "That was my first in eight years. I came close a couple of years ago when Andy [Robustelli] hit Bobby Layne and made him fumble. I ran about 45 yards and had a 10-yard lead on Tom Tracy. Then I tried to get cute and cut. I stumbled over the high grass."[3]

NOTABLE ACHIEVEMENTS

- Ranks third all-time on Giants' "unofficial" sack list with 96½.
- Three-time Pro Bowl selection.
- Two-time First-Team All-Pro selection (1961, 1963).
- 1962 Second-Team All-Pro selection.
- Two-time All-Conference selection (1964, 1966).
- Six-time NFL Eastern Division champion.
- 1956 NFL champion.

GEORGE MARTIN

The career of George Martin spanned two distinct periods in Giants history. Martin, who played left defensive end for the Giants from 1975 to 1988, spent his first nine seasons playing for teams that posted a winning record just once, compiling an overall mark during that time of only 45–85–1. However, the Giants posted a composite record of 49–30 in Martin's final five seasons, capturing the NFL Championship in 1986, Martin's 12th year in the league. Through it all, Martin remained a pillar of strength within the Giants organization, earning the admiration and respect of all his teammates with his wisdom, calm demeanor, and outstanding leadership qualities. During his time in New York, Martin became the team's player representative, chapel leader, and drug-abuse consultant. He and his wife even became the regular hosts for the team's annual Thanksgiving dinner. More than just an exceptional team leader, though, Martin also established himself during his playing days as one of the finest defensive ends in team history. An outstanding pass-rusher, Martin recorded 96 "unofficial" sacks over the course of his career, placing him fourth on the Giants' all-time list (although his official NFL total is only 46). He also had a knack for making big plays, demonstrating throughout his career that he had a "nose for the football" by scoring an unprecedented six touchdowns by a defensive lineman.

Born in Greenville, South Carolina, on February 16, 1953, George Dwight Martin began his professional playing career inauspiciously, being told by then-Giants head coach Bill Arnsparger when he showed up to his first minicamp in 1975 with a dislocated kneecap, "There's no way you're going to be a professional football player. Go home."[1] However, showing the determination that helped make him a significant contributor to the Giants throughout his career, the 11th-round draft pick (262nd overall) out of Oregon worked his way back into shape and ended up winning a starting job as a rookie. Martin remained the team's starting left end his first six years in the league, establishing himself during that time as one of the

In addition to recording an unofficial total of 96 quarterback sacks in his 14 seasons with the Giants, George Martin scored six defensive touchdowns. Courtesy of SportsMemorabilia.com

NFL's top pass-rushers. He also showed his penchant for being in the right place at the right time by recovering seven fumbles and intercepting one pass, which he returned 30 yards for a touchdown.

Nevertheless, the Giants continued to flounder as a team throughout that period, posting an overall mark of just 29–61. The difficult times Martin and his teammates experienced his first several years in the league remained fresh in his mind the remainder of his career, causing him to impress upon his younger teammates in future years the thin line that exists between winning and losing. After the Giants turned things around later in his career, Martin said:

> I attempt to have a conversation every day with at least one of my teammates about the past. I tell them what it's like to be so low you have to look up to see the bottom, that fans are burning tickets and you're embarrassed to wear a Giants emblem anywhere. You're trying to get through the season so you can go home and watch the playoffs on TV. That's really a bad situation. I tell them sometimes how grateful they should be that it's all turned around. And I want

them to know that success is a fleeting thing, and you've got to grab it while you can.[2]

The Giants made the playoffs for the first time in 18 years in 1981, a season in which Martin became a pass-rush specialist. He continued to fill that role for five seasons, during which time he recovered five more fumbles, intercepted another pass, and scored three more touchdowns. However, Martin suddenly found himself pressed into full-time duty again in 1986, after run-stopping specialist Curtis McGriff injured himself during training camp. Despite often being outweighed nearly 50 pounds by opposing offensive linemen, the 255-pound Martin played extremely well throughout the 1986 championship campaign, recording three sacks and an interception, which he returned 78 yards for a touchdown in one of the season's most memorable plays.

Taking note of the 33-year-old veteran's strong performance over the course of the campaign, rookie defensive end Eric Dorsey stated, "He's amazing. He's as fresh in the fourth quarter as he is in the first."[3]

Meanwhile, Giants head coach Bill Parcells said of Martin, "He's a tremendous example for young players, and he inspires me. He can inspire greatness in other people just by his behavior, so he's terrific. I hope he plays five more years."[4]

Commenting on his own performance, Martin suggested, "It's always served as a motivational tactic for me to go out and try to keep up with the younger guys. But, also, I've been endowed with an awful lot of pride, and I will not settle for anything less than my very best."[5]

Martin played two more years for the Giants, accumulating 12½ more sacks before retiring at the conclusion of the 1988 campaign with 46 "official" career sacks, and an "unofficial" total of 96. He missed only six games in his 14 seasons in New York, placing him behind only Eli Manning and Michael Strahan on the team's all-time list, with 201 games played. Martin also scored seven touchdowns over the course of his career, scoring three times on interception returns, twice on fumble recovery returns, once on a lateral return following a blocked field goal, and once on an offensive pass reception. His six defensive touchdowns remained an NFL record for defensive linemen until 2006, when Miami's Jason Taylor established a new mark by notching his seventh TD after intercepting a Brad Johnson pass.

Looking back during the latter stages of his career at the time he spent in a Giants uniform, Martin said, "It's so unbelievable to realize the entire scope of it. I keep thinking I'm going to wake up and we'll be 3–12–1. All

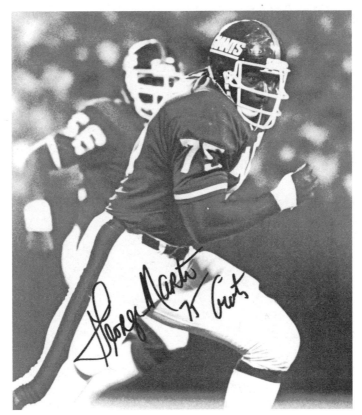

Martin ranks third in franchise history with 201 games played.
Courtesy of PristineAuction.com

these years we always heard how we were heirs to a dynasty. There were years when people thought we were the pits, and rightfully so. Hopefully now the torch has been passed."[6]

Following his playing career, Martin spent several years serving as the executive director and president of the NFL Alumni Association, an organization dedicated to assisting former players. He remained in that position until 2012, when he resigned following allegations of widespread financial mismanagement of the NFLAA. While still in office, he embarked on what became known as the "Journey for 9/11," seeking to raise money for medical care for the first responders to the September 11, 2001, terrorist attacks by walking from New York City's George Washington Bridge all the way to San Francisco's Golden Gate Bridge. The journey, which lasted from September 16, 2007, to June 21, 2008, covered more than 3,000 miles and ended up raising roughly $2 million.

CAREER HIGHLIGHTS

Best Season

Since Martin served as the Giants' full-time starter at the left end position from 1975 to 1980, he quite possibly played his best all-around football for them in one of those seasons. However, the NFL did not record sacks as an official statistic until 1982. That being the case, I elected to go with Martin's 1985 campaign, one in which he registered a career-high 10 "official" sacks, recovered a fumble, and intercepted one pass, which he returned 56 yards for a touchdown.

Memorable Moments/Greatest Performances

Martin scored the first touchdown of his career on September 18, 1977, helping the Giants defeat the Washington Redskins 20–17 in the season opener by intercepting a Billy Kilmer pass and returning it 30 yards for New York's first score of the year. He achieved a major milestone eight years later, returning an interception 56 yards for a touchdown during a 34–3 victory over the St. Louis Cardinals on November 24, 1985. The touchdown, Martin's fifth of his career, made him the NFL's all-time leader in touchdowns scored by a defensive lineman. The game against St. Louis represented arguably the finest all-around effort of Martin's career, since he also recorded three sacks and recovered a fumble during the contest.

However, Martin turned in the two most memorable plays of his career during the Giants' 1986 championship campaign, making both of them against the Denver Broncos. During New York's 19–16 home win against Denver in week 12, Martin turned a 6–3 second-quarter deficit into a 10–6 Giants lead by intercepting a John Elway pass and returning it 78 yards for the longest touchdown of his career. With the Broncos in possession of the ball deep in Giants territory, Martin showed great anticipation by sniffing out a short Elway pass into the right flat. He then displayed outstanding athleticism by stepping in between Elway and his intended receiver, leaping in the air near the 20-yard line, gathering in the ball with his left hand, rumbling down the sideline, breaking an attempted tackle by Elway at the Denver 45, and hurdling over another attempted tackler at the 15, before carrying the ball into the end zone, where an exuberant Lawrence Taylor finally brought him down with a neck-high tackle. Martin again proved to be a thorn in the side of the Broncos in the Super Bowl, tackling Elway in the end zone for a safety late in the first half, thereby reducing Denver's lead to just one point at halftime. The Giants subsequently dominated the third quarter, en route to posting a 39–20 victory that gave them their first NFL championship in 30 years.

NOTABLE ACHIEVEMENTS

- Recorded 10 quarterback sacks in 1985.
- Scored seven career touchdowns.
- Ranks second all-time in NFL among defensive linemen with six defensive touchdowns.
- Ranks third all-time on Giants with 201 games played.
- Ranks fourth all-time on Giants' "unofficial" sack list with 96.
- Ranks eighth all-time on Giants with 46 "official" sacks.
- 1985 Week 12 NFC Defensive Player of the Week.
- 1986 NFC champion.
- Super Bowl XXI champion.

ARNIE WEINMEISTER

The dominant defensive tackle of his time, Arnie Weinmeister played at such a high level that he eventually gained admittance to the Pro Football Hall of Fame even though he competed professionally for only six seasons. After spending his first two years with the New York Yankees of the All-America Football Conference, Weinmeister joined the Giants, with whom he earned First-Team All-Pro honors in each of the next four seasons. During that time, the 6'4", 235-pound Weinmeister made a lasting impression on everyone he competed against, as can be evidenced by the following description the Pro Football Hall of Fame gave of him in an article it published on its members: "Arnie Weinmeister was a steam engine on the field. Players would flip a coin to decide who would have to face the menacing defensive tackle head-on."[1] Yet, surprisingly, Weinmeister never anticipated playing football professionally, with the relative brevity of his career resulting primarily from his keen interest in the business world.

Born in Rhein, Saskatchewan, in Canada, on March 23, 1923, Arnold George Weinmeister entered the University of Washington in 1941 on a football scholarship even though his future plans did not include competing at the professional level. Although Weinmeister performed extremely well for the Huskies at offensive end as a sophomore, he instead chose to focus most of his attention on earning a degree in either math or economics. However, he put his education on hold in 1942, when he dropped out of school to join the military. Weinmeister spent the next three years serving primarily as an artillery officer with General George Patton's forces in France and Germany.

Having added 30 pounds of muscle to his frame during his time in the service, Weinmeister returned to the Huskies bigger and stronger than ever following his discharge in 1946. The added bulk prompted head coach Ralph Welch to move Weinmeister from end to fullback, a position he always wanted to play. Weinmeister excelled at his new position, making such a favorable impression on former Washington State/Gonzaga player

Arnie Weinmeister was the NFL's premier defensive tackle of his era.
Courtesy of SportsMemorabilia.com

Ray Flaherty on one particular occasion that the latter described him as "the best-looking fullback prospect in the country."[2] On the basis of their head coach's scouting report, the New York Yankees of the All-American Football Conference (an NFL rival from 1946 to 1949) immediately acquired Weinmeister's draft rights.

Unfortunately, Weinmeister suffered a serious knee injury the very next week that required surgery to repair. Speaking of the injury years later, Weinmeister stated, "They didn't have knee operations perfected as they do today. It took me about a year to recover."[3]

Upon his return to the Huskies, Weinmeister shifted positions once more, this time moving to defensive tackle as a means of putting less stress on his surgically repaired knee. Although he played well as a senior, Weinmeister continued to express little interest in turning pro, telling the *Seattle Times* in April of 1948, "I want to graduate in June and then get busy in the business world. Football is great fun and the experience in professional football would be something to have, but, after all, I have had enough play. It is about time for me to settle down to work."[4]

Despite Weinmeister's statements to the contrary, Flaherty, who had selected him in the 17th round of the 1945 AAFC Draft with the 166th overall pick, continued to pursue the prize lineman, finally convincing him to join his New York Yankees for at least one year by offering him an $8,000 contract that no NFL team matched. Commenting years later on his decision to temporarily forgo a career in business, Weinmeister revealed, "If it hadn't been for the two leagues, I wouldn't have played pro ball. The salaries they were paying before [the bidding war between the two leagues] wouldn't have interested me. It was a good thing for the players, and, in a way, for pro football, too. It brought a lot of fellows into the game who wouldn't have considered it otherwise."[5]

Once in the fold, Weinmeister became an instant star in the AAFC, excelling on both the offensive and defensive lines en route to earning Second-Team All-League honors as a rookie. Ed Strader, who replaced the fired Flaherty as New York's head coach during the season, said of Weinmeister, "He's the greatest tackle I've ever seen. He has amazing speed. Except for Buddy Young [a fleet-footed running back], he's the fastest player on the team."[6]

Weinmeister earned First-Team All-AAFC honors in his second season, before the league collapsed at the end of the year. The Giants subsequently acquired the negotiating rights to him and several other ex-Yankees, including Otto Schnellbacher and Tom Landry.

After joining the Giants, it didn't take Weinmeister long to establish himself as the NFL's premier defensive tackle. Fitting in perfectly with the team's newly devised "umbrella defense" that emphasized pressure up the middle and man-to-man coverage of all potential pass receivers, Weinmeister used his speed, strength, and intelligence to dominate opposing offensive linemen.

Dante Lavelli, the Cleveland Browns' star end who went up against Weinmeister in both the AAFC and the NFL, said of his former foe, "It was a wonder to see him on the field. He was one of the first big men who could move that quickly."[7]

Buck Shaw, head coach of the San Francisco 49ers, was another who admired Weinmeister, stating, "Weinmeister is the outstanding tackle in the NFL. One man can't handle him."[8]

Even Weinmeister's New York Giants teammates stood in awe of him. Commenting on the defensive tackle's ability to analyze plays, Tom Landry remarked, "If you wanted to know where the opponent's ball was, all you had to do was look for Arnie's jersey number."[9]

Meanwhile, Giants Hall of Fame offensive tackle Roosevelt Brown, who was also noted for his quickness, discussed the difficulties he encountered during practice whenever he pulled out and attempted to cut off the

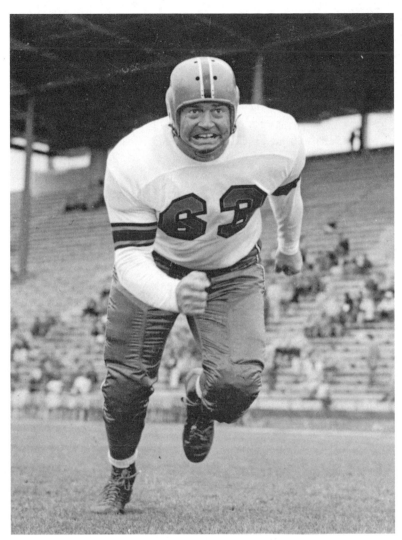

Weinmeister (seen here as a member of the B.C. Lions in 1954) earned
First-Team All-Pro honors in each of his four seasons with the Giants.
Public domain via Wikipedia

inside defender, suggesting, "With Weinmeister, it was impossible. He was
very, very fast himself, and one of the toughest to go up against. Fortunately, I only had to do that in practice."[10]

Weinmeister's exceptional all-around ability enabled him to earn four
straight unanimous First-Team All-Pro selections with the Giants. However, in spite of the incredible success he experienced on the playing field,

Weinmeister continued to contemplate retirement each off-season, later revealing, "At the end of every season, I'd tell myself that's the last one. And then, when July starts to roll around and the camps are opening again, I start getting the fever again."[11]

After serving as Giants co-captain in 1953, Weinmeister finally elected to call it quits at the end of the year when the team replaced longtime head coach Steve Owen with Jim Lee Howell. However, when an anticipated offer to replace the fired Howie Odell as head coach at Washington never materialized, Weinmeister signed a one-year deal to play for the Canadian Football League's Vancouver Lions. Although the Giants subsequently took him to court, suing him for breach of contract, Weinmeister ultimately prevailed, spending the final two years of his playing career in Canada, before retiring from the game for good at the conclusion of the 1955 campaign.

After leaving football, Weinmeister spent the next 36 years in various roles within the Teamsters union, negotiating contracts for health and welfare coverage, pensions, and higher pay. He surrendered his post in 1992, retiring to Seattle, Washington, where he passed away from congestive heart failure on June 28, 2000, at the age of 77.

GIANT CAREER HIGHLIGHTS

Best Season

With the availability of individual defensive statistics being as limited as they are for players who competed during Weinmeister's time, it is extremely difficult to ascertain in which of his four seasons with the Giants he played his best ball. However, New York's defense allowed the opposition a total of 298 points in 1949, the year before Weinmeister arrived. In 1950, the Giants surrendered only 150 points to the opposition, en route to finishing the season with a superb 10–2 record. Since that time, no Giant defense has allowed so few points over the course of a full season. Therefore, although other players came over from the defunct AAFC that year as well, it would seem that Weinmeister made his biggest impact on the Giants in his first NFL season of 1950.

Memorable Moments/Greatest Performances

The Cleveland Browns lost only two games in 1950, with the Giants handing them both defeats. Led by the brilliant mind of Paul Brown and the exceptional quarterbacking of Otto Graham, Cleveland compiled an overall mark of 54–4 in the AAFC from 1946 to 1949. However, after proving to be just as dominant in the NFL by outscoring their opponents by a combined margin of 66–10 in their first two games of 1950, the Browns found themselves unable to register a single point against the Giants in a 6–0 loss in their third contest. Unveiling their famed "umbrella defense" for the first time, the Giants swarmed all over Graham and his receivers, intercepting the Cleveland quarterback three times and allowing no passes to be completed the entire first half. With defensive tackles Weinmeister and Al DeRogatis applying constant pressure to Graham, and New York's innovative four-man secondary bottling up Cleveland's receivers, the Browns barely crossed midfield the entire day. As the anchor of New York's defense, Weinmeister had as much to do with that as anyone. Therefore, although he also registered a safety and made a pass reception in his years with the Giants, Weinmeister's performance during the 6–0 shutout of Cleveland would have to be considered his finest moment.

NOTABLE ACHIEVEMENTS

- Four-time Pro Bowl selection.
- Four-time First-Team All-Pro selection.
- Elected to Pro Football Hall of Fame in 1984.

35

ODELL BECKHAM JR.

Although he has spent just three full seasons in New York, Odell Beckham Jr.'s dynamic playmaking ability enabled him to earn a spot on this list. Proving to be one of the NFL's most prolific wide receivers since he first entered the league in 2014, Beckham has made more than 90 receptions, amassed more than 1,300 receiving yards, and scored at least 10 touchdowns in each of his first three full seasons, earning in the process three trips to the Pro Bowl and two All-Pro nominations. Destined to become the greatest wide-out in franchise history if he can stay healthy and chooses to remain in New York, Beckham needs only to display a greater level of maturity and more of a team-first mentality for him to claim a significantly higher place in these rankings.

Born in Baton Rouge, Louisiana, on November 5, 1992, Odell Cornelious Beckham Jr. attended Isidore Newman High School in New Orleans, where he lettered in football, basketball, and track. In addition to earning All-District honors for his performance on the hardwood in his junior and senior years, Beckham excelled in numerous track-and-field events, recording a personal best of 6.83 meters in the long jump, while also competing in the 100- and 200-meter dashes. Even more proficient on the gridiron, Beckham played wide receiver, quarterback, running back, and cornerback for the Greenies football team, performing so well that he earned District 9-2A Offensive MVP honors and a spot on *The Advocate*'s Super Dozen.

Regarded as a four-star recruit by both Rivals.com and Scout.com, Beckham fielded scholarship offers from several major programs, including Ole Miss, Nebraska, and Tulane, before finally choosing to remain close to home at Louisiana State University. He then spent the next three years starring at wide receiver for LSU, combining with Jarvis Landry to give the Tigers arguably the top receiver tandem in all of college football. Performing especially well as a junior in 2013, Beckham made 57 receptions for 1,117 yards and eight touchdowns, earning in the process First-Team All-Southeastern Conference honors. Choosing to forego his final year of

Odell Beckham Jr. has topped 90 receptions, 1,300 receiving yards, and 10 touchdowns in each of his three full seasons with the Giants.
Public Domain via Wikipedia

college eligibility, Beckham entered the 2014 NFL Draft, where the Giants selected him in the first round with the 12th overall pick.

After missing virtually all of training camp, the entire preseason, and the first four games of the regular season with a hamstring injury, Beckham quickly established himself as the Giants' most potent offensive weapon once he took the field for the first time in week 5. Making his professional debut with a four-catch, one-touchdown effort against Atlanta, Beckham subsequently went on to make 91 receptions for 1,305 yards and 12 touchdowns, with his exceptional play earning him Pro Bowl and NFL Offensive

Rookie of the Year honors. Particularly effective during a seven-game stretch that lasted from November 3 to December 14, Beckham set a league record for NFL rookies by making 61 catches over the course of those seven contests, with the highlight of the streak coming against Dallas on November 23, when he wowed a national television audience by making a remarkable one-handed touchdown reception that pundits later called the "catch of the year." Amazingly, Beckham accomplished all he did while performing at less than 100 percent, revealing following the conclusion of the campaign that he suffered from a pair of hamstring injuries the entire year. In discussing his plight, Beckham admitted, "I was never fully healthy. I was just trying to manage it and maintain it. It's still not right. I'm still working on it." Fully recovered by the start of 2015 training camp, Beckham followed up his brilliant rookie campaign with an equally impressive sophomore season, making 96 receptions for 1,450 yards and 13 touchdowns, en route to earning his second straight trip to the Pro Bowl and Second-Team All-Pro honors.

Blessed with outstanding speed and superb acceleration that make him a threat to score any time he touches the ball, Beckham possesses game-changing ability, frequently turning 10- or 12-yard receptions made on simple slant patterns into lengthy touchdown jaunts. And, even though he stands just 5'11" tall and weighs only 198 pounds, he has huge hands that often enable him to haul in passes with just one arm extended.

Yet, despite his immense talent and exceptional play over the course of the 2015 campaign, Beckham drew a considerable amount of criticism for his behavior during a week 15 loss to the Carolina Panthers, when he engaged in multiple confrontations with cornerback Josh Norman. Flagged for three personal foul penalties, including one that drew him a one-game suspension from the league office for violating safety-related playing rules, Beckham exhibited throughout the contest a volatile temperament that at times makes him his own worst enemy. Prone to conducting himself in an unprofessional manner that includes losing control of his emotions, attempting to draw attention to himself by behaving childishly on the sidelines, and antagonizing his opponents with ludicrous touchdown celebrations, Beckham sometimes fails to focus properly on the task at hand, occasionally making him a detriment to his team.

Beckham's unique skill-set has often prompted everyone within the Giants organization to look the other way in such instances, causing a lack of discipline to gradually develop on the team, which compiled a disappointing record of 6–10 in 2015. However, even though Beckham continued to behave childishly at times in 2016, all seemed well when the Giants posted a record of 11–5 that earned them a spot in the playoffs, with

Beckham is among the NFL's most explosive wide receivers.
Courtesy of Erik Drost

the speedy receiver once again earning Pro Bowl and Second-Team All-Pro honors by making 101 receptions for 1,367 yards and 10 touchdowns. Nevertheless, the season ended on a sour note when the Giants suffered a 38–13 defeat at the hands of the Green Bay Packers in the opening round of the postseason tournament, just six days after Beckham and fellow wide-outs Victor Cruz, Sterling Shepard, and Roger Lewis flew to Miami to celebrate the team's first playoff appearance since 2011. Beckham, who found himself being criticized in the media more than anyone else for the ill-advised trip, continued to be censured after he caught just four passes for 28 yards during the loss.

Beckham's troubles continued in 2017, when, after injuring his left ankle during the preseason, he fractured the same ankle during a week 5 loss to the Los Angeles Chargers, forcing him to undergo season-ending surgery. Beckham finished the year with just 25 receptions, 302 receiving yards, and three TD catches, giving him, as of this writing, career totals of 313 receptions, 4,424 receiving yards, and 38 touchdown receptions. Beckham will enter the 2018 campaign with one year remaining on his contract. If he chooses to re-sign with the Giants at season's end, he will likely go on to set numerous franchise receiving records. However, he will need to do a better job of controlling his emotions if he truly wishes to get the very most out of his ability and help create a winning atmosphere in New York.

CAREER HIGHLIGHTS

Best Season

Beckham performed brilliantly in each of his first three seasons with the Giants, ranking among the NFL leaders in receptions, receiving yards, and touchdown receptions all three years. In addition to catching 91 passes and scoring 12 touchdowns as a rookie in 2014, Beckham amassed a career-high 1,511 all-purpose yards. Two years later, he made a career-high 101 receptions and caught 10 TD passes. Although either of those campaigns would have made an excellent choice, I ultimately settled on 2015, since, in addition to catching 96 passes, Beckham established career-high marks in receiving yards (1,450) and touchdown receptions (13).

Memorable Moments/Greatest Performances

Beckham scored the first touchdown of his career during a 30–20 victory over the Atlanta Falcons on October 5, 2014, when he hooked up with Eli Manning on a 15-yard scoring play early in the fourth quarter that put the Giants ahead to stay. He finished the game with four catches for 44 yards and that one TD.

Although the Giants lost their November 3, 2014, Monday Night meeting with the Indianapolis Colts by a score of 40–24, Beckham surpassed 100 receiving yards for the first time, concluding the contest with eight receptions for 156 yards.

Beckham thrust himself into the national spotlight three weeks later, when, during a 31–28 Sunday Night home loss to the Dallas Cowboys, he made 10 receptions for 146 yards and two touchdowns, one of which came on a sensational 43-yard, one-handed grab in the right corner of the end zone that subsequently became known simply as "The Catch." Snaring the ball while diving backwards, with full extension of his right arm, Beckham made his remarkable reception with only three fingers, prompting many onlookers to identify it as the greatest catch they ever saw.

Beckham continued his exceptional play on December 7, 2014, helping the Giants record a lopsided 36–7 victory over Tennessee by making 11 receptions for 130 yards and one touchdown, which came on a 15-yard connection with Eli Manning late in the first quarter that gave the Giants an early 10–0 lead. Beckham had another huge game one week later, making 12 catches for 143 yards and three touchdowns during a 24–13 win over the Washington Redskins. He followed that up with two more outstanding performances, leading the Giants to a 37–27 win over the St. Louis Rams on December 21 by making eight receptions for 148 yards and two TDs, one of which covered 80 yards, before catching 12 passes, amassing 185 receiving yards, and scoring one touchdown during a 34–26 loss to Philadelphia in the regular-season finale.

Beckham contributed to a 30–27 victory over San Francisco on October 11, 2015, by making seven receptions for 121 yards and one touchdown, which came on a 17-yard hookup with Eli Manning late in the third quarter that gave the Giants a 20–13 lead.

Although the Giants lost a 52–49 shoot-out with the New Orleans Saints three weeks later, Beckham starred in defeat, making eight catches for 130 yards and three touchdowns, the longest of which covered 50 yards. He had another big day when the Giants lost to the Patriots by a score of 27–26 on November 15, 2015, making four catches for 104 yards and one TD, which came on a career-long 87-yard catch-and-run. Beckham topped that performance, though, on December 14, 2015, when he helped lead the Giants to a 31–24 win over the Miami Dolphins by catching seven passes, amassing 166 receiving yards, and scoring a pair of touchdowns, with the second of those being an 84-yard connection with Eli Manning early in the fourth quarter that provided the margin of victory.

Beckham earned NFC Offensive Player of the Week honors for the first time for his performance during a 27–23 win over the Baltimore Ravens on October 16, 2016, when he made eight receptions for a career-high 222 yards and two touchdowns, which came on plays that covered 75 and 66 yards. Beckham scored his second TD with only 1:24 left in the fourth quarter, giving the Giants the victory.

NOTABLE ACHIEVEMENTS

- Has surpassed 90 receptions three times, topping 100 catches once (101 in 2016).
- Has surpassed 1,300 receiving yards three times, topping 1,400 yards once (1,450 in 2015).
- Has surpassed 10 touchdown receptions three times.
- Finished third in NFL with 101 receptions and 1,367 receiving yards in 2016.
- Has led Giants in pass receptions and receiving yards three times each.

- Holds share of Giants single-season record for most touchdown receptions (13 in 2015).
- Ranks among Giants career leaders with 313 pass receptions (10th) and 38 touchdown receptions (5th).
- 2014 Associated Press NFL Offensive Rookie of the Year.
- 2014 Pro Football Writers Association NFL Offensive Rookie of the Year.
- Week Six 2016 NFC Offensive Player of the Week.
- Three-time Pro Bowl selection (2014, 2015, 2016).
- Two-time Second-Team All-Pro (2015, 2016).

36

DICK LYNCH

A New York Giant to the core, Dick Lynch spent nearly half a century affiliated with the Giants in one capacity or another. After being traded to New York from the Washington Redskins after his rookie season of 1958, Lynch started at right cornerback for the Giants for the next eight years. During that time, he established himself as one of the NFL's top cornerbacks, earning one Pro Bowl selection and one First-Team All-Pro nomination, leading the league in interceptions twice, and scoring seven touchdowns—four on interception returns and three on fumble returns. Following his retirement from the game at the conclusion of the 1966 campaign, Lynch assumed a position in the Giants broadcast booth for the next 42 years, entertaining fans of the team with his conversational style and friendly, down-to-earth demeanor.

Born in Oceanside, New York, on April 29, 1936, Richard Dennis Lynch attended Notre Dame University, where he starred as a halfback on offense and a defensive back on defense. As a senior in 1957, Lynch scored the only touchdown in Notre Dame's 7–0 win over the University of Oklahoma that ended the Sooners' 47-game winning streak.

A childhood fan of the Giants while growing up on Long Island, Lynch never expected to play pro football. "I never gave pro football a thought," he said. "When I was at Notre Dame, that was the last thing on my mind."[1]

Selected by the Washington Redskins in the sixth round of the 1958 NFL Draft with the 66th overall pick, Lynch spent his first year in the league seeing spot duty for the Redskins, appearing in all 12 games and intercepting two passes. During Lynch's time in Washington, though, Giants defensive coordinator Tom Landry kept a watchful eye on him, assessing how he might be able to incorporate the young cornerback into New York's defensive scheme. Impressed with what he saw, Landry urged the Giants to acquire Lynch's services, which they did after the latter served a six-month hitch in the Army at Fort Monmouth in New Jersey during the subsequent off-season. Extremely pleased with the trade that sent him

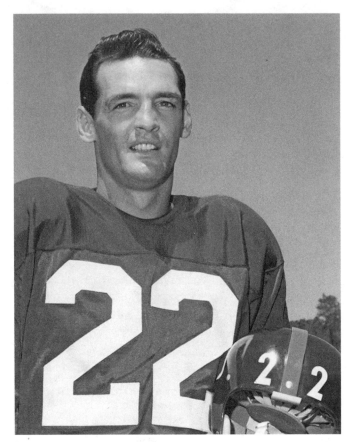

Dick Lynch led the NFL in interceptions twice.
Public domain (author unknown)

from Washington to New York, Lynch later recalled, "It was huge for me, especially being a New Yorker and always a Giant fan."[2]

Taking over at starting right cornerback for the Giants, Lynch went on to have a successful career in New York. After intercepting a total of four passes in his first two years with the Giants, Lynch had his first big season in 1961, leading the league with nine interceptions, while also recovering two fumbles. He followed that up with a solid 1962 campaign in which he intercepted five passes and scored two defensive touchdowns. Lynch had the finest season of his career in 1963, when, in addition to leading the NFL with nine interceptions for the second time, he finished first in the league with three interception returns for touchdowns and 251 total interception return yards. His outstanding performance earned him his only Pro Bowl and First-Team All-Pro selections.

Unfortunately, the Giants began their downward spiral after that 1963 campaign, failing to make the playoffs in any of the next 17 seasons. Nevertheless, Lynch played well for them the next two seasons, intercepting four passes in both 1964 and 1965, before losing his starting job in 1966 and subsequently announcing his retirement. Lynch concluded his Giants career with 35 interceptions, tying him for fourth on the team's all-time list. He appeared in four NFL Championship Games during his time in New York.

Looking back at his playing days with the Giants, Lynch said, "I had a great career. I played with the best group of men you could play with, offensively and defensively. We hung together. In those days you went out there with 11 people. You didn't go out there by yourself. It wasn't just Sam Huff and 10 other guys. It was the defense."[3]

After spending a brief amount of time selling government bonds following his retirement, Lynch joined the Giants' radio broadcast team, where he spent the next 42 years sharing his strategic insight and knowledge of the game with listeners in the New York/New Jersey area, while simultaneously entertaining them with his occasional unrelated stories about his playing days and greetings to his family and friends. Often prone to mispronouncing names, Lynch had a particularly difficult time saying the name of former Giants kicker Brad Daluiso. Meanwhile, his frequent

After starring for the Giants at cornerback for eight seasons, Lynch spent the next 42 years serving the team as a radio announcer.
Public domain (author unknown)

malapropisms included spending nearly an entire broadcast referring to the Houston Texans as the Houston Astros and mispronouncing the name of former quarterback Trent Dilfer, referring to him instead as Kent Dilfer.

Lynch's unpretentious and affable nature, occasional miscues, and Giants pedigree made him a true fan favorite, enabling him to establish a following among several generations of Giants fans. He also became extremely popular with Giants players over the years, developing a particularly close relationship with the team that upset New England in Super Bowl XLII. Speaking of the unbridled joy Lynch felt at the conclusion of that contest, Bob Papa, who shared the broadcast booth with him for 13 seasons, stated, "I think it was an unbelievable joy for him. Dick really bonded with this team. I think it reminded him of the championship teams he played on that lost. At the end of the game, there was a look of tremendous satisfaction on his face. He looked almost proud."[4]

Sadly, Super Bowl XLII turned out to be the last game Lynch ever announced. He died from leukemia less than eight months later on September 24, 2008, passing away at his home in the Douglaston section of Queens at the age of 72.

GIANT CAREER HIGHLIGHTS

Best Season

Although Lynch played very well in 1961, leading the NFL with nine interceptions and recovering two fumbles, he had easily his finest season in 1963, when he earned the only Pro Bowl and First-Team All-Pro nominations of his career by finishing first in the league with nine interceptions, three interception returns for touchdowns, and 251 total interception return yards. The last figure tied him with Emlen Tunnell for the Giants' single-season record.

Memorable Moments/Greatest Performances

Lynch scored his first career touchdown in the final game of the 1960 campaign, returning an interception 16 yards to open the scoring in what turned out to be a 48–34 defeat at the hands of the Cleveland Browns.

Nevertheless, Lynch turned in the most memorable performances of his career in his two best seasons of 1961 and 1963. On October 8, 1961, he intercepted three passes during a 24–9 win over the St. Louis Cardinals that improved the Giants' record to 3–1. Lynch recorded another interception during a 31–10 victory over Dallas the following week, enabling him to tie the Giants' franchise record with four picks in two games. He bettered that mark later in the year, intercepting three passes against the Eagles in week 9, before recording another two interceptions against the Steelers the following week. Lynch's total of five picks in two games still stands as a Giants record.

Lynch's fabulous 1963 campaign also resulted in a number of extraordinary efforts. After sparking a 37–14 Giants win over the Eagles on September 29 by intercepting three passes, Lynch returned an interception 47 yards for a touchdown two weeks later during a 35–24 loss to the Cleveland Browns. Lynch was at it again the very next week, sealing a 37–21 Giants victory over Dallas by closing out the scoring in the fourth quarter with an 82-yard interception return that represented the longest of his career. He recorded his third touchdown of the year on December 8, intercepting two passes and returning one of them 42 yards for a score during a 44–14 win over Washington that improved New York's record to 10–3.

NOTABLE ACHIEVEMENTS

- Led NFL in interceptions twice, interception return yardage once, TD interceptions once, fumble return yardage once, and non-offensive touchdowns twice.
- Tied for fourth on Giants all-time list with 35 career interceptions.
- Shares Giants single-season record for most interception return yardage (251 in 1963).
- Holds Giants record for most interceptions in two consecutive games (5).
- 1963 Pro Bowl selection.
- 1963 First-Team All-Pro selection.
- 1961 Second-Team All-Pro selection.
- 1965 First-Team All-Conference selection.
- Four-time NFL Eastern Division champion.

OSI UMENYIORA

any NFL scouts viewed the Giants' second-round selection of Osi Umenyiora in the 2003 NFL Draft as something of a reach, especially when they considered the fact that several more-accomplished defensive ends from larger schools still remained on the board when the Giants selected Umenyiora at number 56 overall. In making the graduate of Troy State University their second pick of that year's draft, New York bypassed more heralded ends such as Florida State's Alonzo Jackson, Louisville's Dewayne White, Texas's Cory Redding, and Ohio State's Kenny Peterson. Yet the members of the Giants' front office clearly knew what they were doing since, with the exception of Terrell Suggs, whom the Baltimore Ravens selected 10th overall in the first round, Umenyiora ended up surpassing every other player available at his position in terms of his overall production at the NFL level. A two-time Pro Bowler and one-time First-Team All-Pro, Umenyiora recorded 75 sacks in his nine years in New York, placing him fourth on the Giants' all-time official sack list. Meanwhile, his outstanding pass-rushing skills helped the Giants earn five trips to the postseason and two Super Bowl victories.

Born to Nigerian parents in London, England, on November 16, 1981, Ositadimma "Osi" Umenyiora moved with his family to Nigeria as a youngster before eventually migrating to Auburn, Alabama, where he started playing football in his final year of high school. In spite of his relative lack of experience, Umenyiora gradually developed into one of college football's top defensive ends at Troy State, being named honorable mention All-American after starting every game at right defensive end as a senior.

Still viewed very much as a project when the Giants selected him in the second round of the 2003 NFL Draft, Umenyiora saw very little action as a rookie, starting only one game and registering just one sack. However, he earned a starting job by the middle of his second season, after which he went on to record seven sacks, force three fumbles, and make four fumble recoveries, one of which he returned for a touchdown. Umenyiora

Osi Umenyiora ranks fourth on the Giants' all-time with 75 quarterback sacks.
Courtesy of Andy Kronen

developed into a star the following year, earning Pro Bowl and First-Team All-Pro honors by finishing second in the NFL with 14½ sacks. He also forced four fumbles, recovered two others, and registered 70 tackles (48 of them solo). Injuries limited Umenyiora to only 11 games and six sacks in 2006. But he rebounded the following year, helping the Giants advance to the Super Bowl by finishing fifth in the league with 13 sacks. He also forced five fumbles, recovered two others, made 52 tackles, and scored the second touchdown of his career.

Standing 6'3" and weighing close to 260 pounds, Umenyiora had decent size and strength for a defensive end. However, the thing that made him such an outstanding pass-rusher was his tremendous quickness, which he used to outmaneuver the bigger and less-athletic offensive tackles he typically faced. Umenyiora's speed and agility often put opposing linemen in awkward positions, enabling him to overpower them with his patented "bull rush." More often than not, though, he took an outside route to get to the quarterback, creating more than his fair share of turnovers by slapping the ball out of the QB's hand just as he reached him. Early in his career, Umenyiora also played the run well, recording more than 50 tackles on three separate occasions.

A left knee injury suffered during a preseason game against the New York Jets forced Umenyiora to sit out the entire 2008 campaign. After undergoing surgery to repair a torn lateral meniscus, Umenyiora returned to the Giants in 2009 to record seven sacks in his 11 starts. Back in top form by the start of the 2010 season, he recorded 11½ sacks, tying him with Justin Tuck for the team lead in that category. The two teammates also combined for 16 forced fumbles, with 10 of those being credited to Umenyiora, who established a new single-season NFL record in the process.

Umenyiora's outstanding performance in 2010 prompted him to ask general manager Jerry Reese to renegotiate the seven-year, $41 million contract extension he had signed five seasons earlier. However, after Reese balked at the idea, an upset Umenyiora filed an affidavit in conjunction with the NFLPA's lawsuit against the league during the NFL lockout in 2011. Essentially calling Reese a liar in the affidavit, Umenyiora claimed that the Giants general manager reneged on a promise to either give him a huge raise or trade him to a team that would. When the lockout ended, an angry Umenyiora staged a one-day holdout, demanded a trade, and even told friends he never intended to speak to Reese again. Reese, who continued to conduct himself in a strictly professional manner throughout the entire ordeal, never succumbed to Umenyiora's demands, although he eventually renegotiated a deal with him that enabled the unhappy defensive end to earn a few extra million dollars in 2012.

Through it all, though, Umenyiora continued to perform well for the Giants, albeit in a somewhat reduced role. After undergoing arthroscopic surgery on his right knee shortly before the beginning of the 2011 regular season, Umenyiora missed the first several games. Upon his return to the team at midseason, he assumed the role of a pass-rushing specialist, surrendering his starting right defensive end job to second-year phenom Jason Pierre-Paul. Umenyiora ended up recording nine sacks in only nine games, en route to helping the Giants return to the Super Bowl, where they once again defeated the New England Patriots.

Umenyiora holds Giants career records for most fumble-return yards (224) and most forced fumbles (32).
Courtesy of Mike Morbeck

Umenyiora spent one more year in New York, registering six sacks and forcing two fumbles in 2012 before signing a two-year free-agent deal worth $8.55 million with the Atlanta Falcons at season's end. He played well for the Falcons in 2013, recording 7½ sacks and the first interception of his career, which he returned 68 yards for a touchdown. Before leaving the Giants, though, Umenyiora placed a telephone call to Jerry Reese, after which he stated, "Me and Jerry are cool, man. We've always been cool. Jerry's my guy. Obviously, if it wasn't for him, I probably wouldn't even be here [Atlanta], because obviously the team did a comprehensive amount of research on me and my background because of some of the things that have been reported. They wanted to know what type of person I was. So, obviously, they had to talk to Jerry Reese as well as my coach, and they had nothing but positive things to say."[1]

Umenyiora remained in Atlanta for one more season, making just 2½ sacks in a backup role in 2014 before announcing his retirement following the conclusion of the campaign. He ended his career with 85 sacks, 435 tackles, five defensive touchdowns, 35 forced fumbles, 14 fumble recoveries, and 310 fumble-return yards, which represents the second-highest total in NFL history. In addition to sacking opposing quarterbacks a total of 75 times as a member of the Giants, Umenyiora recorded 376 tackles, scored three touchdowns, forced 32 fumbles, and recovered 13 others during his time in New York. Spending his first five seasons playing alongside Michael Strahan may have caused Umenyiora to be somewhat overlooked at times. Nevertheless, he certainly would have to be considered one of the top defensive ends in Giants history.

GIANT CAREER HIGHLIGHTS

Best Season

Umenyiora had an outstanding season in 2010, recording 11½ sacks and setting an NFL record by forcing 10 fumbles. However, he had his best all-around year in 2005, when he earned his only First-Team All-Pro selection by making a career-high 14½ sacks and 70 tackles. Umenyiora's sack total placed him second in the league to Oakland's Derrick Burgess, who sacked opposing quarterbacks 16 times. Umenyiora also forced four fumbles and recovered two others.

Memorable Moments/Greatest Performances

Umenyiora's outstanding athleticism enabled him to return three fumbles for touchdowns during his Giants career. He scored for the first time on December 12, 2004, returning a recovered fumble 50 yards during a 37–14 loss to the Baltimore Ravens. Umenyiora scored his second touchdown some three years later, on October 21, 2007, putting on display for all to see his unique skill set that made him one of the NFL's premier defensive ends. After forcing a fumble while sacking San Francisco quarterback Trent Dilfer, Umenyiora rose quickly to his feet, scooped up the loose ball, and galloped 75 yards into the end zone, in helping the Giants defeat the 49ers 33–15. Umenyiora crossed the goal line for the final time on September 13, 2009, recovering a fumble and returning it 37 yards for a touchdown during a 23–17 victory over the Washington Redskins.

Umenyiora played the greatest game of his career on September 30, 2007, setting a Giants record by sacking beleaguered Philadelphia quarterback Donovan McNabb six times during a 16–3 Giants home win. New York sacked McNabb a total of 12 times over the course of the game.

Umenyiora also played well in that year's Super Bowl, making four tackles and recovering a fumble during the Giants' 17–14 upset win over New England.

Umenyiora put together his greatest stretch of games in October of 2010, earning NFC Defensive Player of the Month honors by recording 18 tackles (10 solo), seven sacks, and six forced fumbles in the Giants' four victories that month.

NOTABLE ACHIEVEMENTS

- Finished in double-digits in sacks three times (2005, 2007, 2010).
- Finished second in NFL with 14½ sacks in 2005.
- Ranks fourth all-time on Giants' "official" list with 75 quarterback sacks.
- Made 70 tackles (48 solo) in 2005.
- Scored three defensive touchdowns.
- Holds Giants career records for most fumble-return yards (224) and most forced fumbles (32).
- Holds Giants single-game record for most sacks (six vs. Philadelphia on September 30, 2007).
- Holds single-season NFL record with 10 forced fumbles in 2010.
- Ranks second all-time in NFL with 310 fumble-return yards.
- Three-time NFC Defensive Player of the Week.
- NFC Defensive Player of the Month for October 2010.
- Two-time Pro Bowl selection (2005, 2007).
- 2005 First-Team All-NFC selection.
- 2005 First-Team All-Pro selection.
- 2010 Second-Team All-Pro selection.
- Two-time NFC champion (2007, 2011).
- Two-time Super Bowl champion (XLII, XLVI).

38

— STEVE OWEN —

Perhaps the most impactful figure in the history of the New York Giants franchise other than Wellington Mara, Steve Owen spent 23 seasons serving as the Giants' head coach, during which time the team compiled an overall record of 153–100–17, winning in the process eight Eastern Conference championships and two NFL titles. Particularly successful under Owen from 1933 to 1946, the Giants appeared in eight NFL Championship games over the course of those 14 seasons, emerging victorious in both 1934 and 1938. Establishing himself as a father figure to many within the organization during his years in New York, Owen drew praise from Wellington Mara, who stated, "Steve Owen was really the rock that we built on. He was like my second father…I admired him, was greatly attached to him, and respected him. He kind of brought me up in the football business."

Yet, before Owen assumed the coaching reins in New York, he spent several seasons starring for the Giants as a tackle on both sides of the ball, earning three All-Pro selections and a spot on the NFL 1920s All-Decade Team. And, with Owen serving as team captain, the Giants dominated their opponents in 1927, compiling a record of 11–1–1 that earned them their first league championship.

Born in Cleo Springs, Oklahoma, on April 21, 1898, Stephen Joseph Owen grew up in an area known as the Cherokee Strip, where his father had claimed land when the region first opened to settlers. Acquiring the nickname "Stout Steve" as a teenager due to his burly 5'10", 220-pound frame, Owen spent his summers working in the Texas oil fields and his winters wrestling for his high school team. Looking back at that period in his life, Owen recalled, "Outside of wrasslin', we didn't have any time for sports. We were too busy with chores and schoolin' and watchin' the marshals chase outlaws across the Cimarron River."

After enrolling at Phillips University in Enid, Oklahoma, Owen competed in several sports, proving to be particularly proficient as a tackle on

Steve Owen served as captain of the Giants when they won their first NFL title in 1927.
Public domain

the gridiron, with former teammate Everett Shelton commenting years later, "For five years, I played defensive halfback behind him, and I never had to make a tackle. Big Steve took care of everything." Acquiring from his own college coach the "down in the dirt" mentality toward football that he later tried to instill in his players, Owen recalled being told by his mentor, "Son, you now have the secret. It's a rough game and you'll get hurt if you let the other fellow hit you harder than you hit him. That's why football is a good game. It won't let a man play easy. You'll learn the rule fast enough. Just remember this: respect every other boy on this squad and work with him. Never lose respect for your opponent or he'll hit you harder than you hit him." While in college, Owen also wrestled professionally under the alias "Jack O'Brien" in order to protect his amateur standing and enlisted in the Student Army Training Corps following the nation's entry into the First World War.

After spending one year coaching at Phillips University following his graduation, Owen went to work in the oil fields in various parts of the Southwest before finally beginning his career in pro football in 1924 as a member of the NFL's Kansas City Cowboys. He subsequently split the ensuing campaign between the Cowboys and the Cleveland Bulldogs before being acquired by the Giants for $500 prior to the start of the 1926 season. Commenting on the deal that sent him to New York, Owen later said, "I had seen a lot of fat hogs go for more than they paid for me. But, in those days, a fat hog was a lot more valuable than a fat tackle. I was going to New York even if I had to walk there."

Quickly establishing himself as one of the Giants' top players upon his arrival in New York, Owen earned Second-Team All-Pro honors in his first year with his new team by starring at left tackle on both offense and defense. After being named team captain prior to the start of the 1927 campaign, Owen helped lead the Giants to their first league championship, earning First-Team All-Pro honors by anchoring a defense that set a single-season NFL record by surrendering just 20 points to the opposition all year. Although the Giants failed to repeat as NFL champions in any of the next three seasons, Owen continued to excel on both sides of the ball, gaining First-Team All-Pro recognition once again in 1929.

Owen, who stood somewhere between 5'10" and six-feet tall and weighed somewhere in the 240- to 260-pound range, depending on the source, proved to be a pillar of strength for the Giants, both on and off the field. Playing 60 minutes every game, Owen did an exceptional job of blocking for the team's running backs on offense, while also dominating his opponent at the line of scrimmage on defense. A brutal tackler, Owen once proclaimed, "If a boy isn't willing to get off the ground and hit back a little harder than he was hit, no coach can help him."

Meanwhile, in discussing the style of play teams employed at that time, Owen noted, "Football was a different game then. The ball was bigger and harder to pass, you couldn't pass from closer than five yards behind the line of scrimmage, and, in 1928, they moved the goal posts back 10 yards from the goal line. But the big difference was the way we played the game. We were pretty much a smash-and-shove gang. We were bone crushers, not fancy Dans."

An exceptional team leader, Owen spent the final two games of the 1930 season and the entire 1931 campaign functioning in the dual role of player-coach before retiring as an active player prior to the start of the 1932 season. Recalling his initial impression of Owen, Giants Hall of fame center/linebacker Mel Hein said, "Steve Owen was the Giants' head coach when I joined the team in 1931. It was his first full year as head coach. Actually, Steve was player-coach that year, but he only suited up for about three games. He was about 33 or 34 then. Steve was a very good coach, though, and all the players respected him."

Owen ended up coaching the Giants for the next 23 years, working under nothing more than a handshake agreement with team owner Tim Mara during that time, with journalist and author Gerald Eskenazi later writing, "Life and football were similar to Owen. Neither was complicated. Appearances were not deceiving. He judged a man by his actions, and it was as simple as that."

In addition to leading the Giants to 153 victories, eight conference titles, and two NFL championships, Owen proved to be a pioneer of sorts, inventing the A-formation offense, the umbrella defense, and the two-platoon system. He also became the first head coach to emphasize defense, with legendary Chicago Bears head coach George Halas stating, "Steve was the first to stress the importance of defense and the advantage of settling for field goals instead of touchdowns. Every team strives today to do what Owen was doing 20 years ago."

In discussing his philosophical approach to the sport, Owen suggested, "Football is a game played down in the dirt, and it always will be. There's no use getting fancy about it."

While Owens's somewhat simplistic coaching philosophy helped make the Giants perennial contenders throughout much of his stay in New York, it began to lose some of its luster when the team posted a winning record just four times between 1945 and 1953. Feeling that the game had passed Owen by, Giants ownership elected to relieve him of his duties following the conclusion of the 1953 campaign, replacing him at the helm with Jim Lee Howell. Revealing how difficult it was to part ways with Owen, Wellington Mara stated, "It was like telling your father you're putting him out of your home."

Although Owen remained with the Giants briefly as a scout, he moved on before long, with Mara saying, "He was hurt and wanted no part of that." After spending most of the next two seasons coaching in college, Owen returned to the NFL, where he spent the 1956 and 1957 campaigns serving as an assistant on the coaching staff of the Philadelphia Eagles.

Following the conclusion of his playing career, Owen spent 23 years coaching the Giants.
Public domain

From Philadelphia, he moved on to the Canadian Football League, where he coached four different teams between 1959 and 1963 before returning to the Giants as a scout early in 1964. Stricken with a terminal cerebral hemorrhage in May 1964, Owen passed away eight days later, on May 17, 1964, at 66 years of age. The Pro Football Hall of Fame opened its doors to him two years later.

Following his passing, Arthur Daley of the *New York Times* wrote, "It was only fitting that stout Steve should have been a member of the Giant organization when he died yesterday. . . . It is quite possible that no professional coach ever inspired more love, devotion, and admiration among his players than did Steve. The only counterpart was Knute Rockne at Notre Dame. A might stout fella was Owen. The Giants and all professional football owe him much for his contributions."

GIANT CAREER HIGHLIGHTS

Best Season

With Owen starring on both sides of the ball for the NFL champion Giants in 1927, they outscored their opponents by a combined margin of 197–20, establishing in the process a league record by notching 10 shutouts. Serving as team captain, Owen earned First-Team All-Pro honors for the first of two times, making the 1927 campaign his finest all-around season.

Memorable Moments/Greatest Performances

Owen helped the Giants dominate the line of scrimmage on both offense and defense throughout most of 1927, performing particularly well during a 19–0 win over the Pottsville Maroons on October 9, a 27–0 victory over the Frankford Yellow Jackets on October 23, and a 25–0 win over the Providence Steam Roller on November 8.

NOTABLE ACHIEVEMENTS

- Two-time First-Team All-Pro (1927, 1929).
- 1926 Second-Team All-Pro.
- NFL 1920s All-Decade Team.
- 1927 NFL champion.
- Elected to Pro Football Hall of Fame in 1966.

39

JEREMY SHOCKEY

Impulsive, crude, obscene, rebellious, outspoken, self-gratifying, and unconventional are all words that could be used to describe Jeremy Shockey's behavior during his six years in New York. A player who marched to the beat of a different drum, Shockey flouted convention, displaying a disdain for authority while following his own set of rules. He argued with his superiors, clashed with teammates, made lewd comments, and laughed in the face of those who suggested he toe the company line. However, Shockey also possessed a considerable amount of talent, explaining why the usually conservative Giants displayed so much patience with someone whose bearing represented the very antithesis of the image the organization typically projected. A naturally gifted athlete who possessed too much speed for linebackers to cover and too much size for cornerbacks to tackle, Shockey proved to be one of the NFL's most difficult individual matchups for opposing defenses his first few years in the league, before injuries began to take their toll on him. An excellent receiver and outstanding open-field runner from the time he first entered the NFL, Shockey gradually developed into a solid blocker as well, making him one of the league's best all-around tight ends. Shockey's varied skill set earned him four Pro Bowl nominations and one First-Team All-Pro selection, before a clash of personalities prompted the Giants to part ways with him after just six seasons.

Born in Ada, Oklahoma, on August 18, 1980, Jeremy Charles Shockey attended Ada High School, where he played basketball and football, starring at wide receiver and outside linebacker on the gridiron all four years. After being rejected as too small by Oklahoma Sooners head football coach Bob Stoops following his graduation from Ada, Shockey enrolled at tiny Northeastern Oklahoma A&M, a junior college, where he grew two inches and gained 30 pounds of muscle in three months. Having dominated the competition he faced there, Shockey subsequently transferred to the University of Miami. He spent the next two years at Miami, helping the

Jeremy Shockey proved to be a polarizing figure during his time in New York.
Courtesy of Rick Sparacino

Hurricanes capture the national championship and earning All-America honors in 2001 before declaring himself eligible for the ensuing NFL Draft.

Selected by the Giants in the first round of the 2002 NFL Draft with the 14th overall pick, Shockey had a big first year in New York, making 74 receptions, for 894 yards and two touchdowns, en route to earning Pro Bowl and First-Team All-Pro honors. Although the 6'5", 253-pound tight end occasionally dropped passes at critical times, he also displayed a penchant for making sensational grabs at other crucial moments. Once he gathered in the ball, though, Shockey ran as well as any other tight end in the league. In addition to possessing surprising speed for a man his size, Shockey had outstanding strength and excellent moves in the open field, making him a nightmare for opposing linebackers and defensive backs. Along with Tiki Barber, the Giants made Shockey the focal point of their offense, attempting to get the ball into his hands as often as possible.

Shockey suffered through an injury-marred 2003 campaign that limited him to only nine games and 48 receptions. However, he rebounded the following season to begin a successful three-year run during which he surpassed 60 receptions each season. He also scored a total of 20 touchdowns during that time. Particularly effective in 2005, Shockey concluded the campaign with 65 receptions, for 891 yards and seven touchdowns.

Shockey's volatile personality finally forced the Giants to part ways with him.
Courtesy of Alexa Scordato via Flickr

Thriving on competition and viewing the opposition as his enemy, Shockey brought with him to the field each week a warlike mentality. In discussing the attitude with which he approached each contest, Shockey explained, "You're always one play away from never playing, so I want to do as much as I can as soon as possible."[1] He added, "It's a war out there, and either they're going to hurt you or you're going to hurt them. I just go out there and play with my heart. . . . Everybody who's ever done anything bad to me, anything that ever went wrong, I try to take it out on somebody—every game. It's like when you see Michael Jordan's highlights and your hair sits up on your arms. I'm like that the whole game."[2]

Supremely confident in his own abilities, Shockey proclaimed, "I don't want to sound arrogant, but the defense might shut me down on one or two out of five plays, but I'll make them pay eventually."[3]

Giants players and fans initially appreciated the spark that Shockey brought to their team. An extremely emotional player, the tight end played with tremendous passion, pumping his fist in the air after making a big play, trash-talking opponents, and waving his arms to stir up the home crowd. Yet his unbridled enthusiasm also proved to be a liability at times. In Shockey's rookie campaign of 2002, the Giants squandered a 38–14 third-quarter lead to San Francisco in the playoffs, allowing the 49ers to score 17 unanswered points in the final period. Before the 49ers began their comeback, Shockey dropped what appeared to be a sure touchdown pass in the end zone that would have sealed the victory for New York. TV cameras subsequently caught him making an obscene gesture to a member of the 49er defense. Then, as the Giants' lead evaporated in the fourth quarter, Shockey expressed his frustration by hurling a cup of ice over his shoulder and into the stands, where it struck two children.

Jim Fassel, who coached the Giants during Shockey's first two years in New York, tolerated the tight end's emotional outbursts, explaining:

> You can't have it both ways. You can't have a bunch of choirboys and expect them to go out and fight their ass off on the field. As a coach, what you're trying to figure out is, are they a bad person, or are they a good person that just kind of drifts a little bit? Shockey is a good guy. But you're gonna have to live with the edge in Shockey if you want him to be the player he is. You don't like that edge, then don't have him on your team. Me, I want him on my team in the worst way.[4]

However, the conservative and extremely regimented Tom Coughlin didn't prove to be nearly as tolerant of Shockey after he took over as head coach in New York in 2004. Coughlin didn't approve of the manner in which Shockey and wide receiver Plaxico Burress spent their off-seasons practicing in Florida instead of joining the rest of the team up north. He found particularly objectionable a comment Shockey made following a loss to Seattle in week 3 of the 2006 campaign in which the tight end stated, "We got outplayed, and we got outcoached. Write that down."[5]

Such comments also eventually began to wear thin on Giants fans, especially when the outspoken tight end dropped an ever-increasing number of passes as his career in New York wore on. Shockey also antagonized fans of the team with a number of ill-advised remarks he made to the press, including a particularly offensive statement he made about women.

Shockey finally reached a point of no return with the Giants and their fans during the championship campaign of 2007. After making 57 receptions for 619 yards and three touchdowns over the course of the first 13 games, Shockey suffered a fractured fibula and damage to his ankle during a 22–10 loss to Washington in week 15. Forced to miss the rest of the season, Shockey could only watch as the Giants went on to win the NFL championship, with Eli Manning appearing far more comfortable in his absence. Speculation subsequently arose as to whether the Giants might be better off without Shockey, prompting the self-absorbed tight end to exclude himself from numerous team celebrations, including a White House tribute for the new Super Bowl champions. Although rumors surfaced prior to the 2008 NFL Draft that the Giants wished to trade Shockey, they failed to consummate such a deal, prompting the disgruntled tight end to display his unhappiness by separating himself from the rest of the team during June minicamp. He finally bought a ticket out of New York by engaging in an on-field shouting match with general manager Jerry Reese during the camp. The Giants traded Shockey to the New Orleans Saints for a pair of draft picks one month later, ending their six-year association with the controversial tight end. Shockey left New York having made a total of 371 receptions, for 4,228 yards and 27 touchdowns. He ranks fourth in team history in receptions.

Shockey subsequently spent three semi-productive, injury-marred years in New Orleans, helping the Saints win the NFL Championship in 2009 by making 48 receptions, for 569 yards and three touchdowns during the regular season. After being released by the Saints on February 22, 2011, Shockey joined the Carolina Panthers, for whom he made a career-low 37 catches in 2011. Unsigned at the end of the year, Shockey expressed an interest in returning to the Giants, prompting NFL commentator Amani Toomer to lash out at his former teammate by writing on Twitter, "No!! Shockey 'I will never play for you again!' he yelled at Jerry Reese in 2008. Let him keep his word. Bad teammate, worse person."[6]

The Giants showed no interest in having Shockey rejoin them, and no other NFL team chose to sign him to a contract either. As a result, he spent all of 2012 and 2013 sitting on the sidelines before finally announcing his retirement. Shockey ended his career with 547 receptions, 6,143 receiving yards, and 37 touchdowns.

GIANT CAREER HIGHLIGHTS

Best Season

Shockey played very well in 2005, making 65 receptions for 891 yards and seven touchdowns. He also averaged a career-high 13.7 yards per catch. But Shockey made his biggest overall impact as a rookie in 2002, establishing career highs with 74 receptions and 894 receiving yards, en route to earning his lone First-Team All-NFL selection.

Memorable Moments/Greatest Performances

Shockey had his first truly big game as a professional on November 17, 2002, helping the Giants defeat the rival Washington Redskins by a score of 19–17 by making 11 receptions for 111 yards. He had another big day five weeks later against Indianapolis, catching seven passes for 116 yards during a 44–27 Giants win over the Colts. Shockey followed that up by making 10 receptions for 98 yards and a touchdown during New York's 10–7 overtime win over Philadelphia in the regular season finale that earned the Giants a spot in the playoffs. He made arguably his most important catch as a member of the Giants midway through the fourth quarter of that contest, leaping high in the end zone to outfight Eagles defensive back Brian Dawkins for a Kerry Collins seven-yard pass that tied the score at 7–7.

Although the Giants ended up losing in overtime to the Dallas Cowboys by a score of 16–13 on October 16, 2005, Shockey had one of the biggest days of his career, making five catches for 129 yards and a touchdown. Included in his five receptions was a 59-yard catch-and-run—his longest play from scrimmage as a member of the Giants. Shockey turned in another exceptional effort against Seattle six weeks later, catching 10 passes for 127 yards and one touchdown. Unfortunately, the Giants once again lost in overtime, this time by a score of 24–21. Shockey had his last big game for the Giants on November 11, 2007, making 12 receptions for 129 yards and one touchdown during a 31–20 loss to Dallas.

NOTABLE ACHIEVEMENTS

- Caught more than 60 passes four times, topping 70 receptions once (74 in 2002).
- Ranks fourth all-time on Giants with 371 career receptions.
- Diet Pepsi 2002 NFL Rookie of the Year.
- NFL Alumni 2005 Tight End of the Year.
- 2002 Week 17 NFC Offensive Player of the Week.
- Four-time Pro Bowl selection (2002, 2003, 2005, 2006).
- 2002 First-Team All-Pro selection.
- 2002 First-Team All-NFC selection.
- 2007 NFC champion.
- Super Bowl XLII champion.

RON JOHNSON

Playing for mostly bad teams with below-average offensive lines prevented Ron Johnson from receiving as much notoriety and gaining as much yardage on the ground as he likely would have had he been fortunate enough to perform for any number of other NFL teams. Those two factors also kept Johnson from finishing any higher than 40th in these rankings, even though his skill set surpassed that of several of the other running backs that appear before him on this list. Nevertheless, Johnson, who played halfback for the Giants from 1970 to 1975, established himself during his time in New York as one of the finest all-around backs in team history. An outstanding runner and exceptional receiver out of the backfield, Johnson surpassed 1,600 all-purpose yards twice, en route to becoming the first Giants player to rush for more than 1,000 yards in a season. A true workhorse, Johnson led all NFL running backs in touches and rushing attempts two times each, while also finishing first in the league in touchdowns scored once. In the process, Johnson helped lead the Giants to their only two winning seasons between 1964 and 1980.

Born in Detroit, Michigan, on October 17, 1947, Ronald Adolphis Johnson earned High School All-America honors at Detroit's Northwestern High School before enrolling at the University of Michigan. While at Michigan, Johnson excelled both on and off the football field, receiving the Big 10 Medal, which is awarded to the most outstanding scholar-athlete in the school. He also earned All-American honors as a senior in 1968, finishing sixth in the Heisman Trophy voting after setting a school record that still stands by rushing for 347 yards against Wisconsin.

Subsequently selected by the Cleveland Browns in the first round of the 1969 NFL Draft with the 20th overall pick, Johnson soon found himself playing second fiddle in the Cleveland backfield to perennial All-Pro fullback, Leroy Kelly. Although Johnson scored seven touchdowns as a rookie, he carried the ball only 138 times, gaining just 472 yards on the ground.

Ron Johnson helped lead the Giants to their only two winning seasons between 1964 and 1980.
Courtesy of RMYAuctions.com

However, Johnson's situation soon changed when the Browns found a suitable trading partner in the Giants.

Seeking to obtain a quality wide receiver to replace Paul Warfield, whom they earlier dealt to Miami, the Browns contacted the Giants to inquire about Homer Jones. The Giants, in turn, asked for "Johnson," referring to Walter Johnson, the star defensive tackle of the Browns. Thinking that the Giants desired their second-year running back by the same name, the Browns quickly agreed on a deal with them. After the two sides eventually cleared up the misunderstanding, they settled on a trade that sent Jones to Cleveland for defensive tackle Jim Kanicki, linebacker Wayne Meylan, and the "other" Johnson on the Browns roster. Speaking of the 3-for-1 deal, Giants coach Alex Webster later noted, "We wanted another runner, but the main thing we wanted was another big defensive tackle."[1]

While Kanicki helped solidify the middle of the Giants' defensive line, Johnson gave them more than they bargained for at the halfback position. After starting off the season slowly, Johnson developed into a tremendous threat out of the backfield. Blessed with exceptional balance and good speed and strength, the 6'1", 205-pound Johnson gave the Giants the running game they previously lacked. Running behind a smallish and somewhat suspect offensive line, Johnson rushed for 1,027 yards and eight touchdowns, becoming in the process the first Giants player to reach the 1,000-yard plateau in a season. He also proved to be an outstanding target for Fran Tarkenton coming out of the backfield, making 48 receptions, for another 487 yards and four touchdowns. Johnson ended up leading the NFL with 1,514 yards from scrimmage and 263 carries, en route to earning First-Team All-Pro and First-Team All-Conference honors.

Expressing his appreciation at one point during the season for the added dimension Johnson brought to the Giants' offense, Tarkenton gushed, "Johnson's the best halfback in football today . . . period! He does everything. He catches the ball. He blocks. He runs inside and outside, and he makes the big plays. All the great ones make the big plays."[2]

Asked to describe which running back he patterned himself after, Johnson stated, "You can't model yourself after anybody. You have to go with the assets you have yourself. Of course, I've had idols—Jimmy Brown when I was younger, and now Gale Sayers."[3]

Johnson's outstanding 1970 campaign helped the Giants compile a record of 9–5, giving them high hopes for the following season. However, those hopes were dashed when a serious knee injury forced Johnson to miss all but two games in 1971, relegating New York to a 4–10 finish.

Healthy again by the start of the ensuing campaign, Johnson led the Giants to a record of 8–6 in 1972 by rushing for 1,182 yards and nine touchdowns, while also catching 45 passes, for 451 yards and five touchdowns. His 14 touchdowns led the NFL. Johnson also led the league in rushing attempts for the second time, carrying the ball a total of 298 times, en route to earning Second-Team All-Conference honors.

Johnson's exceptional all-around play prompted former Giants head coach Jim Lee Howell to express his admiration for the third-year running back by saying, "As I look at the Giants today, Ron Johnson is truly one of the outstanding ball-carriers. That knee injury knocked him out in '71, but his play the year before was sensational . . . over 1,000 yards rushing.

In 1970, Johnson became the first Giants running back to rush for more than 1,000 yards in a season.
Courtesy of SportsMemorabilia.com

He doesn't need much of a hole . . . just a little wiggle and he'll get by with great balance. He'll keep going after being hit."[4]

Johnson had another solid year in 1973, rushing for 902 yards, making 32 receptions, and scoring nine touchdowns. However, injuries slowed him considerably the following year, limiting him to only 97 carries and 218 yards rushing, and allowing Doug Kotar to beat him out for the starting halfback job. Reduced to the role of a backup by 1975, Johnson rushed for only 351 yards, although he managed to make 34 receptions and score six touchdowns. He retired at the end of the year, ending his career with 4,308 yards rushing, 55 touchdowns, and 213 receptions, for 1,977 yards. In his six seasons with the Giants, he rushed for 3,836 yards, scored 48 touchdowns, and made 189 receptions, for a total of 1,813 yards. Johnson ranks among the Giants' all-time leaders in rushing, rushing touchdowns, and total touchdowns.

During his playing days, Johnson embarked on a career as a real estate executive and entrepreneur, allowing him to move seamlessly into the business world following his retirement. In 1983, he founded the Rackson Corporation, a food service company that currently operates 24 KFC franchises in New Jersey, Tennessee, and Michigan. In 2006, Johnson was named chairman of the National Football Foundation and College Hall of Fame, becoming just the fifth person to hold that position in the 59-year history of the organization. Unfortunately, he was diagnosed with Alzheimer's disease just two years later, prompting his son Christopher to take over as his business manager, and ultimately forcing him to move into a residential care facility in New Jersey, where he currently resides. Johnson's wife of nearly 40 years, Karen, has expressed the belief that the hits her husband took as a football player contributed to the early onset of his illness. She also maintains that there will soon be a growing need for more facilities to care for more patients like her longtime husband, former NFL standout Ron Johnson.

GIANT CAREER HIGHLIGHTS

Best Season

Johnson performed exceptionally well for the Giants in both 1970 and 1972, compiling extremely similar numbers over the course of those two campaigns. In the first of those years, he rushed for 1,027 yards, caught 48 passes for another 487 yards, scored 12 touchdowns, and averaged 3.9 yards per carry. In 1972, he accumulated 1,182 yards on the ground, made 45 receptions for another 451 yards, scored a league-leading 14 touchdowns, and averaged 4.0 yards per carry. Johnson earned Pro Bowl honors both years. Clearly, either one of those seasons would have made a good choice.

Still, Johnson earned more individual accolades in 1970, being named First-Team All-Pro and First-Team All-Conference; he only made Second-Team All-Conference in 1972. He also led the NFL with 1,514 yards from scrimmage in 1970. But Johnson actually gained slightly more yardage in 1972 (1,633), and he also scored two more touchdowns, en route to leading the league in the last category. Furthermore, the fact that Johnson failed to earn All-NFL honors in 1972 had less to do with his own performance than the emergence of O. J. Simpson and Larry Brown as the league's top two running backs.

In the end, I elected to go with 1972 for the simple reason that the Giants faced a higher level of competition that season than they did two years earlier. Although the Giants finished 9–5 in 1970, they played only five games against teams that ended up posting a winning record. Meanwhile, in compiling a record of 8–6 in 1972, the Giants played eight games against teams with a winning mark, including the Miami Dolphins, who finished the regular season with a perfect 14–0 record. Surely, that has to count for something.

Memorable Moments/Greatest Performances

After rushing for a total of only 129 yards in the first three games of 1970, Johnson had his first big game as a member of the Giants in the season's fourth contest. Playing against the Philadelphia Eagles at Yankee Stadium on October 11, 1970, Johnson carried the ball 18 times, for 142 yards and two touchdowns, in leading the Giants to a 30–23 win that marked their first victory of the season. Johnson's touchdown runs covered 68 and 34 yards, with the last one providing the margin of victory.

Johnson also played a huge role in two memorable comebacks later in the year. With the Giants trailing the Dallas Cowboys 20–9 late in the third quarter on November 8, Johnson pulled his team to within four points by scoring on a four-yard run. The Giants still trailed 20–16 with just over three minutes remaining in the contest, when Johnson got a step on All-Pro cornerback Mel Renfro and gathered in a 13-yard slant-in pass from Fran Tarkenton for the game-winning touchdown. Johnson concluded the game with 140 yards rushing and four receptions for another 59 yards. The Giants' 23–20 victory put their record at 5–3, tying them with Dallas for second place in the NFC East, just one game behind the first-place St. Louis Cardinals.

The Giants mounted an even more stirring comeback just one week later against Washington. Trailing the Redskins by a score of 33–14 at the start of the fourth quarter, the Giants scored three touchdowns in the final period to come away with a stunning 35–33 victory. Johnson scored the first and third touchdowns of the quarter, going over from five and nine yards out, respectively. He finished the day with 106 yards on the ground, and another 49 through the air.

Johnson had another huge game two years later, scoring all four touchdowns for the Giants during a 27–12 victory over the Philadelphia Eagles on Monday night, October 2, 1972. After opening the scoring in the first quarter with a 16-yard touchdown reception on a pass from Norm Snead, Johnson scored twice in the second period, once on a five-yard run, and, again, on a nine-yard pass completion. He closed out the evening's scoring in the fourth quarter by hooking up again with Snead, this time from 15 yards out. Johnson finished the game with 124 yards rushing, five receptions for 60 yards, and four touchdowns, which represented a new Giants record.

NOTABLE ACHIEVEMENTS

- Rushed for more than 1,000 yards twice (1970, 1972).
- Caught more than 40 passes twice (1970, 1972).
- Scored more than 10 touchdowns twice (1970, 1972).
- First Giants player to rush for more than 1,000 yards in a season (1,027 yards in 1970).
- Led all NFL running backs in rushing attempts twice (1970, 1972).
- Led NFL with 14 touchdowns in 1972.
- Led NFL with 1,514 yards from scrimmage in 1970.
- Finished second in NFL with 1,633 yards from scrimmage in 1972.
- Finished second in NFL in rushing in 1970.
- Finished third in NFL in rushing in 1972.
- Ranks among Giants all-time leaders in rushing yardage (7th), rushing touchdowns (8th), and total touchdowns scored (10th).
- Shares Giants record with four touchdowns in one game (October 2, 1972).
- Two-time Pro Bowl selection (1970, 1972).
- 1970 First-Team All-Pro selection.
- 1970 First-Team All-Conference selection.
- 1972 Second-Team All-Conference selection.

41

HOMER JONES

Traded for the man who immediately preceded him on this list, Homer Jones established himself as arguably the NFL's most potent offensive weapon during his time in New York. Averaging better than 20 yards per reception in five of his six years with the Giants, Jones ended up posting a career average of 22.3 yards per catch that represents the highest in NFL history for players with at least 200 receptions. The fleet-footed wide receiver also surpassed 1,000 receiving yards three consecutive times, en route to earning Pro Bowl and First-Team All-Conference honors two times each, and All-Pro honors once. Jones presented opposing defenses with such a dangerous threat on the outside that he scored 33 of his 38 career touchdowns from more than 30 yards out. He also registered 11 scoring plays of at least 70 yards. Only a chronically bad knee prevented Jones from sustaining his level of dominance for a longer period of time, thereby relegating him to a lower spot in these rankings than he most certainly would have received otherwise.

Born in the small rural community of Pittsburg, Texas, on February 18, 1941, Homer Carroll Jones moved to Los Angeles with his family during World War II, before returning to Texas shortly after the war ended. After focusing most of his attention on playing the saxophone his first two years in high school, Jones finally elected to try out for his school's football team in his senior year. Starting at fullback for his squad, Jones displayed the tremendous breakaway speed for which he later became well known by running for an 80-yard touchdown the first time he carried the ball. Although Jones played extremely well in his first year of organized ball, the unwritten rules of the day kept the large white universities situated in the South from offering him an athletic scholarship. Subsequently choosing from the nine black southern universities that made him an offer, Jones ultimately settled on Texas Southern College, located in nearby Houston.

Excelling not only in football but also in track and field at Texas Southern, Jones specialized in the 100- and 200-yard dashes, posting a personal

Homer Jones topped 1,000 receiving yards three straight
times for the Giants.
Courtesy of EACGallery.com

best of 9.2 seconds in the first event. Meanwhile, he eventually found a
home at flanker on the gridiron, after spending his first two seasons splitting his time between linebacker and halfback. Particularly adept at running
reverses from his flanker position, Jones often used his great speed to pick
up huge chunks of yardage. However, doing so caused him to injure his
knee in his next-to-last game at Southern, hurting his stock heading into
the pro football draft.

Selected by the Houston Oilers in the fifth round of the 1963 AFL Draft, and by the Giants in the 20th round of the 1963 NFL Draft (#278 overall), Jones elected to sign with the Oilers. However, Houston lost interest in him after he re-injured his knee during a pickup game prior to reporting to his first training camp. Cut by the Oilers, Jones contacted the Giants, who brought him to New York, where team doctor Anthony Pisani operated on his injured knee. After spending the entire 1963 season in rehab, Jones joined the Giants late in 1964, appearing in three games for them and making four receptions for 82 yards.

Fully healthy by the start of the 1965 campaign, Jones became a huge contributor in his first full season, catching 26 passes, for 709 yards and six touchdowns. One of his touchdowns went for 89 yards, which represented the longest scoring play of the year in the NFL. En route to compiling an astounding average of 27.3 yards per reception over the course of the campaign, Jones also made TD grabs that covered 79, 74, and 72 yards.

Firmly entrenched as the Giants' starting split end by the opening of the 1966 season, Jones built on the success he experienced the previous year by making 48 receptions, for 1,044 yards and eight touchdowns. He finished fourth in the NFL in receiving yards and placed third in the league with an average of 21.8 yards per reception. Jones proved to be one of the few bright spots for a Giants team that finished the season with a record of just 1–12–1.

Joined in New York the following year by Fran Tarkenton, Jones developed a special connection with his team's new quarterback. While Tarkenton's scrambling tendencies made him a unique signal-caller for his time, Jones's unusual physical gifts allowed him to similarly separate himself from the other wide receivers of the day. In addition to possessing world-class speed, Jones had great size and strength. Standing 6'2" and weighing 225 pounds, he simply overpowered those defensive backs he found himself unable to run away from. Jones also had huge hands, which, combined with his blinding speed, prompted Tarkenton to once say, "He is like a man on a motorcycle waving a butterfly net high up in the air."[1]

Further elaborating on Jones's unique skill set years later, Tarkenton stated, "He was the fastest receiver I have ever seen, and he weighed 235 pounds. Once he got the football in his hands, there's never been a receiver who could run like he could run. He was unbelievable. And they were starting to do the bump-and-run back in those days. He'd go by the bump-and-run like it wasn't there."[2]

The combination of Tarkenton and Jones helped lead the Giants to a 7–7 record in 1967, with both men earning Pro Bowl honors. For his

Jones (seen here with Fran Tarkenton) rivaled Bob Hayes as the top deep threat of his time.
Public domain (author unknown)

part, Jones made 49 receptions, for 1,209 yards and 13 touchdowns. He also rushed for another score, giving him an NFL-leading 14 touchdowns on the year. Meanwhile, his average of 24.7 yards per reception placed him second in the league rankings.

Jones's exceptional play made for an interesting sidebar at that year's Pro Bowl. In an attempt to boost interest in the annual contest, the *Los Angeles Herald* announced its intent to stage a pregame 100-yard race between Jones and Dallas Cowboys wide receiver Bob Hayes, widely considered to be the world's fastest human being. The winner was to receive the then ridiculously high sum of $25,000. However, concerned that the race might create too much of a carnival-like atmosphere at the Pro Bowl, Giants owner Wellington Mara urged Jones not to participate, offering him a $5,000 bonus to withdraw from the contest. Jones reluctantly agreed, although he believed he would have come out on top. Asked repeatedly throughout the remainder of his career if he felt he would have won the race, Jones invariably responded, "What hurts more, getting hit by a 22-caliber bullet [Hayes wore number 22 for Dallas and stood just 5'11" and weighed only 185 pounds] or a 45-caliber bullet [Jones wore number 45 and weighed 40 more pounds than Hayes]?"[3]

Jones had another outstanding year in 1968, earning his second straight Pro Bowl selection by catching 45 passes, for 1,057 yards and seven touchdowns. He finished third in the NFL in pass receiving yardage, and he also placed second in the league with an average of 23.5 yards per catch.

After opening up the 1969 campaign with a 54-yard touchdown grab against the Minnesota Vikings during a 24–23 Giants win, Jones entered into a mysterious and prolonged slump that saw him go the rest of the year without crossing the opponents' goal line again. Although Jones finished the season with 42 catches, his 744 receiving yards, one touchdown, and 17.7 yards-per-reception average represented easily his lowest marks since he first became a full-time starter four years earlier.

While Giants fans speculated as to the cause of Jones's decreased productivity, those within the organization knew that his old knee injury had degenerated to the point that he no longer possessed the same cutting ability and game-changing speed. Aware that the wide receiver's best days were clearly behind him, the Giant front office subsequently dealt him to the Cleveland Browns for a package of players that included second-year running back Ron Johnson.

The Browns soon discovered that Jones had very little left in the tank. Although he experienced one more brief moment of glory in the 1970 season opener by returning the second-half kickoff 94 yards for a touchdown against the Jets in the first ever *Monday Night Football* game, Jones ended up catching only 10 passes, for 141 yards and one touchdown over the course of the season. Traded to the Cardinals at the end of the year, Jones never played another down in the NFL. With the condition of his knee having worsened even more, Jones announced his retirement prior to the start of the 1971 campaign. He concluded his career with 224 receptions, for 4,986 yards and 36 touchdowns. Jones scored another two times, once on a reverse, and once on the aforementioned kickoff return. His average of 22.3 yards per reception remains the highest in NFL history for players with at least 200 catches.

Jones also has the distinction of being the originator of the "spike," a touchdown celebratory gesture that subsequently led to far more elaborate celebrations by more recent generations of NFL players. Having observed early in his career how players such as Frank Gifford and Green Bay's Paul Hornung typically tossed the ball to fans in the stands after scoring a touchdown, Jones decided to come up with his own post-touchdown maneuver. That being the case, he invented the "spike," a move that saw him throw the football down hard into the end zone after crossing the opponents' goal line. Modern scoring celebrations, including "touchdown dances," are said to have evolved from Jones's invention of spiking the ball.

Although Jones created a permanent legacy for himself in NFL annals with his celebratory gesture, Giants fans fortunate enough to see him play will never forget the thrills he gave them with one of his long touchdown grabs. Rivaling Odell Beckham Jr. as the most exciting wide receiver in team history, Jones terrorized opposing defenses with his mere presence on the field. With 19 career touchdown receptions of more than 50 yards, Jones averaged an amazing 47.8 yards per touchdown catch over the course of his career. Giants fans are not likely to ever see anyone else like him.

GIANT CAREER HIGHLIGHTS

Best Season

Although Jones also played very well in 1966 and 1968, he clearly had his best season in 1967, when he established career highs with 49 receptions, 1,209 receiving yards, and a league-leading 14 touchdowns. In addition to finishing second in the NFL in receiving yards and yards per reception (24.7), Jones placed third in the league with 1,269 yards from scrimmage. His total of 13 TD receptions ties him with Odell Beckham Jr. for the highest single-season mark in franchise history. Amazingly, Jones crossed the opponents' goal line one out of every four times he touched the ball, scoring from 70, 69, 68, 66, 63, 52, and 45 (twice) yards out at different times.

Memorable Moments/Greatest Performances

Jones made his mark as a member of the Giants for the first time on October 17, 1965, helping them improve their record to 3–2 by gathering in an Earl Morrall pass and going 89 yards for his first career touchdown during a 35–27 win over the Philadelphia Eagles. The catch-and-run represented the longest scoring play in the NFL the entire year. He was at it again four weeks later, scoring from 79 yards out during a 34–21 loss to the Cleveland Browns. Jones had his biggest game of the year, though, against the Washington Redskins in week 13, making three receptions, for 182 yards and two touchdowns, in leading the Giants to a 27–10 victory. His scoring plays covered 74 and 72 yards.

Jones began the 1966 campaign in style, hooking up with Earl Morrall on scoring plays of 75 and 98 yards during a 34–34 tie with the Pittsburgh Steelers in the season opener. Jones's 98-yard TD reception remained a Giants record until Victor Cruz scored from 99 yards out against the Jets 45 years later.

However, Jones put together the most memorable streak of his career early the following year, beginning the 1967 campaign by scoring two touchdowns in each of the first three contests. He helped the Giants register a 37–20 victory over the Cardinals in the season opener by making five receptions, for 175 yards and two touchdowns, one of which covered 70 yards. He followed that up by scoring on a 52-yard pass play and a 46-yard run during a 38–24 loss to the Cowboys in week 2. Although New York's record fell to 1–2 the following week with a 38–34 loss to Washington, Jones made four receptions, for 196 yards and two touchdowns. His two scoring plays covered 35 and 68 yards. Jones had another huge game later in the year against the Vikings, gathering in four Fran Tarkenton passes, for 149 yards and two touchdowns, during a 27–24 loss to Minnesota. Tarkenton and Jones connected from 66 and 45 yards out. Jones once again burned the Cardinals' secondary in the season finale, helping the Giants even their record at 7–7 by making five receptions, for 125 yards and one touchdown, which came on a 69-yard hookup with Tarkenton.

Jones also had several big games in 1968, the first of which came against the Redskins in week 3. During that contest, Jones helped lead the Giants to a 48–21 win by making five receptions, for 179 yards and two touchdowns. His scoring plays came on 82- and 56-yard connections with Fran Tarkenton. He recorded four receptions, for 116 yards and one touchdown, the following week during a 38–21 victory over the Saints that improved New York's record to 4–0. Jones had his last truly big game for the Giants in the next-to-last game of the season, on December 8, 1968. Although the slumping Giants lost to the Cardinals by a score of 28–21, Jones made four receptions, for 142 yards and one touchdown, which covered 73 yards.

NOTABLE ACHIEVEMENTS

- Caught more than 40 passes four times (1966–1969).
- Surpassed 1,000 receiving yards three times (1966–1968).
- Averaged more than 20 yards per reception five times (1964–1968).
- Scored more than 10 touchdowns once (14 in 1967).

- Led NFL with 13 touchdown receptions and 14 touchdowns scored in 1967.
- Finished second in NFL with 1,209 receiving yards in 1967.
- Finished second in NFL in yards per reception average twice (1967, 1968).
- Finished third in NFL in receiving yards once, yards per reception once, and yards from scrimmage once.
- Holds NFL record for highest lifetime yards per reception average (minimum 200 receptions; 22.3).
- Ranks among Giants all-time leaders in pass reception yardage (5th) and touchdown receptions (tied—6th).
- Holds share of Giants single-season record with 13 touchdown receptions in 1967.
- Two-time Pro Bowl selection (1967, 1968).
- 1967 Second-Team All-Pro selection.
- Two-time First-Team All-Conference selection (1967, 1968).

42

DEL SHOFNER

el Shofner, Y. A. Tittle's favorite target during the time the two men spent together in New York, proved to be one of the NFL's most potent offensive weapons his first three seasons with the Giants. The speedy receiver amassed more than 1,000 pass-receiving yards each year from 1961 to 1963, leading the league in total touchdown receptions and average gain per reception during that time. Shofner averaged 62 receptions, 1,146 yards, and 11 touchdowns over the course of those three seasons, earning Pro Bowl and First-Team All-Pro honors each year. He and Tittle helped the Giants advance to the NFL Championship Game in each of those campaigns, with Shofner's contributions to the team during that period eventually earning him a spot on the NFL's 1960s All-Decade Team. Only illness and injuries prevented him from establishing an even greater legacy that might have enabled him to earn a place in the Pro Football Hall of Fame when his playing days were over.

Born in Center, Texas, on December 11, 1934, Delbert Martin Shofner developed a reputation during his time at Baylor University as one of the greatest all-around athletes in school history. A member of the college's baseball and basketball teams, as well as a sprinter on the track team, Shofner made an even bigger name for himself on the gridiron, where he starred on both offense and defense. Playing wide receiver on offense and safety on defense, the versatile Shofner also punted and returned punts and kickoffs. After witnessing Shofner lead Baylor to a 13–7 victory over Tennessee in the 1957 Sugar Bowl, the Los Angeles Rams selected him in the first round of the 1957 NFL Draft with the 11th overall pick.

Although Shofner spent his first NFL season serving as a member of the Rams' defensive secondary, he moved to the offensive side of the ball the following year. Excelling in his new role, the lanky 6'3", 186-pound receiver caught 51 passes, scored eight touchdowns, and led the league with 1,097 pass receiving yards in 1958, en route to earning Pro Bowl and First-Team All-Pro honors for the first of two straight times. He also doubled as

Del Shofner teamed up with Y. A. Tittle to form the NFL's most dangerous passing combination during the early 1960s.
Courtesy of SportsMemorabilia.com

the team's punter, continuing to serve in that capacity in each of the next two seasons as well. Shofner's performance made such a strong impression on veteran teammate Elroy "Crazy Legs" Hirsch that the future Hall of Fame receiver, responding to a question about his future retirement plans, pointed to Shofner and said, "That young man is going to retire me."[1]

However, instead of retaining Shofner's services, the Rams engineered a blockbuster trade with the Giants at the conclusion of the 1960 campaign that sent the speedy receiver to New York for a first-round draft pick.

Arriving in New York the same time as Y. A. Tittle, Shofner spent the next three seasons forming one-half of the NFL's most feared offensive tandem. Serving as New York's primary deep threat, Shofner gave the Giants the type of dangerous offensive weapon they previously lacked. In discussing his favorite target, Tittle said that former 49ers teammate Billy Wilson had the best hands of all the receivers he played with, and that Frank Gifford was the smartest. But he added that Shofner "was the best and most dangerous of all"[2] because he had the ability to score from anywhere on the field. Throwing short to Shofner, Tittle said, was like asking Mickey Mantle to bunt.

Frank Gifford, who came out of retirement in 1962 and spent the final three years of his career playing alongside Shofner at the flanker position, also had high praise for the speedy wide-out, calling him the "perfect target for Tittle." He added, "When you have a receiver with the kind of speed I had, it's wonderful having a Del Shofner around because he would clear the whole barn for you. He always commanded double coverage because he was the guy who could hit from 65 or 70 yards out."[3]

After making 68 receptions for 1,125 yards and 11 touchdowns his first year in New York, Shofner caught 53 passes for 1,133 yards and 12 touchdowns in 1962. He followed that up by making 64 receptions for

Shofner earned Pro Bowl and First-Team All-Pro honors three straight times from 1961 to 1963.
Courtesy of SportsMemorabilia.com

1,181 yards and nine touchdowns in 1963. Shofner earned Pro Bowl and First-Team All-Pro honors all three years, helping the Giants advance to the NFL Championship Game each season. However, injuries and illness limited him to only six games in 1964, holding him to just 22 receptions, 323 yards, and no touchdowns. After suffering a deep knee bruise in a preseason game, Shofner stepped in a hole during practice, causing him to pull a hamstring muscle that kept him out of the season opener. His string of bad luck continued on October 25 against Cleveland, when he landed hard on his thumb after catching a pass from Tittle. However, the worst had yet to come. Describing the events that took place just prior to the start of the November 8 game against Dallas, Shofner revealed, "All I did was run from our dugout to the bench. Suddenly, I was so tired, I felt as if I had played a whole game."[4] He later discovered that he had been suffering from a bleeding ulcer.

Although Shofner eventually recovered from his illness, he failed to return to top form in subsequent seasons. After making only 32 catches and scoring just three touchdowns his final three years in New York, he announced his retirement at the conclusion of the 1967 campaign. Shofner ended his career with 349 receptions, for 6,470 yards and 51 touchdowns. His numbers with the Giants include 239 catches, for 4,315 yards and 35 touchdowns. Shofner averaged 18.5 yards per reception over the course of his career. He appeared in a total of five Pro Bowls and made First-Team All-Pro five times. Jerry Rice and Terrell Owens are the only other "modern-era" NFL wide receivers to earn as many as five First-Team All-Pro selections.

GIANT CAREER HIGHLIGHTS

Best Season

Shofner played exceptionally well in each of his first three years in New York, and any of those seasons would have made a good choice. He caught a career-high 68 passes in 1961, amassed 1,125 receiving yards, and scored 11 touchdowns. Two years later, Shofner made 64 receptions, compiled a career-best 1,181 receiving yards, and scored nine touchdowns. He finished in the league's top five in receptions and receiving yardage both years. Shofner also placed among the leaders in touchdowns in 1961 and yards from scrimmage in 1963.

Nevertheless, I ultimately chose to identify 1962 as Shofner's finest season. Although his total of 53 receptions left him just ninth in the NFL, he accumulated 1,133 receiving yards and scored a career-high 12 touchdowns, placing him near the top of the league rankings in both categories. Meanwhile, Shofner's average of 21.4 yards per reception represented the second-highest mark posted by any player in the league.

Memorable Moments/Greatest Performances

Despite playing in three NFL Championship Games, Shofner never had a signature performance that would have raised him to exalted status among Giants fans. He recorded just three receptions for 41 yards during Green Bay's 37–0 thrashing of the Giants in the 1961 title contest. Swirling winds and an icy field conspired against him the following year, taking away the deep pass and limiting him to five catches and 69 yards during the Giants' 16–7 loss to the Packers. Meanwhile, Chicago's stifling defense prevented Shofner from catching a single pass during the Bears' 14–10 win over the Giants in the 1963 Championship Game. Shofner complicated matters further by dropping a sure touchdown pass in the end zone.

Still, Shofner turned in a number of memorable regular-season performances in his years with the Giants. On November 5, 1961, he caught six passes for 122 yards during a 53–0 mauling of the Redskins, scoring on touchdown plays of 35, 13, and 32 yards. Shofner scored three touchdowns again just five weeks later, doing so during a 28–24 victory over Philadelphia that put the Giants in first place to stay in the Eastern Conference.

Shofner turned in another pair of three-touchdown performances the following year, accomplishing the feat for the first time on November 11, 1962, when he helped the Giants defeat Dallas by a score of 41–10 by scoring from 19, 23, and 41 yards out. He finished the day with six receptions for 158 yards. Shofner duplicated his earlier effort just two weeks later against Washington, recording another three touchdowns during a 42–24 New York win.

However, Shofner played arguably his greatest game as a Giant earlier in the year during Y. A. Tittle's memorable seven-TD performance against the Redskins on October 28. Although Tittle grabbed most of the headlines with his extraordinary effort, Shofner set a new team record by making 11 catches for 269 yards during New York's 49–34 victory over Washington.

NOTABLE ACHIEVEMENTS

- Surpassed 1,000 receiving yards three times (1961–1963).
- Topped 50 receptions three times, surpassing 60-mark twice (1961, 1963).
- Scored more than 10 touchdowns twice (1961, 1962).
- Averaged more than 20 yards per reception once (21.4 in 1962).
- Finished second in NFL with 1,125 receiving yards in 1961.
- Finished second in NFL with 12 touchdown receptions and 21.4 yards per reception average in 1962.
- Finished third in NFL with 68 receptions in 1961.
- Finished third in NFL with 1,181 receiving yards in 1963.
- Ranks among Giants all-time leaders in pass reception yardage (13th) and touchdown receptions (tied—6th).
- Three-time Pro Bowl selection.
- Three-time First-Team All-Pro selection.
- NFL 1960s All-Decade Team.
- Three-time NFL Eastern Division champion.

JUSTIN TUCK

One of the most versatile defensive linemen in team history, Justin Tuck contributed to the success of the Giants in many ways over the course of his nine seasons in New York. After serving primarily as a backup to Pro Bowlers Michael Strahan and Osi Umenyiora his first two years in the league, Tuck began to garner significant playing time in 2007, when he helped the Giants advance to the playoffs by recording 10 sacks in a part-time role. He subsequently established himself as an elite defensive end, earning Pro Bowl and All-Pro honors two times each. Tuck eventually also assumed the role of defensive leader, after being named one of New York's team captains. Excelling against both the pass and the run, Tuck afforded the Giants' coaching staff the luxury of moving him inside to play tackle in those situations that required the deployment of an extra pass-rushing defensive end. Tuck's versatility and leadership helped the Giants advance to the playoffs three times and win two Super Bowls.

Born in Kellyton, Alabama, on March 29, 1983, Justin Lee Tuck grew up rooting for two of the Giants' most bitter rivals—the San Francisco 49ers and the Dallas Cowboys. Beginning his high school football career as a quarterback at Alabama's Central Coosa County, Tuck eventually switched to tight end and defensive end, where he earned Alabama Class 4A Player of the Year honors as a senior in 2000. An outstanding basketball player as well, Tuck won two state championships as a member of the school's basketball team.

After enrolling at the University of Notre Dame, Tuck saw very little action until his junior year. However, he accomplished quite a bit his final two seasons with the Fighting Irish, setting school records for most career sacks (24½), most sacks in a single season (13½), and most career tackles for a loss (43), en route to earning the nickname "The Freak" from his teammates for his raw athleticism.

Justin Tuck's leadership and versatility made him a key contributor to Giant
teams that won two Super Bowls.
Courtesy of John J. Shelmet

Upon his graduation from Notre Dame, Tuck looked forward to turning pro, discussing prior to the 2005 NFL Draft the qualities he intended
to bring with him to whatever team selected him:

Every defensive end who is going to be picked in the first round
is going to be a good pick for whoever they're chosen by; but, if I
had to tell you what sets me apart, that would be my desire and
determination to get better. I know what I need to work on; I know
my weaknesses, but I have that work ethic to improve every day. I
have that want to be the best player at my position, and I have the
belief in myself that one day that will come true.[1]

Despite being projected as a mid-first-round pick, Tuck lasted until the third round of the draft, when the Giants made him the 74th overall selection. He subsequently spent his rookie campaign playing behind Strahan and Umenyiora, recording just one sack in extremely limited action. He also made 31 tackles, with 18 of those coming on special teams. After impressing New York's coaching staff prior to the start of the ensuing campaign, Tuck saw his season end prematurely when he suffered a serious foot injury during an October 23 victory over the Dallas Cowboys. Returning to the team in 2007 after undergoing successful surgery, Tuck played a huge role in the Giants' unexpected run to the Super Bowl, recording 10 sacks and 64 tackles (48 solo) during the regular season, despite starting only two games. In addition to spelling both Strahan and Umenyiora at defensive end throughout the season, Tuck teamed with Mathias Kiwanuka on the inside in obvious passing situations to form a four-man defensive front that proved to be too quick and agile for opposing offensive lines to handle. Defensive coordinator Steve Spagnuolo made particularly good use of the formation throughout the postseason, with the team's "four defensive end front" applying constant pressure to quarterbacks Jeff Garcia, Tony Romo, Brett Favre, and Tom Brady. Particularly effective against New England in the Super Bowl, the Giant defense sacked Brady five times, with Tuck getting to the Patriot quarterback twice.

Promoted to starting defensive end following the retirement of Michael Strahan at the conclusion of the 2007 campaign, Tuck demonstrated that he learned a great deal from the man who mentored him his first few years in the league. In his first year as a full-time starter, Tuck recorded 12 sacks, 66 tackles (52 solo), three forced fumbles, and one interception, en route to earning Pro Bowl and First-Team All-Pro honors.

A shoulder injury he sustained early in 2009 adversely affected Tuck's play the remainder of the year. Nevertheless, he finished second on the team with six sacks, placed third with 60 tackles (46 solo), and forced five fumbles. Healthy again in 2010, Tuck returned to top form, recording 11½ sacks and 76 tackles (48 solo), forcing five fumbles, and recovering five others. His outstanding all-around performance earned him his second trip to the Pro Bowl and Second-Team All-Pro honors.

Injuries and inconsistent play hampered Tuck in both 2011 and 2012, limiting him to totals of only nine sacks and 86 tackles over the course of those two seasons. Yet he still managed to perform extremely well throughout the 2011 postseason, accumulating 3½ sacks, two of which came in the Giants' Super Bowl win over New England.

Tuck recorded four sacks of Tom Brady in the Giants' two Super Bowl wins over New England.
Courtesy of Mike Morbeck

After struggling early in 2013, Tuck rebounded during the season's second half, concluding the campaign with 11 sacks, 63 tackles (41 solo), two forced fumbles, and the second interception of his career. However, after becoming a free agent at season's end, Tuck elected to sign with the

Oakland Raiders. He left New York having recorded a total of 60½ sacks, placing him sixth on the Giants' "official" all-time sack list. Tuck also registered 456 tackles (324 solo), 18 forced fumbles, and six fumble recoveries as a member of the Giants.

Tuck ended up spending two years in Oakland, recording just six sacks and 57 tackles for the Raiders in 2014 and 2015 before announcing his retirement prior to the start of the 2016 campaign and signing a one-day contract with the Giants that allowed him to retire as a member of the team.

CAREER HIGHLIGHTS

Best Season

Tuck earned First-Team All-Pro honors for the only time in 2008, when he recorded a career-high 12 sacks, made 66 tackles (52 solo), forced three fumbles, and returned an interception for a touchdown. However, he had his finest all-around season two years later, when he made Second-Team All-Pro by registering 11½ sacks and 76 tackles (48 solo), forcing five fumbles, and recovering five others.

Memorable Moments/Greatest Performances

Tuck turned in one of his most memorable performances in just his second game as a full-time starter. After opening up the 2008 campaign one week earlier by sacking Washington quarterback Jason Campbell on the season's first play, Tuck led the Giants to a 41–13 victory over the St. Louis Rams in week 2 by sacking quarterback Marc Bulger twice and returning an interception 41 yards for the only touchdown of his career. Tuck also started off the 2009 season extremely well, leading the Giants to a 23–17 win over the Redskins by recording 1½ sacks, making two tackles behind the line of scrimmage, and deflecting a pass, en route to earning NFC Defensive Player of the Week honors.

Tuck turned in one of his most dominant performances on October 3, 2010, against the Chicago Bears. Leading an overpowering Giants defense that sacked Bears quarterbacks a total of 10 times, Tuck recorded three sacks and a forced fumble during a 17–3 New York victory. He performed magnificently again on December 1, 2013, recording a career-high four sacks during a 24–17 win over the Washington Redskins.

Nevertheless, Tuck likely will always be remembered most for the efforts he turned in against New England in Super Bowls XLII and XLVI. Sacking Patriots quarterback Tom Brady twice in each of those contests, Tuck played particularly well in Super Bowl XLII, applying constant pressure to Brady and also forcing a fumble. Discussing his outstanding performance following the game, Tuck stated, "I just wanted it more. This was my time to shine, and I was going to do everything I could to make the most of it. In a game like this, you have to leave it all on the field, and that's exactly what I did."[2]

NOTABLE ACHIEVEMENTS

- Finished in double-digits in sacks four times (2007, 2008, 2010, 2013).
- Ranks sixth all-time on Giants' official list with 60½ quarterback sacks.
- Surpassed 60 tackles five times, topping the 70 mark once (76 in 2010).
- Two-time NFC Defensive Player of the Week.
- Two-time Pro Bowl selection (2008, 2010).
- 2008 First-Team All-Pro selection.
- 2010 Second-Team All-Pro selection.
- Two-time NFC champion (2007, 2011).
- Two-time Super Bowl champion (XLII, XLVI).

44

─ RED BADGRO ─

One of the National Football League's finest all-around athletes of the early 1930s, Morris "Red" Badgro excelled as a wide receiver and defensive back for the Giants from 1930 to 1935, after earlier spending two years pursuing a career in Major League Baseball. A talented receiver, excellent blocker, and sure-tackling defender, Badgro did an outstanding job for the Giants on both sides of the ball, enabling him to earn four All-Pro selections. In the process, Badgro helped the Giants win three consecutive NFL Eastern Division titles and capture their second league championship in 1934.

Born in Orillia, Washington, on December 1, 1902, Morris Hiram Badgro excelled in baseball, football, and basketball in high school before enrolling at the University of Southern California on a basketball scholarship. Although Badgro continued to play all three sports while in college, he ultimately decided to join the NFL's New York Yankees after graduating from USC. However, after spending all of 1927 and part of 1928 returning kicks, catching passes, and playing defense for the Yankees, Badgro decided to try his hand at baseball, leaving the NFL during the early stages of the 1928 campaign to join a minor league team in Tulsa, Oklahoma. He subsequently spent the 1929 and 1930 seasons serving as a backup outfielder for the American League's St. Louis Browns, hitting two home runs, driving in 45 runs, scoring 57 others, and compiling a batting average of .257 in a total of 143 games and 382 official at-bats.

Realizing that his skill set made him better suited to play in the NFL, Badgro elected to return to football after hitting just .239 for the Browns in 1930. With the Yankees having disbanded during his absence, Badgro signed with the Giants, with whom he spent the next six seasons. Able to truly focus all of his attention on the gridiron for the first time, Badgro soon established himself as one of the NFL's premier players. An outstanding two-way performer, Badgro developed a reputation as a superior defender and a big-play receiver. Although the league did not begin to officially

Red Badgro recorded the first TD reception in NFL
Championship Game history in 1933.
Public domain

record statistics of any kind until 1932, Badgro earned Second-Team
All-NFL honors in 1930 before being awarded a spot on the First Team
the following year. He made First-Team All-Pro again in 1933 and 1934,
helping the Giants finish first in the NFL's Eastern Division both years, and
leading them to the league championship in the second of those campaigns
by finishing fifth in the NFL with 206 receiving yards and tying for the
league lead with 16 receptions. Although the Giants lost the 1933 NFL title
game to the Chicago Bears, Badgro gained a measure of immortality during
that contest by making the first touchdown reception in championship

game history. After helping the Giants capture their third straight Eastern Division title in 1935, Badgro joined football's version of the Brooklyn Dodgers, with whom he spent his final year before retiring at the conclusion of the 1936 campaign.

Following his retirement, Badgro spent many years coaching at the University of Washington before leaving the game for good and moving to the town of Kent, close to his original hometown of Orillia. He earned one final honor before passing away at the age of 95 on July 13, 1998, becoming in 1981, at 78 years of age, the oldest person to be inducted into the Pro Football Hall of Fame, a distinction he held until 2012, when 83-year-old Jack Butler gained induction. Upon Badgro's admittance to Canton, the legendary Red Grange, who competed against him in the NFL Championship Games of 1933 and 1934, called his former opponent "one of the best half-dozen ends I ever saw."[1]

CAREER HIGHLIGHTS

Best Season

Although Badgro earned First-Team All-Pro honors in 1931 and 1933 as well, the 1934 season would have to be considered the finest of his career. In addition to establishing career highs with 206 receiving yards and a league-leading 16 pass receptions, Badgro helped lead the 8–5 Giants to a stunning 30–13 victory over the previously unbeaten Chicago Bears in the NFL Championship Game that later became known as the "Sneakers Game."

Memorable Moments/Greatest Performances

Badgro made many key catches for the Giants over the course of his career, with one of his biggest being a 15-yard reception that helped put the Giants in position to score the only points in a 3–0 win over the Bears that enabled them to clinch the Eastern Division title in 1933. He also turned in a number of big plays on defense, including blocking a punt, which he returned for the go-ahead touchdown during a win over the Boston Redskins in 1935.

However, Badgro will always be remembered mostly for being the first player to score a touchdown in the NFL Championship Game series that began in 1933. He earned that distinction by hauling in a 29-yard TD pass from quarterback Harry Newman that gave the Giants an early 7–6 lead. Yet, Badgro's most vivid memory of that contest through the years remained his failure to cross the Chicago goal line with what would have been the winning touchdown on the game's final play. Some 60 years later, Badgro described in a 1994 interview the events that took place after he hauled in a pass and headed for the Chicago end zone: "If I had gotten by Red Grange, I would have scored. Grange had me around the middle . . . his arms were around the ball, and I couldn't get rid of it. If I get by him, we win the game. . . . I wish I had the ball again."[2] Grange ended up bringing Badgro down just short of the goal line, ending the game and preserving Chicago's 23–21 victory over New York.

NOTABLE ACHIEVEMENTS

- Led NFL with 16 receptions in 1934.
- First player to score a touchdown in NFL Championship Game history (1933).
- Three-time First-Team All-Pro selection (1931, 1933, 1934).
- 1930 Second-Team All-Pro selection.
- Three-time NFL Eastern Division champion.
- 1934 NFL champion.
- Elected to Pro Football Hall of Fame in 1981.

45

JOE MORRISON

E arning the nickname "Old Dependable" during his time with the Giants for his tremendous versatility, Joe Morrison garnered significant playing time at six different positions over the course of his 14 seasons in New York. At different times from 1959 to 1972, the University of Cincinnati graduate lined up at fullback, halfback, flanker, split end, tight end, and strong safety. Although Morrison spent the vast majority of his time either running the ball out of the backfield or catching passes as a wide-out, he never became associated with one particular position but was instead identified simply as a football player. In fact, Morrison's willingness to help his team by manning almost any spot on the field once prompted his longtime coach Allie Sherman to quip, "We've got a problem, but I know Joe can handle it. We need a guard."[1]

Even though Morrison built his reputation largely on his adaptability and selfless attitude, he did an outstanding job wherever the Giants put him. In addition to retiring as the team's all-time leading pass receiver (395 receptions), he ranked second in receiving yardage (4,993), fifth in rushing yardage (2,474), and second in touchdown receptions (47). He even intercepted two passes while playing safety in 1961. Morrison's career spanned two entirely different periods in Giants history. While Morrison spent his first five seasons playing for winning teams, the Giants posted an overall record of just 51–71 in his final nine years in New York.

Born in Lima, Ohio, on August 21, 1937, Joseph R. Morrison played quarterback at Lima South High School before attending the University of Cincinnati, where he displayed the versatility for which he later became so well noted by splitting his time between halfback and quarterback on offense, while also playing defense during his three varsity seasons. Subsequently selected by the Giants in the third round of the 1959 NFL Draft with the 34th overall pick, Morrison spent most of his rookie season serving as a backup running back and returning punts and kickoffs. After garnering more playing time on offense in his second year in the league, Morrison

Joe Morrison played six different positions for the Giants during his time in New York.
Courtesy of RMYAuctions.com

moved to the defensive side of the ball in 1961, recording the only two interceptions of his career as a safety.

Morrison saw very little action in 1962, but he became a starter on offense for the first time the following year, rushing for a career-high 568 yards, making 31 receptions for another 284 yards, and scoring 10 touchdowns. Morrison moved to wide receiver in 1964, a season in which he surpassed 40 receptions and 500 receiving yards for the first of five times. Although he remained at flanker in three of the next five seasons, Morrison also spent one year at halfback and another at fullback, posting his best overall numbers while manning those positions in 1966 and 1969, respectively. Morrison established career highs with 46 receptions and 724 yards in the first of those campaigns, while also rushing for 275 yards out of the backfield. New York's lack of a running game forced Morrison to move from flanker to fullback at the beginning of 1969, after which he rushed for 387 yards, made 44 receptions for 647 yards, and scored a career-high 11 touchdowns.

Morrison did a solid job wherever he played even though he lacked superior athletic ability. Standing 6'1" and weighing 215 pounds, he possessed only average size. Meanwhile, he had below-average speed, especially for a wide receiver. Yet Morrison possessed outstanding intelligence and excellent instincts, and he knew how to separate himself from his defender. Speaking of Morrison, Allie Sherman recalled, "He understood football, and he understood himself."[2] At the same time, Morrison's versatility endeared him to his coaches, his teammates, and the fans who cheered his pregame dash down the Giants' sideline into the left-field corner at Yankee Stadium.

The arrival of Ron Johnson in 1970 relegated Morrison to a backup role—one he assumed his last three years in the league. Morrison retired at the conclusion of the 1972 campaign with career totals that continue to place him in the Giants' top 10 in most statistical categories.

Morrison's tremendous versatility earned him the nickname "Old Dependable."
Courtesy of MearsOnlineAuctions.com

Following his retirement, Morrison became a head football coach at the collegiate level, directing the University of Tennessee at Chattanooga from 1973 to 1979, the University of New Mexico from 1980 to 1982, and the University of South Carolina from 1983 to 1988. By leading the Gamecocks to a 10–2 record in 1984, Morrison earned National Coach of the Year honors.

The future looked bright for South Carolina after the Gamecocks posted consecutive 8–4 records under Morrison in 1987 and 1988. However, the 51-year-old head coach passed away prior to the start of the 1989 campaign, collapsing after playing racquetball at Williams-Brice Stadium, and dying on February 5, 1989, from congestive heart failure. Following Morrison's passing, longtime Giants owner Wellington Mara said, "He was the ultimate team player. He would do anything you asked him. Run the ball, catch, play on special teams—anything."[3]

CAREER HIGHLIGHTS

Best Season

Morrison had his best year as a running back in 1963, when he rushed for 568 yards and posted a career-high 4.8-yard rushing average. He also scored 10 touchdowns and gained another 284 yards on pass receptions, giving him a total of 852 yards from scrimmage. Even though the Giants won only one game in 1966, Morrison established career highs in receptions (46) and receiving yardage (724). He also gained another 275 yards on the ground, leaving him just one yard short of the magical 1,000-yard mark in total yardage. Yet Morrison had his finest all-around season in 1969, when he rushed for 387 yards, made 44 receptions for 647 yards, and scored a career-high 11 touchdowns. In his final year as a starter, the 32-year-old Morrison surpassed 1,000 total yards for the only time in his career, accumulating 1,034 yards from scrimmage.

Memorable Moments/Greatest Performances

Morrison scored the first two touchdowns of his career in the final game of his rookie season, gathering in a nine-yard TD pass from Charlie Conerly and scoring on a one-yard run during a 24–10 victory over the Washington Redskins on December 13, 1959. However, Morrison didn't have his first really big game until 1963, when he helped the Giants defeat the Eagles

37–14 in week 3 by rushing for 120 yards and scoring three touchdowns. Morrison's touchdowns included a career-long 70-yard run that closed out the scoring in the fourth quarter. He again scored three touchdowns in the final game of the regular season, making two TD catches and scoring on a one-yard run during a 33–17 win over the Steelers that clinched the Eastern Division title for the Giants.

Morrison surpassed 100 receiving yards for the first time in his career on November 1, 1964, helping the Giants defeat the Cardinals 34–17 by making six receptions for 122 yards and one touchdown. He had an even bigger game against the Browns in the final game of the regular season, making eight catches for 147 yards during a 52–20 loss to the eventual NFL champions.

Morrison had a huge day against Pittsburgh on October 15, 1967, helping the Giants defeat the Steelers, 27–24, by making six receptions for 125 yards and two touchdowns, including a season-long 59-yarder that put the Giants ahead to stay late in the fourth quarter.

Morrison scored three touchdowns for the final time in his career on December 7, 1969, crossing the opponents' goal line three times during a 49–6 pasting of the Cardinals that ended a seven-game losing streak for the Giants. Morrison ran for one score and caught two TD passes, finishing the game with 132 total yards. He had his last big game for the Giants two weeks later in the regular season finale, making six receptions for 134 yards, gaining another 25 yards on the ground, and scoring two touchdowns during a 27–14 win over the Browns.

NOTABLE ACHIEVEMENTS

- Caught at least 40 passes five times.
- Surpassed 500 receiving yards five times, topping 700 yards once (724 in 1966).
- Scored at least 10 touchdowns twice (1963, 1969).
- Surpassed 1,000 yards from scrimmage once (1,034 in 1969).
- Finished third in NFL with 11 touchdowns in 1969.
- Ranks among Giants' all-time leaders in pass receptions (3rd), pass reception yardage (4th), touchdown receptions (3rd), and touchdowns scored (3rd).
- Four-time NFL Eastern Division champion.

VICTOR CRUZ

The Giants struck gold when they signed Victor Cruz to a free-agent contract just one day after all 32 NFL teams bypassed the former University of Massachusetts wide receiver in the 2010 NFL Draft. Seeking to add depth to their receiving corps, the Giants swooped in, hoping that Cruz might prove to be a suitable backup to starters Hakeem Nicks and Steve Smith. However, they ended up getting much more than they originally bargained for, with Cruz eventually developing into arguably the league's best slot receiver. After spending virtually all of his rookie season on the injured reserve list, Cruz burst upon the NFL scene in 2011, setting a new Giants record by amassing 1,536 receiving yards. He followed that up with another 1,000-yard season in 2012, making him just the fifth player in team history to surpass 1,000 receiving yards in back-to-back seasons.

Born to an African American father and a Puerto Rican mother in Paterson, New Jersey, on November 11, 1986, Victor Cruz attended Paterson Catholic High School, where he starred at wide receiver and defensive back. After enrolling at the University of Massachusetts, Cruz initially struggled academically, finding it particularly difficult to focus on his studies after his father committed suicide in 2007. However, after being sent home twice for academic reasons, Cruz displayed the resolve that later helped him become an elite NFL receiver by graduating with a degree in African American studies. Before completing his coursework, he also found time to excel on the football field, even though he didn't start a game until his junior season. Cruz concluded his college career with 11 touchdowns and just under 2,000 receiving yards.

Cruz subsequently signed with the Giants after all 32 NFL teams passed on him in the 2010 draft. Given little chance of earning a roster spot at the start of training camp, Cruz nevertheless made a strong impression on New York's coaching staff during the preseason, leading all NFL wide-outs with 297 receiving yards and four touchdown catches. Particularly impressive against the Jets during a Monday night preseason contest, Cruz finished the game with six receptions, for 145 yards and three touchdowns. Largely on

Victor Cruz proved to be arguably the NFL's best slot receiver his first few seasons in New York.
Courtesy of Scott Mecum

the strength of that performance, the Giants placed him on their 53-man regular season roster. However, Cruz pulled a hamstring while practicing for the season opener, enabling him to appear briefly in only three games before being placed on injured reserve for the remainder of the year.

Returning to the Giants fully healthy at the start of 2011, Cruz began the season as the team's fourth wide receiver. However, injuries to Mario Manningham and Domenik Hixon soon forced him to assume a more prominent role in New York's offense. Responding well to the challenge, Cruz displayed the sort of ability that earned him the permanent starting spot opposite Hakeem Nicks. Blessed with soft hands, outstanding speed, and excellent quickness, Cruz proved to be the perfect complement to Nicks as the team's slot receiver. Demonstrating a tremendous feel for the game, he also excelled at finding openings in the opposing defense, making him an exceptional third-down target for Eli Manning. Speaking of the comfort level he soon reached with Cruz, the Giants quarterback stated, "He's a guy that has a natural feel for the game, how to get open, where defenders are, what the coverage is, and what he needs to do to get open."[1]

Coach Tom Coughlin also expressed his satisfaction with the young receiver's play when he said, "If you're good enough and quick enough to get yourself in the middle of the field when the safeties divide, you provide the quarterback with an awful lot of weaponry. In Victor Cruz, you have the same kind of young guy who has exceptional quickness and is learning as he goes along here, and has had an exceptional year as he learns more about how to play at an NFL level."[2]

As Cruz evolved into an elite receiver over the course of his first full season, he also developed a huge fan base, with his patented touchdown celebratory salsa dance making him a cult hero of sorts. Yet Cruz remained grounded, explaining that he did his dance as a way of honoring his deceased grandmother, who taught him how to dance salsa and loved touchdown celebrations.

Cruz had an opportunity to dance in the opponent's end zone a total of nine times in 2011, scoring nine TDs, while also making 82 receptions for a franchise record 1,536 yards. Although he dropped more passes than he would have liked the following year, Cruz had a similarly productive 2012 campaign, catching 86 passes, for 1,092 yards and 10 touchdowns. While the Giants struggled throughout most of 2013, Cruz remained one of the team's few bright spots, making 73 receptions for 998 yards and four touchdowns, with only a concussion and injured left knee that kept him out of the final two contests preventing him from surpassing 1,000 receiving yards for the third consecutive season.

Cruz's total of 1,536 receiving yards in 2011 represents a single-season franchise record.
Courtesy of Dave Kopp via Flickr

Having signed a five-year contract extension worth nearly $46 million on July 8, 2013, Cruz was expected to remain with the Giants through 2017. Yet, even though the lengthy contract negotiations that precipitated Cruz's signing caused Giants fans to feel a bit anxious, NFL followers spent much of that time debating his true value as a slot receiver. Speaking of Cruz's worth on the NFL Network's *Total Access*, former Giants center Shaun O'Hara stated:

> He is absolutely elite. Everybody talks about slot receivers having to have 100-catch seasons. To me, it's not about quantity, it's about quality. And, when you look at Victor Cruz the last two seasons, he has led the NFL in production on third down. So I look at Victor Cruz as elite because he does a number of things. Yes, we compare him to Wes Welker. He runs great routes. He's very precise getting out and creating separation. . . . He has the speed that most slot receivers don't. . . . Victor Cruz brings certain abilities that not all slot receivers have. I think back to the Jets game in 2011—the play

that vaulted the Giants into their Super Bowl run. He made guys miss, not a lot of slot receivers can do that.[3]

Unfortunately, Cruz suffered a torn patellar tendon in Game 6 of the 2014 campaign that ended his season prematurely and essentially ended his days as a top-flight receiver. Although he attempted to mount a comeback in 2016 after missing the entire 2015 season as well, Cruz failed to display the same quickness and acceleration he had possessed prior to his injury, making only 39 receptions for just 586 yards and one touchdown. Released by the Giants on February 13, 2017, Cruz failed to catch on with any other NFL team, leaving him to wonder if his playing days had come to an end at only 31 years of age. Over parts of six seasons with the Giants, he caught 303 passes, amassed 4,549 receiving yards, and scored 25 touchdowns.

CAREER HIGHLIGHTS

Best Season

Although Cruz made four more receptions and scored one more touchdown in 2012, he had his best season one year earlier. In addition to finishing third in the NFL and establishing a Giants single-season record by amassing 1,536 receiving yards in 2011, Cruz ranked among the league leaders with 82 receptions and nine touchdown catches. He also finished third in the league with an average of 18.7 yards per reception, which bettered by six yards the average he posted in 2012.

Memorable Moments/Greatest Performances

Cruz had his breakout game against Philadelphia on September 25, 2011, making three receptions for 110 yards and scoring the first two touchdowns of his career during a 29–16 Giants win over the Eagles. Cruz's TD receptions covered 74 and 28 yards. Although the Giants lost to Seattle two weeks later, Cruz once again proved to be a huge factor, making eight receptions for 161 yards, including a 68-yard touchdown catch off a tipped pass. He had another big game against New Orleans on November 28, making nine receptions for 157 yards and two touchdowns, one of which went for 72 yards, during a 49–24 loss to the Saints. Cruz also came up big in the regular season finale against Dallas. With the Giants and Cowboys squaring off in a game to determine the NFC East champion, Cruz opened the scoring with a 74-yard TD reception. Later in the contest, he made a key 44-yard catch on third down that put the Giants in position to kick a field goal. Cruz concluded New York's 31–14 victory with six receptions, for 178 yards and one touchdown. He subsequently played well in the NFC title game, making 10 catches for 142 yards during the Giants' 20–17 overtime win over San Francisco.

Cruz had his biggest day of the 2012 campaign in week 2, helping the Giants defeat Tampa Bay 41–34 by making 11 receptions for 179 yards and one touchdown, which went for 80 yards.

Yet the seminal moment of Cruz's career occurred on December 24, 2011, against the New York Jets. With the 7–7 Giants needing victories in their final two contests to have any hope of making the playoffs, they trailed the Jets late in the first half by a score of 7–3 when Cruz took a short pass from Eli Manning and turned it into a 99-yard touchdown—the longest in franchise history. Cruz's 89 yards after the catch represent the most in NFL history by any receiver on a 99-yard reception. The play provided much of the impetus for the Giants to dominate the Jets the rest of the game, as they went on to defeat their New York counterparts by a final score of 29–14. They never looked back from that point on, winning their five remaining contests as well, en route to capturing the NFL championship.

NOTABLE ACHIEVEMENTS

- Surpassed 1,000 receiving yards twice (2011, 2012).
- Made more than 70 receptions three times, surpassing 80 catches twice (2011, 2012).
- Scored 10 touchdowns in 2012.
- Finished third in NFL with 1,536 receiving yards and average of 18.7 yards per reception in 2011.
- Holds Giants record for longest touchdown reception (99 yards vs. Jets on December 24, 2011).
- Holds Giants single-season record with 1,536 receiving yards in 2011.
- Ranks among Giants career leaders in receptions (11th) and receiving yards (10th).
- 2012 Pro Bowl selection.
- 2011 Second-Team All-Pro selection.
- 2011 NFC champion.
- Super Bowl XLVI champion.

HAKEEM NICKS

hortly after the Giants released Plaxico Burress on April 3, 2009, due to his problems with the law, it became quite evident to them that they needed to replace his offensive production at wide receiver. With Amani Toomer also announcing his retirement at the conclusion of the 2008 campaign, the Giants suddenly found themselves in desperate need of someone capable of stretching opposing defenses. Although Steve Smith showed promise as a slot receiver, the team lacked a legitimate deep threat. The Giants filled that void when they made Hakeem Nicks their first selection in the 2009 NFL Draft. Establishing himself as a starter midway through his rookie season, Nicks averaged nearly 17 yards per reception his first year in the league, making 47 catches for 790 yards and six touchdowns. Over the course of the next four seasons, he surpassed 75 receptions and 1,000 receiving yards twice each, more than making up for the loss of Burress. Indeed, in 2011 and 2012 Nicks teamed up with Victor Cruz to give the Giants one of the most dynamic wide-receiver tandems in the NFL.

Born in Charlotte, North Carolina, on January 14, 1988, Hakeem Nicks starred in football at local Independence High School, where he earned a top-10 rating among all North Carolina players by both Super-Prep and Rivals.com. Leading his high school team to an undefeated record during his time there, Nicks made 94 receptions for 1,819 yards and 20 touchdowns as a senior.

Upon graduating from high school, Nicks decided to remain in his home state, accepting a scholarship offer to attend the University of North Carolina. As a sophomore at UNC, he set a single-season school record by making 74 catches. His 958 receiving yards also represented the third-highest total in school history. Nicks continued to excel as a junior, making 68 receptions, scoring 12 touchdowns, and becoming the school's first 1,000-yard receiver by amassing 1,222 yards through the air. Nicks concluded the campaign with 14 school records, including career receptions (181), career receiving yards (2,580), and career touchdowns (21). He

Hakeem Nicks teamed up with Victor Cruz to give the Giants one of the NFL's most dynamic wide-receiver tandems.
Courtesy of Mike Cassella

subsequently ended his college career in style at the 2008 Meineke Car Care Bowl, making eight receptions for a bowl record 217 yards, and scoring on touchdown plays of 73, 66, and 25 yards.

After announcing his intention to turn pro following his junior year, Nicks received high praise from his coach at UNC, Butch Davis, who previously served on the Dallas coaching staff from 1989 to 1994. Davis likened the young wide receiver's skill set to that of someone he coached with the Cowboys, suggesting, "You don't want to put this burden on a kid coming into his rookie year, but a lot of his physical attributes are very similar to Michael Irvin. Hakeem is big, he's physical, he catches the ball over the middle, and he's got that ability to play physical when people are draped all over him, as they're going to be in the National Football League."[1]

Davis went on to say that Nicks has "as good a set of hands catching the ball as anybody I've ever been around."[2] He added, "The thing that I liked about him is, the bigger the game, it seemed like the better that he plays. The game he had in the bowl game, he was so geeked about wanting to play well. He knew it was a national audience. And how could you have played any better than he did in that game?"[3]

Having observed the degree to which Nicks dominated his opposition at the collegiate level, the Giants selected him in the first round of the 2009

Nicks topped 1,000 receiving yards twice for the Giants.
Courtesy of Mike Cassella

NFL Draft with the 29th overall pick. Although it subsequently took Nicks some time to earn a starting spot on New York's offense, he made significant contributions from the very beginning, scoring a touchdown in each of the four games New York played during the month of October.

Over the course of his rookie campaign, Nicks displayed the many qualities that prompted his former coach at UNC to liken him to Michael Irvin. An extremely physical receiver, the 6'1", 210-pound Nicks demonstrated his ability to catch balls in traffic. His thickness and huge hands often allowed him to outwrestle defensive backs for passes thrown into tight spaces. And, although Nicks was not considered to have blinding speed coming out of college, defenders rarely managed to catch him from behind once he got his hands on the ball.

Despite being limited by injury to 13 games in his sophomore campaign of 2010, Nicks improved upon his numbers significantly, making 79 receptions for 1,052 yards and 11 touchdowns. Victor Cruz joined Nicks in the Giants' receiving corps the following year, giving the team a lethal combination on the outside. While Cruz's rapid rise to stardom captured much of the media attention, Nicks had another outstanding year, making 76 catches for 1,192 yards and seven touchdowns. Injuries held down Nicks's production in 2012, limiting him to 13 games, 53 receptions, 692 yards, and only three touchdowns. Despite remaining healthy throughout most of 2013, Nicks again failed to perform at an elite level, making just 56 receptions, for 896 yards and no touchdowns. Seeking a long-term contract extension similar to the one the Giants gave Cruz prior to the start of the campaign, Nicks often appeared disinterested and unmotivated as he joined his teammates in turning in a subpar performance. As a result, the Giants made little effort to retain his services at season's end, allowing him to sign a free agent deal with the Indianapolis Colts. Nicks left New York with career totals of 311 receptions, 4,622 receiving yards, and 27 touchdowns.

Assuming a backup role in Indianapolis in 2014, Nicks failed to distinguish himself with the Colts, making just 38 receptions for 405 yards and four touchdowns. After signing with the Tennessee Titans during the subsequent off-season, Nicks failed to earn a roster spot, prompting him to rejoin the Giants midway through the campaign. Appearing in six games with the Giants in 2015, Nicks caught seven passes for 54 yards and no touchdowns before announcing his retirement after being waived by the New Orleans Saints on July 27, 2016. He ended his career with 356 receptions, 5,081 receiving yards, and 31 touchdowns.

CAREER HIGHLIGHTS

Best Season

Nicks's 79 receptions and 11 touchdowns in 2010 both represent career highs. However, he caught only three fewer passes the following year, accumulated 140 more receiving yards, and averaged 2.4 more yards per reception (15.7 to 13.3). It's an extremely close call, but the critical role Nicks played in New York's march to the NFL title made the 2011 campaign his best all-around year. The Giants' most potent offensive weapon throughout the postseason, Nicks made 28 receptions for 444 yards and four touch-downs during the Giants' four victories.

Memorable Moments/Greatest Performances

Nicks first demonstrated his ability to make big plays in the fourth week of his rookie season of 2009, taking a screen pass and going 54 yards for his first career touchdown during a 27–16 Giants victory over Kansas City. Nicks scored a touchdown in each of the next three games as well, becom-ing in the process the first Giants rookie in 48 years to score a touchdown in four straight games. Among his TD receptions were a 37-yarder against New Orleans and a 62-yarder against Arizona. Nicks also recorded a season-long 68-yard reception against the Oakland Raiders in week 5. His outstanding performance during the month of October earned him NFL Offensive Rookie of the Month honors.

Nicks had a big day in the 2010 season opener, catching four passes for 75 yards and scoring three touchdowns during a 31–18 win over the Carolina Panthers. He had another huge game four weeks later, making a career-high 12 receptions for 130 yards and two touchdowns, in helping the Giants defeat the Houston Texans by a score of 34–10. Nicks also came up big against Dallas in week 7, making nine receptions for 108 yards and two touchdowns during a 41–35 victory over the Cowboys. Two weeks later, Nicks caught six passes for 128 yards and one touchdown during a 41–7 pasting of the Seattle Seahawks.

Nicks turned in his first dominant performance of the 2011 campaign against Arizona in week 4, making 10 receptions for 162 yards and one touchdown during a 31–27 Giants win over the Cardinals. He had another big game later in the year, helping the Giants defeat Dallas for the first of two times by making eight receptions for 163 yards during a memorable 37–34 come-from-behind road win.

Yet Nicks reached the high point of his career during the 2011 post-season, when he turned in epic performances against Atlanta in the wild card round, Green Bay in the divisional championship round, and New England in the Super Bowl. Nicks began his extraordinary run by making six receptions for 115 yards and two touchdowns during the Giants' 24–2 win over the Falcons. One of his scores was a career-long 72-yarder. Nicks followed that up by catching seven passes for 165 yards and another two touchdowns, including a 37-yard Hail Mary reception just before halftime, in helping the Giants defeat the top-seeded Packers by a score of 37–20. He continued his dominance against the Patriots in Super Bowl XLVI, making 10 receptions for 109 yards during New York's 21–17 victory.

NOTABLE ACHIEVEMENTS

- Surpassed 1,000 receiving yards twice (2010, 2011).
- Made more than 70 receptions twice (2010, 2011).
- Finished fourth in NFL with 11 touchdown receptions in 2010.
- NFL Offensive Rookie of the Month for October 2009.
- NFL Alumni 2011 Wide Receiver of the Year.
- 2012 Week 2 NFC Offensive Player of the Week.
- 2011 NFC champion.
- Super Bowl XLVI champion.

48

PLAXICO BURRESS

Plaxico Burress proved to be a huge headache to Giants head coach Tom Coughlin during his time in New York. The enigmatic wide receiver showed up late for meetings, occasionally failed to show up for practice at all, and complained about his contract. He often lost focus during contests when Eli Manning didn't target him as much as he would have liked. Many people believe that Burress sabotaged the Giants' chances of repeating as NFL champions in 2008 with his irresponsible actions that eventually landed him in prison. Coughlin himself has gone on record as saying that he feels the Giants would have won the Super Bowl again that year had they not been distracted by Burress's troubles with the law. Nevertheless, Burress contributed significantly to the success of the Giants during his 3½ years in New York, serving as their primary deep threat and a tremendous weapon inside the red zone. In addition to amassing more than 1,000 receiving yards in two of his three full seasons with the Giants (he had 988 yards the other year), Burress made 33 touchdown receptions as a member of the team, placing him among the franchise's all-time leaders in that category. And in spite of his off-field transgressions, Burress created a permanent place for himself in Giants lore by making the winning touchdown grab in Super Bowl XLII.

Born in Norfolk, Virginia, on August 12, 1977, Plaxico Burress excelled at football while attending Green Run High School in Virginia Beach, Virginia, earning a spot on *Parade* magazine's All-America football team. After spending a postgraduate year at Fork Union Military Academy in Fork Union, Virginia, Burress enrolled at Michigan State University, where he set a school record in his first year for the most passes caught in a single season (65). He went on to establish himself as one of the university's all-team leaders in career receptions (131), touchdown catches (20), and receiving yards (2,155), doing so in just two seasons. Burress led the Spartans to victory in his final college game by making 13 receptions for 185 yards and three touchdowns against Florida in the 2000 Citrus Bowl.

Plaxico Burress proved to be an outstanding target for Eli Manning inside the red zone during his time in New York.
Courtesy of Rick Sparacino

Subsequently selected by the Pittsburgh Steelers in the first round of the 2000 NFL Draft with the eighth overall pick, Burress suffered a wrist injury as a rookie that limited him to just 12 games and 22 receptions. After undergoing surgery during the off-season, he returned to the Steelers in 2001 to win the starting job opposite Hines Ward. Burress played extremely well the next two seasons, having the most productive year of his career in 2002, when he made 78 receptions for 1,325 yards and seven touchdowns.

Before long, though, Burress began to develop a reputation for being someone who had a difficult time respecting authority. After being suspended by the Steelers in May 2004 for failing to attend a team practice, the NFL levied four fines against him later in the year for committing the following violations:

- Postgame comments he made regarding officiating.
- Unsportsmanlike conduct—specifically, verbal abuse of the head linesman.
- Throwing the ball into the stands.
- Slapping a referee in the face.

Burress's indiscretions ended up costing him a significant amount of playing time in 2004, limiting him to only 11 games and 35 receptions. More importantly, he subsequently found his options limited when he became a free agent at season's end. With the Steelers electing not to re-sign him, Burress received few offers from other teams due to the reputation he built in Pittsburgh. However, the Giants, in desperate need of a deep threat, finally came through with a six-year, $25 million offer that Burress eventually accepted after a considerable amount of haggling.

Burress had an outstanding first year in New York, making 76 receptions for 1,214 yards and seven touchdowns, in helping the Giants compile a record of 11–5 that earned them the NFC East title. His lanky 6'5", 225-pound frame made him an inviting target for Eli Manning, who leaned heavily on Burress in his first full season as the Giants starting quarterback. The two men worked extremely well together, with Manning often looking to Burress when he needed a big play. The receiver knew how to use his height and long arms to his advantage, frequently out-leaping opponents for passes intentionally thrown to him on an arch. Yet he possessed surprising strength as well, also knowing how to use his body to create separation between himself and his defender.

Burress had a somewhat less-productive 2006 season in which he caught 63 passes for 988 yards and 10 touchdowns, despite struggling with a groin injury for much of the year. He returned to top form in 2007, making 70 receptions for 1,025 yards and a career-high 12 touchdowns, even though an ailing ankle prevented him from practicing the entire season. Burress subsequently cemented his Giants legacy by having a memorable postseason during which he dominated the Green Bay secondary in the NFC Championship Game and scored the winning touchdown against New England in the Super Bowl.

Yet, in spite of the outstanding on-field contributions that Burress made to the Giants, he often tested the patience of Coach Tom Coughlin, who grew weary over time of the receiver's penchant for showing up late for meetings and occasionally missing practices altogether. The Giants' hierarchy finally reached a point early in 2008 when it began to weigh the pros and cons of having Burress on the team. After earlier threatening not to participate in May mini-camp as a result of his dissatisfaction with his contract, Burress practiced very little when the team assembled for training camp some two months later, claiming that he had an injured ankle. Shortly after the regular season began, Burress failed to show up for work one Monday, after which he could not be reached by phone for two days. The Giants subsequently suspended him for their October 5 game against

Burress scored the game-winning touchdown of Super Bowl XLII.
Courtesy of SportsMemorabilia.com

Seattle for a violation of team rules. Less than two months later, the wide receiver made his last appearance in a Giants uniform in a game against the Arizona Cardinals. Just five nights after that November 23 contest, Burress committed an error in judgment that nearly ended his playing career and unquestionably changed his life forever.

On the night of November 28, 2008, Burress and teammate Antonio Pierce decided to frequent a Manhattan nightclub, with the former carrying an illegal handgun in the waistband of his pants. As the gun started to slip down his leg, Burress grabbed for it, accidentally causing it to discharge and shooting himself in the thigh. After initially receiving treatment for the wound at a local hospital and trying to conceal the incident from authorities, Burress turned himself in to police two days later to face charges of criminal possession of a handgun. New York mayor Michael Bloomberg urged that Burress be prosecuted to the fullest extent of the law, saying that any punishment short of the minimum 3½ years for unlawful carrying of a handgun would be "a mockery of the law."[1]

Upon learning of the incident, the Giants fined Burress and suspended him for the remainder of the season. They later released him on April 3, 2009, when it became apparent to them that his court case would take longer than expected to resolve.

Meanwhile, Burress asked a Manhattan grand jury for sympathy during two hours of testimony on July 29, 2009. Less than one week later, the jury indicted him on two counts of criminal possession of a weapon in the second degree, and a single count of reckless endangerment in the second degree. On August 29, Burress accepted a plea deal that ended up putting him in prison for 20 months.

After being released from jail in June of 2011, Burress got himself reinstated with the NFL. He subsequently signed a one-year deal with the New York Jets, making 45 receptions for 612 yards and eight touchdowns with them over the course of the 2011 campaign. Although Burress failed to receive an offer from any NFL team prior to the start of the 2012 season, he eventually returned to Pittsburgh, rejoining the Steelers more than halfway through the campaign. On March 12, 2013, Burress signed a one-year deal to remain in Pittsburgh. However, after suffering a torn rotator cuff during training camp, he failed to appear in a single game for the Steelers in 2013. With no NFL teams expressing interest in him when he became an unrestricted free agent at season's end, Burress announced his retirement, ending his career with 553 receptions, 8,499 receiving yards, and 64 touchdowns. His numbers with the Giants include 244 receptions, 3,681 receiving yards, and 33 touchdowns.

GIANT CAREER HIGHLIGHTS

Best Season

Although he scored five more touchdowns two years later, Burress had his best all-around season for the Giants in 2005, when he made 76 receptions for 1,214 yards and seven TDs. Burress gained nearly 200 more yards than he did in 2007, with his average of 16.0 yards per reception proving to be the best of his Giants career.

Memorable Moments/Greatest Performances

Burress had his first big game for the Giants in week 4 of the 2005 campaign, making 10 receptions for 204 yards and two touchdowns during a 44–24 Giants win over the St. Louis Rams. He had another huge day against Philadelphia seven weeks later, catching six passes for 113 yards and one touchdown during a 27–17 victory over the Eagles. His 61-yard TD reception in the fourth quarter put the game out of reach. Burress also came up big in the regular season finale, helping the Giants defeat the Raiders 30–21 by making five receptions for 128 yards, including a career-long 78-yard TD grab.

Burress had his biggest game of the 2006 season in week 2, making six receptions for 114 yards and one touchdown during a 30–24 overtime win over the Eagles. His 31-yard TD catch nearly 12 minutes into overtime gave the Giants the victory.

Although the Giants lost their 2007 season opener to Dallas by a score of 45–35, Burress played extremely well, catching eight passes for 144 yards and three touchdowns, including a season-long 60-yarder. He had another big day against Philadelphia in week 14, helping the Giants defeat the Eagles 16–13 by making seven receptions for 136 yards and one touchdown.

Yet it is the 2007 postseason for which Burress will always be remembered most. Playing under frigid conditions in Green Bay in the NFC Championship Game, Burress turned in a performance for the ages, setting a franchise playoff record by making 11 receptions for 154 yards during a 23–20 Giants overtime victory. He followed that up by catching the game-winning touchdown pass in Super Bowl XLII that made the score 17–14 with only 35 seconds remaining on the clock.

NOTABLE ACHIEVEMENTS

- Surpassed 70 receptions twice (2005, 2007).
- Topped 1,000 receiving yards twice (2005, 2007).
- Scored at least 10 touchdowns twice (2006, 2007).
- Finished in top five in NFL in touchdown receptions twice (2006, 2007).
- Ranks ninth all-time on Giants with 33 career touchdown receptions.
- 2005 Week 4 NFC Offensive Player of the Week.
- 2007 NFC champion.
- Super Bowl XLII champion.

49

BOB TUCKER

Mark Bavaro's grit and determination enabled him to create a permanent place for himself in Giants lore. Meanwhile, Jeremy Shockey drew constant attention to himself during his time in New York with his colorful persona. However, more than 40 years after he played his last game for the Giants, Bob Tucker remains the most underrated and overlooked tight end in team history. A sure-handed receiver and solid blocker, Tucker spent almost 7½ years in New York, playing for teams that compiled an overall record of 35–67–1 during that time. Persevering through several coaching and quarterback changes, the 6'3", 230-pound undrafted free agent out of tiny Bloomsburg University in Pennsylvania distinguished himself as one of the few outstanding players on mostly dreary teams. After joining the Giants in 1970, Tucker went on to amass more receiving yards (4,376) than any other tight end in Giants history. The first player at his position to lead the NFC in pass receptions, Tucker also caught more passes than any other tight end during the 1970s. Only a poor supporting cast in most seasons likely prevented Tucker from accomplishing a considerable amount more, which would have earned him a higher place in these rankings.

Born in Hazleton, Pennsylvania, on June 8, 1945, Robert Louis Tucker garnered little interest from the NFL when he graduated from Bloomsburg University, forcing him to spend his first few professional seasons playing for the Pottstown Firebirds of the Atlantic Coast League. Discovered by the Giants prior to the start of the 1970 campaign, Tucker earned the team's starting tight end job in his first training camp, wresting it away from New York's longtime starter at the position, Aaron Thomas.

Tucker quickly developed a tremendous rapport with Fran Tarkenton, rapidly gaining his quarterback's trust in establishing himself as the team's "go-to" receiver in short- and medium-yardage passing situations. Although Tucker lacked breakaway speed, he ran well, had outstanding moves in the open field, and possessed exceptional hands. The tight end also did a good

Bob Tucker caught more passes during the 1970s than any other tight end in
the league.
Courtesy of RMYAuctions.com

job of blocking at the point of attack, excelling in particular at the "crack-
back" block.

Tucker caught 40 passes, for 571 yards and five touchdowns as a
rookie, in helping the Giants nearly make the playoffs with a record of 9–5.
Although the team posted a mark of just 4–10 the following year, Tucker
improved upon his performance, making 59 receptions, for 791 yards and
four touchdowns. Tucker's 59 catches enabled him to become the first tight
end to lead the NFC in receptions.

Unfortunately, the Giants' poor showing prevented Tucker from earning either Pro Bowl or All-NFL honors in his second season. But, while he remained one of the league's most overlooked players in subsequent years, he continued to perform well for the Giants, even after they dealt Tarkenton back to Minnesota at the conclusion of the 1971 campaign. Whether catching passes from Norm Snead, Randy Johnson, or Craig Morton, Tucker remained New York's most reliable receiver, making in excess of 40 receptions four more times between 1972 and 1976. He performed particularly well in the first of those years, catching 55 passes, for 764 yards and four touchdowns, en route to earning Second-Team All-NFL honors for the only time in his career.

Tucker found himself surrounded by a great deal of instability during his years with the Giants, playing for them at four different home stadiums—Yankee Stadium, the Yale Bowl, Shea Stadium, and Giants Stadium. He also saw the team go through numerous coaching and quarterback downgrades that dragged Wellington Mara's flagship franchise to the depths of the NFL. However, through it all, Tucker remained an outstanding player and a true professional. Speaking of the former tight end years later, John Mara said, "No doubt, Bob was revolutionary for his time. He wasn't the fastest, but he had such great hands and a knack for finding openings and knocking people over. He was one of the greatest players we had during some very lean years for our franchise."[1]

For his part, Tucker chose to put a positive spin on the time he spent in New York, expressing his fondness for longtime Giants owner Wellington Mara by saying, "Listen, Wellington always tried to do the best for his team. But he was loyal to a fault: He was such a good guy, if you played for him a number of years, he wasn't going to throw you out. He didn't have the heart to cut you, but you took up a spot from a young player."[2]

Yet, at the same time, Tucker acknowledged the many mistakes that the Giants organization made during his time there, adding, "And our drafting—we never got much out of it; Rocky Thompson, Eldridge Small, Dave Tipton . . . they didn't measure up or last very long. So we didn't get the influx of talent we expected, and we had high draft choices, too. But that's the football business."[3]

Tucker finally grew weary of the Giants' constant failures, asking the team to trade him shortly after the 1977 season got underway. Management obliged five games into the campaign, sending him to Minnesota, where he reunited with his old Giants teammate Fran Tarkenton. Spending the final 3½ years of his career with the Vikings, Tucker never again experienced the same level of individual success he had in New York. Yet he found his time

Tucker led the NFC with 59 pass receptions in 1971.
Courtesy of SportsMemorabilia.com

in Minnesota far more gratifying since the Vikings reached the playoffs three times in his four years with them.

Tucker retired at the conclusion of the 1980 campaign with 422 career receptions, for 5,421 yards and 27 touchdowns. Only two NFL players caught more passes during the 1970s. Tucker's numbers as a member of the Giants include 327 receptions, 4,376 receiving yards, and 22 touchdowns.

A victim of bad timing, Tucker had the misfortune of joining the Giants in the middle of the darkest period in team history. He also left them just a few years before George Young helped resurrect the team by drafting players such as Phil Simms and Lawrence Taylor.

GIANT CAREER HIGHLIGHTS

Best Season

Although Tucker earned All-NFL honors for the only time in his career in 1972 by making 55 receptions, for 764 yards and four touchdowns, he performed slightly better one year earlier. By catching 59 passes, for 791 yards and four touchdowns in 1971, Tucker not only became the first tight end to lead the NFC in pass receptions, but he also finished second in the entire league. Meanwhile, his 791 receiving yards placed him ninth in the league rankings.

Memorable Moments/Greatest Performances

Tucker had his breakout game in his rookie season of 1970 against the St. Louis Cardinals on October 25, making six receptions, for 150 yards and two touchdowns during a 35–17 Giants win that evened their record at 3–3. Tucker's touchdown grabs covered 41 and 17 yards.

However, he saved most of his finest performances for the following year, en route to leading the NFC in pass receptions. During a 17–13 loss to the Pittsburgh Steelers on November 21, 1971, Tucker caught five passes for 108 yards. One week later, he recorded the longest play of his career, scoring from 63 yards out on a catch and run during a 24–7 loss to the Cardinals. Tucker had his biggest game, though, on the season's final day, clinching the NFC pass-receiving title by making eight receptions, for 116 yards and one touchdown during a 41–28 loss to Philadelphia.

NOTABLE ACHIEVEMENTS

- Caught more than 50 passes three times (1971, 1972, 1973).
- First tight end to lead NFC in pass receptions (59 in 1971).
- Led Giants in pass receptions five times (1971–1974, 1976).
- Set Giants record (since broken) by catching a pass in 38 straight games (1970–1972).
- Caught more passes than any other tight end during 1970s.
- Third in NFL in pass receptions during 1970s.
- Giants all-time leader among tight ends in pass receiving yards (4,376).
- Ranks among Giants all-time leaders in pass receptions (8th) and pass receiving yardage (12th).
- 1972 Second-Team All-Pro selection.
- 1972 Second-Team All-Conference selection.

50

JASON PIERRE-PAUL

Known for his freakish athletic ability, Jason Pierre-Paul earned a spot in these rankings even though he has been a full-time starter for the Giants in just five of his eight seasons with Big Blue. Blessed with perhaps as much raw talent as any man ever to don a Giants uniform, Pierre-Paul came to New York with little football knowledge. However, he had all the physical tools to become a dominant defensive lineman. In explaining his selection of the inexperienced Pierre-Paul with the 15th overall pick of the 2010 NFL Draft, Giants general manager Jerry Reese stated, "He has the length, number one. He's 6'5" and 270 pounds. The speed he has, the long arms he has, the athletic ability he has . . . those kinds of things; he comes naturally raw, oozing with that kind of talent. The motor he has. It's hard to find a package like that. He has some freakish athletic skills we're excited about trying to hone and get him on a good path toward the quarterback."[1]

Pierre-Paul subsequently rewarded the Giants for taking a chance on him. After accumulating 4½ sacks in a back-up role as a rookie, he took the NFL by storm in 2011, earning Pro Bowl and First-Team All-Pro honors by finishing fourth in the league with 16½ sacks. An outstanding run-defender as well, Pierre-Paul also made 93 tackles (72 solo)—the second most by a Giants lineman since the NFL began recording tackles as an official statistic more than three decades ago. He followed that up with a solid 2012 campaign in which he recorded 6½ sacks and 66 tackles, despite being double- or even triple-teamed on virtually every play. Still, there were those who initially wondered if the Giants made the right decision when they selected Pierre-Paul so early in the draft.

Born to Haitian immigrants in Deerfield Beach, Florida, on February 28, 1989, Jason Pierre-Paul spent most of his youth playing basketball, lettering in that sport while attending Deerfield Beach High School, before finally taking up football in his junior year. Displaying a natural predilection toward his latest undertaking, Pierre-Paul subsequently excelled in his first two years of college football, first as a freshman at California's College

Jason Pierre-Paul earned Pro Bowl and First-Team All-Pro honors in his first year as a starter by recording 16½ sacks and 93 tackles in 2011.
Courtesy of Mike Morbeck

of the Canyons, and then as a sophomore at Fort Scott Community College in Kansas. However, NFL scouts first began to take notice of Pierre-Paul after he transferred to the University of South Florida in 2009. Dominating his opposition on a regular basis, Pierre-Paul earned the nickname "Haitian Sensation," even shocking his coaches with his extraordinary athleticism.

Kevin Patrick, who served as Pierre-Paul's defensive line coach during the latter's only season of major college football, related a story of how his prize protégé sent a 315-pound offensive lineman tumbling sideways onto his ear during a pass-rush drill at his very first practice. Recalling the incident, Patrick said, "It was, 'Oh, my God, did you just see him?' If you watch closely, you'll see him do things and you'll stand back and go, 'Oh, my Lord!'"[2]

Electing to forgo his senior year of college and enter the 2010 NFL Draft, Pierre-Paul similarly wowed pro scouts who watched him on film. After selecting him in the first round, Giants general manager Jerry Reese revealed, "He's a guy that, during the season when I went to South Florida, because they had four senior guys, where you put the tape on and you're saying, 'Wow, who in the world is this guy?' because you don't know anything about him; he just got there. But he made you take notice; he was jumping off the film. So, of course, you track him through the year. He was just a junior, but the way he was playing, it was a very strong indication the guy was going to come out. He wasn't a late riser for us. We had big grades on him throughout the year."[3]

Reese added, "We think the guy has the biggest upside of any player in the draft. We think the sky is the limit."[4]

Reese based his optimism on a number of factors. In addition to standing 6'5" and weighing 270 pounds, Pierre-Paul has outstanding speed (he can run the 40-yard dash in 4.7 seconds), long arms (35 inches), and huge hands. He also has something that cannot be measured in pounds, inches, or seconds: tremendous desire and a motor that never quits. Revealing the passion he takes with him to the field, Pierre-Paul stated on one occasion, "However many snaps I play for, when I'm on the field, I go 120 percent."[5]

Pierre-Paul's rare skill set had him starting on the Giants' defensive line before long. After serving primarily as a backup to Justin Tuck and Osi Umenyiora his first year in the league, Pierre-Paul became a one-man wrecking crew in his second season. With both Tuck and Umenyiora suffering through injury-marred campaigns, Pierre-Paul established himself as New York's dominant defender, placing near the top of the league rankings in sacks, and finishing third on the team in tackles. He continued to excel in the postseason, helping the Giants post victories over Atlanta, Green Bay, San Francisco, and New England, en route to winning the Super Bowl.

Although Pierre-Paul compiled less-impressive numbers in 2012, much of that could be attributed to the constant attention he drew from opposing

Pierre-Paul currently ranks seventh in franchise history with 58½ career sacks.
Courtesy of PristineAuction.com

offensive lines. He also played through a back injury that had to be surgically repaired at season's end. Slowed by the aftereffects of his off-season surgery, Pierre-Paul made little impact in 2013, recording just two sacks and 27 tackles, before sitting out the final few weeks of the campaign with an ailing shoulder. Healthy again in 2014, Pierre-Paul made 77 tackles, forced three fumbles, and ranked among the league leaders with 12½ sacks.

However, Pierre-Paul nearly saw his career come to an end during the subsequent off-season, when he suffered a serious hand injury in a July 4, 2015, fireworks accident that forced him to have his right index finger and parts of two other fingers amputated. Playing with a protective cast on his right hand when he returned to action midway through the 2015 campaign, Pierre-Paul failed to make much of an impact. Yet even though he was unable to re-establish himself as a dominant defender in either of the next two seasons, Pierre-Paul performed well for the Giants, recording a total of 15½ sacks and making 121 tackles before being dealt to the Tampa Bay Buccaneers for a pair of draft picks on March 22, 2018. Leaving the Giants with 58½ career sacks to his credit, Pierre-Paul ranks seventh in team annals in that category. He also recorded 432 tackles (309 solo), forced 13 fumbles, recovered seven others, intercepted two passes, and scored three touchdowns during his time in New York.

CAREER HIGHLIGHTS

Best Season

This was a no-brainer. Pierre-Paul had easily his best season in 2011, when he established career highs with 16½ sacks and 93 tackles. He also successfully defended seven passes, forced two fumbles, and recorded a safety.

Memorable Moments/Greatest Performances

Pierre-Paul returned both of his interceptions for touchdowns, crossing the opponent's goal line for the first time in his career on October 28, 2012, when he helped lead the Giants to a 29–24 victory over the Dallas Cowboys by picking off a Tony Romo pass and returning the ball 28 yards for a TD. He recorded another pick-six on November 17, 2013, when he put the finishing touches on a 27–13 win over the Packers by returning a Scott Tolzien aerial 24 yards for the game's final score. Pierre-Paul scored the last of his three career touchdowns during a 27–13 victory over the Cleveland

Browns on November 27, 2016, when he rumbled 43 yards after recovering a fumble. He also recorded three sacks and seven tackles during the contest, earning in the process NFC Defensive Player of the Week honors for the fourth time in his career.

However, Pierre-Paul turned in his finest all-around performance against the Dallas Cowboys on December 11, 2011. The 6–6 Giants entered the final few moments of the contest leading the 7–5 Cowboys by a score of 37–34, with their season literally hanging in the balance. Having already recorded two sacks and a forced fumble, Pierre-Paul provided further heroics by blocking Dallas placekicker Dan Bailey's last-second 47-yard attempt at a field goal that would have tied the score and sent the game into overtime. By doing so, Pierre-Paul became the first player in NFL history to record a sack, force a fumble, and block a field goal attempt in the same game, earning in the process NFC Defensive Player of the Week honors for the first time. Meanwhile, his extraordinary effort, coupled with the Giants' 29–14 victory over the Jets two weeks later, provided much of the impetus for the team to go on its exceptional postseason run that ended in victory in Super Bowl XLVI.

NOTABLE ACHIEVEMENTS

- Finished fourth in NFL with 16½ sacks in 2011.
- Recorded 93 tackles (72 solo) in 2011.
- Ranks seventh in Giants history with 58½ career sacks.
- Four-time NFC Defensive Player of the Week.
- Only player in NFL history to record a sack, forced fumble, and blocked field goal attempt in same game (vs. Dallas on December 11, 2011).
- Two-time Pro Bowl selection (2011, 2012).
- 2011 First-Team All-Pro selection.
- 2011 NFC champion.
- Super Bowl XLVI champion.

SUMMARY
AND HONORABLE MENTIONS
(THE NEXT 25)

Having identified the 50 greatest players in New York Giants history, the time has come to select the best of the best. Based on the rankings contained in this book, the members of the Giants' all-time offensive and defensive teams are listed below. Our squads include the top player at each position, with the offense featuring the two best wide receivers, running backs, tackles, and guards. Several of the offensive linemen were taken from the list of honorable mentions that will soon follow. Meanwhile, the defense features two ends, two tackles, two inside linebackers, a pair of outside backers, two cornerbacks, and a pair of safeties. Although I included neither a placekicker nor a punter in the top 50, those two positions have been accounted for as well.

OFFENSE	DEFENSE
Player, Position	Player, Position
Eli Manning, QB	Michael Strahan, LE
Frank Gifford, RB	Steve Owen, LT
Tiki Barber, RB	Arnie Weinmeister, RT
Mark Bavaro, TE	Andy Robustelli, RE
Amani Toomer, WR	Brad Van Pelt, LOLB
Kyle Rote, WR	Sam Huff, LILB
Roosevelt Brown, LT	Harry Carson, RILB
Jack Stroud, LG	Lawrence Taylor, ROLB
Mel Hein, C	Mark Haynes, LCB
Chris Snee, RG	Emlen Tunnell, S
Jumbo Elliott, RT	Jimmy Patton, S
Don Chandler, PK	Dick Lynch, RCB
	Dave Jennings, P

Although I limited my earlier rankings to the top 50 players in Giants history, many other fine players have worn a Giants uniform over the years, some of whom narrowly missed making the final cut. Following is a list of those players deserving of an honorable mention. These are the men I deemed worthy of being slotted into positions 51 to 75 in the overall rankings. Where applicable and available, the statistics they compiled during their time in New York are included, along with their most notable achievements while playing for the Giants.

51: IKE HILLIARD (WR: 1997–2004)

Courtesy of SportsMemorabilia.com

Giant Numbers

368 receptions, 4,630 receiving yards, 27 TD receptions.

NOTABLE ACHIEVEMENTS

- Caught more than 50 passes five times, topping 60 catches twice and 70 receptions once (72 in 1999).
- Accumulated 996 receiving yards in 1999.
- Made eight touchdown receptions in 2000.
- Ranks among Giants all-time leaders in pass receptions (5th) and pass reception yardage (9th).
- 2000 NFC champion.

52: JOHN MENDENHALL (DT: 1972–1979)

Courtesy of SportsMemorabilia.com

NOTABLE ACHIEVEMENTS

- Led Giants with 10 sacks and 7 forced fumbles in 1977.
- Led Giants linemen in tackles six times.
- 1974 First-Team All-NFC selection.
- 1974 Second-Team All-Pro selection.

53: RAY FLAHERTY (WR, DB; 1928–1935)

Public domain

NOTABLE ACHIEVEMENTS

- Led NFL with 21 receptions, 350 receiving yards, 5 TD receptions, and average of 16.7 yards per reception in 1932.
- Three-time First-Team All-Pro selection (1928, 1929, 1932).
- Two-time Second-Team All-Pro selection (1933, 1934).
- Three-time NFL Eastern Division champion.
- 1934 NFL champion.
- Elected to Pro Football Hall of Fame in 1976.

54: BART OATES (C; 1985–1993)

Courtesy of SportsMemorabilia.com

NOTABLE ACHIEVEMENTS

- Three-time Pro Bowl selection (1990, 1991, 1993).
- 1987 Second-Team All-NFC selection.
- Two-time NFC champion (1986, 1990).
- Two-time Super Bowl champion (XXI, XXV).

55: JIM BURT (NT; 1981–1988)

Courtesy of SportsMemorabilia.com

Giant Numbers

18 sacks, 550 tackles, 10 fumble recoveries.

NOTABLE ACHIEVEMENTS

- Recorded career-high seven sacks in 1984.
- Led Giants linemen in tackles three times.
- 1986 Pro Bowl selection.
- 1986 First-Team All-NFC selection.
- 1986 NFC champion.
- Super Bowl XXI champion.

56: DAVE JENNINGS (P; 1974–1984)

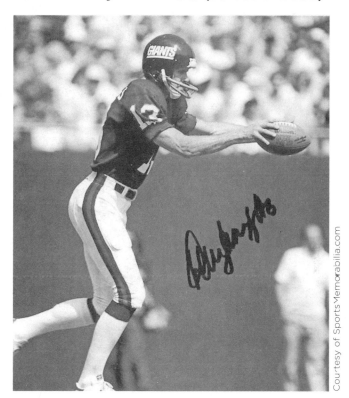

Courtesy of SportsMemorabilia.com

Giant Numbers

Averaged 41.7 yards per punt; career long: 73 yards.

NOTABLE ACHIEVEMENTS

- Averaged better than 40 yards per punt in nine of 11 seasons, posting average in excess of 42 yards five times.
- Led NFL with punting average of 44.8 in 1980.
- Finished second in NFL with punting average of 42.7 in 1979.
- Four-time Pro Bowl selection (1978–1980, 1982).
- Three-time First-Team All-NFC selection (1979, 1980, 1982).
- Three-time Second-Team All-NFC selection (1976, 1978, 1981).
- Two-time First-Team All-Pro selection (1979, 1980).
- Three-time Second-Team All-Pro selection (1978, 1981, 1982).

57: SEAN LANDETA (P; 1985–1993)

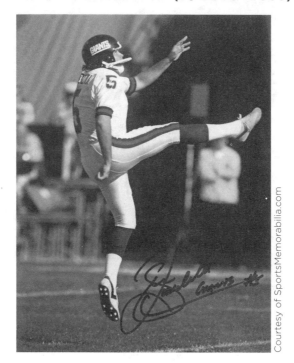

Courtesy of SportsMemorabilia.com

Giant Numbers

Averaged 43.4 yards per punt; career long: 71 yards.

NOTABLE ACHIEVEMENTS

- Averaged better than 42 yards per punt in eight of nine seasons, posting average in excess of 43 yards five times.
- Finished second in NFL with punting average of 44.8 in 1986.
- Two-time Pro Bowl selection (1986, 1990).
- Three-time First-Team All-NFC selection (1986, 1989, 1990).
- 1985 Second-Team All-NFC selection.
- Three-time First-Team All-Pro selection (1986, 1989, 1990).
- NFL 1980s All-Decade Team.
- NFL 1990s All-Decade Team.
- Two-time NFC champion (1986, 1990).
- Two-time Super Bowl champion (XXI, XXV).

58: CHRIS SNEE (OG; 2004–2013)

Courtesy of Alexa Scorcato via Flickr

NOTABLE ACHIEVEMENTS

- Four-time Pro Bowl selection (2008, 2009, 2010, 2012).
- 2008 First-Team All-Pro selection.
- Two-time Second-Team All-Pro selection (2009, 2010).
- Two-time NFC champion (2007, 2011).
- Two-time Super Bowl champion (XLII, XLVI).

59: BRANDON JACOBS (RB; 2005–2011, 2013)

Courtesy of Erica Wines

Giant Numbers

5,094 rushing yards, 60 rushing touchdowns, 82 receptions, 743 receiving yards, 4 TD receptions.

NOTABLE ACHIEVEMENTS

- Rushed for more than 1,000 yards twice (2007, 2008).
- Averaged better than 5 yards per carry three times (2007, 2008, 2010).
- Finished third in NFL in yards per carry twice (2008, 2010).
- Finished third in NFL with 15 touchdowns in 2008.
- NFC Offensive Player of the Month for October 2007.
- Giants all-time leader in rushing touchdowns (60).
- Ranks among Giants all-time leaders in rushing yardage (4th), total touchdowns scored (4th), and yards per carry (3rd).
- Two-time NFC champion (2007, 2011).
- Two-time Super Bowl champion (XLII, XLVI).

60: AHMAD BRADSHAW (RB; 2007–2012)

Courtesy of Adm. Jonathan Greenert

Giant Numbers

4,232 rushing yards, 32 rushing touchdowns, 132 receptions, 1,087 receiving yards, 3 TD receptions.

NOTABLE ACHIEVEMENTS

- Rushed for more than 1,000 yards twice (2010, 2012).
- Averaged better than 5 yards per carry twice (2007, 2008).
- Scored 11 touchdowns in 2011.
- Posted longest run from scrimmage in NFL in 2007 (88 yards).
- NFC Offensive Player of the Week for December 23, 2007.
- Ranks among Giants all-time leaders in rushing yardage (6th), rushing touchdowns (9th), and yards per carry (2nd).
- Two-time NFC champion (2007, 2011).
- Two-time Super Bowl champion (XLII, XLVI).

61: DON CHANDLER (P, PK; 1956–1964)

Courtesy of CollectAuctions.com

Giant Numbers

Averaged 43.8 yards per punt; career long: 74 yards.
Successful on 59 percent of field-goal attempts; scored 525 total points.

NOTABLE ACHIEVEMENTS

- Averaged better than 40 yards per punt nine straight times, posting average in excess of 44 yards five times.
- Led NFL with 106 points scored in 1963.
- Finished second in NFL in punting average three times.
- Finished second in NFL in field goal percentage twice and field goals made once.
- 1964 First-Team All-Conference selection.
- NFL 1960s All-Decade Team.
- Six-time NFL Eastern Division champion.
- 1956 NFL champion.

62: ERICH BARNES (CB; 1961–1964)

Courtesy of Oh o Sports Group

Giant Numbers

18 interceptions, 282 return yards, 3 TD interception returns, 5 touchdowns.

NOTABLE ACHIEVEMENTS

- Intercepted 7 passes in 1961.
- Led NFL with 195 interception-return yards and 2 TD interception returns in 1961.
- Holds Giants record for longest interception return (102 yards: October 15, 1961 vs. Dallas).
- Four-time Pro Bowl selection.
- 1962 First-Team All-NFC selection.
- 1961 First-Team All-Pro selection.
- 1962 Second-Team All-Pro selection.
- Three-time NFL Eastern Division champion.

63: JUMBO ELLIOTT (OT; 1988–1995)

Courtesy of SportsMemorabilia.com

NOTABLE ACHIEVEMENTS

- 1993 Pro Bowl selection.
- 1990 NFC champion.
- Super Bowl XXV champion.

64: WILLIE WILLIAMS (CB; 1965, 1967–1973)

Courtesy of RMYAuctions.com

Giant Numbers

35 interceptions, 462 return yards.

NOTABLE ACHIEVEMENTS

- Led NFL with 10 interceptions in 1968.
- Holds Giants record for most consecutive games with an interception (6 in 1968).
- Ranks fifth in Giants history with 35 career interceptions.
- 1969 Pro Bowl selection.

65: MARK COLLINS (CB; 1986–1993)

Courtesy of SportsMemorabilia.com

Giant Numbers

17 interceptions, 207 return yards, 1 TD interception return, 515 tackles.

NOTABLE ACHIEVEMENTS

- Surpassed 80 tackles twice (1989, 1991).
- 1990 First-Team All-NFC selection.
- Two-time NFC champion (1986, 1990).
- Two-time Super Bowl champion (XXI, XXV).

66: WARD CUFF (RB, DB, PK; 1937–1945)

Courtesy of Richard Albersheim, Albersheims.com

Giant Numbers

1,766 rushing yards, 6 rushing touchdowns, 101 receptions, 1,477 receiving yards, 12 TD receptions, 31 field goals.

NOTABLE ACHIEVEMENTS

- Led NFL in yards per rushing attempt twice (1943, 1944).
- Led NFL with 152 interception-return yards in 1941.
- Led NFL kickers in field goals made three times (1938, 1939, 1943).
- Led NFL kickers in field goal percentage twice (1938, 1943).
- Finished fourth in NFL with 523 yards rushing in 1943.
- Three-time Pro Bowl selection (1938, 1939, 1941).
- Three-time First-Team All-Pro selection (1941, 1943, 1944).
- Two-time Second-Team All-Pro selection (1938, 1939).
- Five-time NFL Eastern Division champion.
- 1938 NFL champion.

67: JACK STROUD (OG, OT; 1953–1964)

Courtesy of FootballCardGallery.com

NOTABLE ACHIEVEMENTS

- Three-time Pro Bowl selection (1955, 1957, 1960).
- 1962 First-Team All-Conference selection.
- Six-time Second-Team All-Pro selection.
- Six-time NFL Eastern Division champion.
- 1956 NFL champion.

68: TOM LANDRY (S, P; 1950–1955)

Courtesy of SportsMemorabilia.com

Giant Numbers

31 interceptions, 360 return yards, 3 TD interception returns, 6 touchdowns. Averaged 40.4 yards per punt; career long: 69 yards.

NOTABLE ACHIEVEMENTS

- Recorded 8 interceptions three times (1951, 1952, 1954).
- Led NFL with 2 TD interception returns in 1951.
- Averaged more than 40 yards per punt five times, posting average in excess of 42 twice.
- Ranks sixth in Giants history with 31 career interceptions.
- 1954 Pro Bowl selection.
- 1954 First-Team All-Pro selection.
- 1950 NFL Eastern Division champion.

69: KEITH HAMILTON (DT, DE; 1992–2003)

Courtesy of SportsMemorabilia.com

Giant Numbers

63 sacks, 513 tackles.

NOTABLE ACHIEVEMENTS

- Recorded at least 10 quarterback sacks twice (1993, 2000).
- Ranks fifth all-time on Giants' "official" sack list with 63.
- 2000 Second-Team All-NFL selection.
- 2000 NFC champion.

70: SHAUN O'HARA (C; 2004–2010)

Courtesy of Alexa Scordato via Wikipedia

NOTABLE ACHIEVEMENTS

- Three-time Pro Bowl selection (2008, 2009, 2010).
- 2008 Second-Team All-Pro selection.
- 2007 NFC champion.
- Super Bowl XLII champion.

71: EDDIE PRICE (RB; 1950–1955)

Public domain (author unknown)

Giant Numbers

3,292 rushing yards, 20 rushing touchdowns, 75 receptions, 672 receiving yards, 4 TD receptions.

NOTABLE ACHIEVEMENTS

- Led NFL with 971 yards rushing in 1951.
- Led NFL in rushing attempts twice (1951, 1952).
- Finished second in NFL with 7 rushing touchdowns in 1951.
- Holds Giants' single-season record for highest rushing average (5.6 yards per carry in 1950).
- Three-time Pro Bowl selection (1951, 1952, 1954).
- Two-time First-Team All-Pro selection (1951, 1952).
- 1950 NFL Eastern Division champion.

72: THOMAS "PEPPER" JOHNSON (LB; 1986–1992)

Courtesy of PristineAuction.com

Giant Numbers

579 tackles, 19 sacks, 10 interceptions, 2 touchdowns.

NOTABLE ACHIEVEMENTS

- Recorded more than 100 tackles three straight years (1990–1992), leading Giants in tackles each time.
- 1990 Pro Bowl selection.
- 1990 First-Team All-NFC selection.
- 1990 First-Team All-Pro selection.
- Two-time NFC champion (1986, 1990).
- Two-time Super Bowl champion (XXI, XXV).

73: ROSEY GRIER (DT; 1956–1962)

Courtesy of MearsOnlineAuctions.com

NOTABLE ACHIEVEMENTS

- Two-time Pro Bowl selection (1956, 1960).
- 1962 First-Team All-Conference selection.
- 1956 First-Team All-Pro selection.
- Two-time Second-Team All-Pro selection (1958, 1959).
- Five-time NFL Eastern Division champion.
- 1956 NFL champion.

74: BENNY FRIEDMAN (QB; 1929–1931)

Courtesy of RMYAuctions.com

Giant Numbers

36 touchdown passes, 10 rushing touchdowns.

NOTABLE ACHIEVEMENTS

- Set NFL single-season record with 20 touchdown passes in 1929.
- Two-time First-Team All-Pro selection (1929, 1930).

75: PETE GOGOLAK (PK; 1966–1974)

Courtesy of EACGallery.com

Giant Numbers

Successful on 57.5 percent of field-goal attempts (126 of 219); scored 646 total points.

NOTABLE ACHIEVEMENTS

- Giants all-time leader in points scored (646) and field goals made (126).

GLOSSARY
ABBREVIATIONS AND STATISTICAL TERMS

C: Center.

COMP %: Completion percentage. The number of successfully completed passes divided by the number of passes attempted.

INTS: Interceptions. Passes thrown by the quarterback that are caught by a member of the opposing team's defense.

LCB: Left cornerback.

LE: Left end.

LG: Left guard.

LILB: Left inside linebacker.

LOLB: Left outside linebacker.

LT: Left tackle.

NT: Nose tackle.

P: Punter.

PK: Place-kicker.

QB: Quarterback.

RB: Running back.

RCB: Right cornerback.

RE: Right end.

RG: Right guard.

RILB: Right inside linebacker.

ROLB: Right outside linebacker.

RT: Right tackle.

S: Safety.

TD PASSES: Touchdown passes.

TD RECS: Touchdown receptions.

TDS: Touchdowns.

TE: Tight end.

WR: Wide receiver.

NOTES

Chapter 1

1. Lawrence Taylor, quoted in *Sports Century: Fifty Greatest Athletes—Lawrence Taylor* (ESPN, 1999). Broadcast, Season 1, episode 11.

2. Harry Carson, quoted in *Sports Century: Fifty Greatest Athletes—Lawrence Taylor*.

3. Beasley Reece, quoted in *Sports Century: Fifty Greatest Athletes—Lawrence Taylor*.

4. Joe Theismann, quoted in *Sports Century: Fifty Greatest Athletes—Lawrence Taylor*.

5. John Madden, quoted in *Sports Century: Fifty Greatest Athletes—Lawrence Taylor*.

6. Dick Butkus, quoted in *Sports Century: Fifty Greatest Athletes—Lawrence Taylor*.

7. Lawrence Taylor, quoted in *LT: Lawrence Taylor* (NFL Films, 1993). VHS.

8. Mike Singletary, quoted in *Sports Century: Fifty Greatest Athletes—Lawrence Taylor*.

9. Lawrence Taylor, quoted in *Giants Forever: History of the New York Giants* (NFL Films Video, 1988). VHS.

10. Bill Parcells, quoted in *Giants among Men: The 1986 New York Giants from Opening Day to the Super Bowl* (NFL Films Video, 1987). VHS.

11. Dan Reeves, quoted in *Giants among Men*.

12. Joe Bugel, quoted in *Giants among Men*.

13. Jay Schroeder, quoted in *Giants among Men*.

14. Taylor, quoted in *Sports Century: Fifty Greatest Athletes—Lawrence Taylor*.

15. Joe Gibbs, quoted in *LT: Lawrence Taylor*.

16. Ron Jaworski, quoted in *LT: Lawrence Taylor*.

17. Bill Parcells, quoted in *LT: Lawrence Taylor*.

18. Bill Parcells, quoted in *Giants Forever*.

19. Taylor, quoted in *Sports Century: Fifty Greatest Athletes—Lawrence Taylor*.

20. Taylor, quoted in *Sports Century: Fifty Greatest Athletes—Lawrence Taylor*.

21. Lawrence Taylor, quoted in Rebecca Leung, "L.T. over the Edge: Former Hall of Famer Reveals Shocking Stories from His Playing Days," *CBS News*, September 10, 2004, www.cbsnews.com/news/lt-over-the-edge-642605 (accessed April 15, 2013).

22. Dave Anderson, quoted in *LT: Lawrence Taylor*.

23. Phil Simms, quoted in *LT: Lawrence Taylor*.

Chapter 2

1. Jim Terzian, *New York Giants: Great Teams' Great Years* (New York: Macmillan, 1973), 130.

2. Harland Svare, quoted in *Blue Diamond: 75 Years of New York Giants Football* (NFL Films, 1999). VHS.

3. Jim Lee Howell, quoted in www.answers.com/topic/emlen-tunnell (accessed April 18, 2013).

4. Terzian, *New York Giants: Great Teams' Great Years*, 129.

5. Frank Gifford, quoted in *Blue Diamond*.

6. Terzian, *New York Giants: Great Teams' Great Years*, 133.

7. Andy Robustelli, quoted in James M. Manheim, "Emlen Tunnell," *Answers.com*, www.answers.com/topic/emlen-tunnell (accessed April 18, 2013).

8. Terzian, *New York Giants: Great Teams' Great Years*, 133.

Chapter 3

1. Jim Terzian, *New York Giants: Great Teams' Great Years* (New York: Macmillan, 1973), 105.

2. Al DeRogatis, quoted in Frank Litsky, "Roosevelt Brown, 71, Dies; Hall of Fame Giants Tackle," *New York Times*, June 11, 2004, www.nytimes.com /2004/06/11/sports/roosevelt-brown-71-dies-hall-of-fame-giants-tackle.html (accessed April 22, 2013).

3. Ernie Accorsi, quoted in Litsky, "Roosevelt Brown, 71, Dies."

4. Frank Gifford, quoted in Litsky, "Roosevelt Brown, 71, Dies."

5. Sam Huff, quoted in Litsky, "Roosevelt Brown, 71, Dies."

6. Accorsi, quoted in Litsky, "Roosevelt Brown, 71, Dies."

7. Roosevelt Brown, quoted in Litsky, "Roosevelt Brown, 71, Dies."

8. Terzian, *New York Giants: Great Teams' Great Years*, 108.

Chapter 4

1. Jim Terzian, *New York Giants: Great Teams' Great Years* (New York: Macmillan, 1973), 113.

2. Al Davis, quoted in Robert McG. Thomas Jr., "Mel Hein, 82, the Durable Center of the New York Football Giants," *New York Times*, February 2, 1992, www.nytimes.com/1992/02/02/us/mel-hein-82-the-durable-center-of-the-new-york-football-giants.html (accessed April 23, 2013).

3. Steve Hirdt, www.youtube.com/watch?v=EXy1BH1cIUY (accessed April 2013).

Chapter 5

1. Jerry Reese, quoted in John Branch, "Super Bowl Ring in Hand, Strahan Says He's Retiring," *New York Times*, June 10, 2008, www.nytimes.com/2008/06/10/sports/football/10strahan.html?ref=Michaelstrahan&_r=0 (accessed June 28, 2013).

2. Ernie Accorsi, quoted in Branch, "Super Bowl Ring in Hand."

Chapter 6

1. Kevin Lamb, *Giants: The Unforgettable Season* (New York: Macmillan, 1987), 48.

2. Lamb, *Giants: The Unforgettable Season*, 48.

3. Peter King, "Hall of Fame Game: Why Carson Finally Made It; NFL-Wide News and Notes," *Sports Illustrated*, February 13, 2006, http://sportsillustrated.cnn.com/2006/writers/peter_king/02/13/mmqb/index.html (accessed June 16, 2013). Also available at http://boards.giants.com/showthread.php?30688-Stopping-the-run.

4. Lamb, *Giants: The Unforgettable Season*, 48.

5. Lamb, *Giants: The Unforgettable Season*, 48.

6. Lamb, *Giants: The Unforgettable Season*, 48.

7. Harry Carson, quoted in King, "Hall of Fame Game."

Chapter 7

1. David Cutcliffe, quoted in "Eli Manning," *JockBio.com*, www.jockbio.com/Bios/EManning/Eli_they-say.html (accessed July 11, 2013).

2. Johnny Vaught, quoted in "Eli Manning."

3. Ernie Accorsi, quoted in "Eli Manning."

4. John Mara, quoted in Ralph Vacchiano, "John Mara: Giants Sticking with Eli Manning," *New York Daily News*, November 14, 2007, www.nydailynews.com /sports/football/giants/john-mara-giants-sticking-eli-manning-article-1.256096 (accessed July 11, 2013).

5. Shaun O'Hara, quoted in "Eli Manning."

6. Kevin Gilbride, quoted in "Eli Manning."

7. Tom Coughlin, quoted in "Eli Manning."

8. Coughlin, quoted in "Eli Manning."

9. Eli Manning, quoted in Matt Ehalt, "Eli Manning: I'm in Class with Tom Brady," *ESPN.com*, August 18, 2011, http://espn.go.com/new-york/nfl/story /_/id/6868654/eli-manning-sees-same-class-new-england-patriots-tom-brady (accessed July 11, 2013).

10. David Diehl, quoted in "Eli Manning."

Chapter 8

1. Frank Gifford, quoted in "Andy Robustelli Dies at Age 85," *ESPN.com*, June 1, 2011, http://sports.espn.go.com/new-york/nfl/news/story?id=6611816 (accessed April 25, 2013).

2. Gifford, quoted in "Andy Robustelli Dies at Age 85."

3. Frank Gifford, quoted in Ralph Vacchiano, "Andy Robustelli, Former Giants Defensive End and Pro Football Hall of Famer, Dead at 85," *New York Daily News*, May 30, 2011, www.nydailynews.com/sports/football/giants/andy -robustelli-giants-defensive-pro-football-hall-famer-dead-85-article-1.142426 (accessed April 25 2013).

4. Jim Terzian, *New York Giants: Great Teams' Great Years* (New York: Macmillan, 1973), 126.

5. Tom Landry, in *Giants Forever: History of the New York Giants* (NFL Films Video, 1988). VHS.

6. Tom Landry, quoted in Richard Goldstein, "Andy Robustelli, Giants' Hall of Fame Defensive End, Dies at 85," *New York Times*, May 31, 2011, www.nytimes .com/2011/06/01/sports/football/andy-robustelli-giants-hall-of-fame-defensive -end-dies-at-85.html (accessed April 25, 2013).

7. George Martin, quoted in "Andy Robustelli Dies at Age 85."

8. Martin, quoted in "Andy Robustelli Dies at Age 85."

9. Martin, quoted in "Andy Robustelli Dies at Age 85."

10. Andy Barral, quoted in Goldstein, "Andy Robustelli."

Chapter 9

1. Frank Gifford, quoted in Mike Puma, "Gifford Was Star in Backfield, Booth," *ESPN.com*, http://espn.go.com/classic/biography/s/Gifford_Frank.html (accessed May 7, 2013).

2. Gifford, quoted in Puma, "Gifford Was Star in Backfield, Booth."

3. Joe Namath, quoted in Puma, "Gifford Was Star in Backfield, Booth."

4. Sam Huff, quoted in Puma, "Gifford Was Star in Backfield, Booth."

Chapter 10

1. Kevin Lamb, *Giants: The Unforgettable Season* (New York: Macmillan, 1987), 54.

2. Lamb, *Giants: The Unforgettable Season*, 54.

3. Lamb, *Giants: The Unforgettable Season*, 54.

4. Lamb, *Giants: The Unforgettable Season*, 54.

5. Joe Morris, quoted in Greg Hanlon, "'As Hard as You Can': A Story about the Indestructibility of Phil Simms," *Capital*, February 1, 2013, www.capitalnewyork.com/article/sports/2013/02/7468317/hard-you-can-story-about-indestructibility-phil-simms?page=all (accessed June 20, 2013).

6. Bill Parcells, quoted in Hanlon, "As Hard as You Can."

7. Phil Simms, quoted in Hanlon, "As Hard as You Can."

8. Lawrence Taylor, quoted in *Giants among Men: The 1986 New York Giants from Opening Day to the Super Bowl* (NFL Films Video, 1987).

9. Phil McConkey, quoted in *Giants among Men*.

10. Lamb, *Giants: The Unforgettable Season*, 54.

11. George Young, quoted in *Giants among Men*.

12. Lamb, *Giants: The Unforgettable Season*, 54.

13. Lamb, *Giants: The Unforgettable Season*, 54.

14. Phil Simms, quoted in Hanlon, "As Hard as You Can."

15. Phil Simms, quoted in *Giants among Men*.

Chapter 11

1. Jim Terzian, *New York Giants: Great Teams' Great Years* (New York: Macmillan, 1973), 118.

2. Terzian, *New York Giants: Great Teams' Great Years*, 118.

3. Terzian, *New York Giants: Great Teams' Great Years*, 118.

4. Terzian, *New York Giants: Great Teams' Great Years*, 119.

5. Jim Brown, quoted in *Giants Forever: History of the New York Giants* (NFL Films Video, 1988). VHS.

6. Sam Huff, quoted in Bob Carter, "The Violent World," *ESPN.com,* http://espn .go.com/classic/biography/s/Huff_Sam.html (accessed May 12, 2013).

7. Terzian, *New York Giants: Great Teams' Great Years*, 119.

8. Terzian, *New York Giants: Great Teams' Great Years*, 120.

Chapter 12

1. Brad Van Pelt, www.starledger.com/sports/football/giants/former-giant-brad -van-pelt-dies-heart-attack (accessed June 4, 2013).

2. Brian Kelley, quoted in Hank Gola, "Giants Pro Bowl Linebacker Brad Van Pelt Dies of Heart Attack at 57," *New York Daily News*, February 18, 2009, www .nydailynews.com/sports/football/giants/giants-pro-bowl-linebacker-brad-van -pelt-dies-heart-attack-57-article-1.390945 (accessed June 4, 2013).

3. Kelley, quoted in Gola, "Giants Pro Bowl Linebacker Brad Van Pelt Dies of Heart Attack."

4. Kelley, quoted in Gola, "Giants Pro Bowl Linebacker Brad Van Pelt Dies."

5. John Mara, quoted in Gola, "Giants Pro Bowl Linebacker Brad Van Pelt Dies."

6. Harry Carson, quoted in Tom Rock, "Giants Great Brad Van Pelt Dies at 57," *Long Island Newsday*, February 18, 2009, www.newsday.com/sports/football /giants/giants-great-brad-van-pelt-dies-at-57-1.890415 (accessed June 4, 2013).

7. Carson, quoted in Rock, "Giants Great Brad Van Pelt Dies at 57."

8. Carson, quoted in Rock, "Giants Great Brad Van Pelt Dies at 57."

Chapter 13

1. Kevin Lamb, *Giants: The Unforgettable Season* (New York: Macmillan, 1987), 50.

2. Lamb, *Giants: The Unforgettable Season*, 50.

3. Lamb, *Giants: The Unforgettable Season*, 50.

4. Lamb, *Giants: The Unforgettable Season*, 50.

5. Lamb, *Giants: The Unforgettable Season*, 50.

6. Lamb, *Giants: The Unforgettable Season*, 50.

7. Leonard Marshall, quoted in Matt Ehalt, "Former Giants Defensive End Leonard Marshall Is Now Professor Sack," *New York Daily News*, August 29, 2009, www.nydailynews.com/sports/football/giants/giants-defensive-leonard-marshall -professor-sack-article-1.394728 (accessed June 7, 2013).

8. Marshall, quoted in Ehalt, "Former Giants Defensive End."

Chapter 14

1. Kevin Lamb, *Giants: The Unforgettable Season* (New York: Macmillan, 1987), 40.

2. Lamb, *Giants: The Unforgettable Season*, 40.

3. Lamb, *Giants: The Unforgettable Season*, 40.

4. Lawrence Taylor, quoted in "Over on the Other Side Is a Giant Linebacker of Note: Carl Banks," *Los Angeles Times*, January 11, 1987, http://articles.latimes .com/1987-01-11/sports/sp-3849_1_carl-banks (18 June 2013).

5. George Martin, quoted in *Giants among Men: The 1986 New York Giants from Opening Day to the Super Bowl* (NFL Films Video, 1987).

6. Carl Banks, quoted in "Over on the Other Side Is a Giant Linebacker of Note."

7. Banks, quoted in "Over on the Other Side Is a Giant Linebacker of Note."

8. Art Shell, quoted in "Over on the Other Side Is a Giant Linebacker of Note."

9. Banks, quoted in "Over on the Other Side Is a Giant Linebacker of Note."

10. Carl Banks, quoted in "Giants Legacy: Carl Banks," *New York Giants*, March 21, 2012, www.giants.com/videos/videos/Giants-Legacy-Carl-Banks/e4b46f86 -60e8-4907-8209-b1cd6d4e6916 (accessed June 18, 2013).

11. Carl Banks, quoted in Jim Corbett, "My Super Bowl: Carl Banks," *USA Today*, February 3, 2013, www.usatoday.com/story/sports/nfl/2013/02/03 /carl-banks-giants-super-bowl-xxi/1886241 (accessed June 18, 2013).

Chapter 15

1. Tiki Barber, quoted in "Barber Unhappy with Strahan's Salary Stance," *ESPN .com*, March 21, 2002, http://static.espn.go.com/nfl/news/2002/0321/1355387 .html (accessed July 9, 2013).

2. Keith Hamilton, quoted in "Barber Unhappy with Strahan's Salary Stance."

3. Tiki Barber, quoted in John Branch, "NBC Gives Barber the Ball, and He Runs with It," *New York Times*, February 14, 2007, www.nytimes.com/2007/02/14 /sports/football/14tiki.html?pagewanted=print&_r=0 (accessed July 9, 2013).

4. Eli Manning, quoted in http://blog.nj.com/ledgergiants/2007/02/eli_responds _to_tiki.html (accessed July 9, 2013).

Chapter 16

1. Amani Toomer, quoted in Michael David Smith, "Amani Toomer on Jeremy Shockey: 'Bad Teammate, Worse Person,'" *NBC Sports.com*, March 15, 2012, http://profootballtalk.nbcsports.com/2012/03/15/amani-toomer-on-jeremy -shockey-bad-teammate-worse-person (accessed June 27, 2013).

2. Amani Toomer, quoted in Ebenezer Samuel, "Eli Manning Able to Laugh Off Amani Toomer's Comments That Tony Romo Is a Better QB Than the NY Giants' Signal Caller," *New York Daily News*, July 23, 2012, www.nydailynews.com /sports/football/giants/eli-manning-laugh-amani-toomer-comments-tony-romo -better-qb-ny-giants-signal-caller-article-1.1120226 (accessed June 27, 2013).

3. Toomer, quoted in Samuel, "Eli Manning Able to Laugh Off."

4. Eli Manning, quoted in Samuel, "Eli Manning Able to Laugh Off."

5. Manning, quoted in Samuel, "Eli Manning Able to Laugh Off."

Chapter 17

1. Carl Banks, quoted in "Giants Chronicles: Mark Bavaro," *New York Giants*, March 27, 2012, www.giants.com/media-vault/videos/Giants-Chronicles-Mark -Bavaro/dfbbd3f0-45ee-40a6-927d-905d38c20988 (accessed June 14, 2013).

2. Kevin Lamb, *Giants: The Unforgettable Season* (New York: Macmillan), 42.

3. Lamb, *Giants: The Unforgettable Season*, 42.

4. Lamb, *Giants: The Unforgettable Season*, 42.

5. Lamb, *Giants: The Unforgettable Season*, 42.

6. Lamb, *Giants: The Unforgettable Season*, 42.

7. Bill Parcells, quoted in "Giants Chronicles: Mark Bavaro."

8. Ron Erhardt, quoted in *Giants among Men: The 1986 New York Giants from Opening Day to the Super Bowl* (NFL Films Video, 1987). VHS.

9. Lamb, *Giants: The Unforgettable Season*, 42.

10. Lamb, *Giants: The Unforgettable Season*, 42.

11. Mark Bavaro, quoted in "Giants Chronicles: Mark Bavaro."

12. Lamb, *Giants: The Unforgettable Season*, 42.

13. Joe Morris, quoted in "Giants Chronicles: Mark Bavaro."

Chapter 18

1. Fran Tarkenton, "Fran Tarkenton: 'In 1961, I Was a Freak.' Today, Running Quarterbacks Embraced," *TwinCities.com*, January 15, 2013, www.twincities.com/sports/ci_22379070/fran-tarkenton-1961-i-was-freak-today-running (accessed May 24, 2013).

2. Fran Tarkenton, quoted in *Blue Diamond: 75 Years of New York Giants Football* (NFL Films, 1999). VHS.

Chapter 19

1. Y. A. Tittle, quoted in "Y. A. Tittle," *Louisiana Sports Hall of Fame*, www.la sportshall.com/inductees/football/y.a.-tittle (accessed May 23, 2013).

2. Pat Summerall, quoted in *Blue Diamond: 75 Years of New York Giants Football* (NFL Films, 1999). VHS.

3. Jim Terzian, *New York Giants: Great Teams' Great Years* (New York: Macmillan, 1973), 91.

4. Tittle, quoted in "Y. A. Tittle."

5. Frank Gifford, quoted in "Y. A. Tittle."

6. Tittle, quoted in "Y. A. Tittle."

Chapter 20

1. Jimmy Patton, "Giants Greatest Defensive Backs," *Giants Beat Forum*, December 30, 2007, http://mbd.scout.com/mb.aspx?s=64&f=1871&t=1739976 (accessed May 11, 2013). Originally published in a 1960 article from *Time Magazine: Playing Safety*.

Chapter 21

1. Ernie Accorsi, quoted in Mark Weinstein, "Remembering Rodney: A Bluenatic's Lament," *Bluenatic.com*, April 24, 2008, http://bluenatic.blogspot.com/2008/04/remembering-rodney.html (accessed June 24, 2013).

2. Hampton, quoted in Weinstein, "Remembering Rodney."

3. Rodney Hampton, quoted in "Former Giants RB Rodney Hampton Gives Back with Hamp's Camp," NJTV Online, July 11, 2012, www.njtvonline.org /njtoday/video/former-giants-rb-rodney-hampton-gives-back-with-hamps-camp (accessed June 24, 2013).

4. Hampton, quoted in Weinstein, "Remembering Rodney."

Chapter 22

1. Jessie Armstead, quoted in *St. Petersburg* (Florida) *Times*, www.sptimes.com /News/012501/SuperBowl2001/At_decisive_ moment_A.shtml (accessed June 23, 2013).

2. Armstead, quoted in *St. Petersburg Times*.

3. Armstead, quoted in *St. Petersburg Times*.

4. Jessie Armstead, quoted in David O'Brien, "Armstead No Small Surprise: Giants' Rookie LB Is a Quick Study," *Sun Sentinel* (Fort Lauderdale, Florida), August 27, 1993, http://articles.sun-sentinel.com/1993-08-27/sports /9308270103_1_giants-10-time-jessie-armstead-giants-special-teams (accessed June 23, 2013).

5. Jessie Armstead, quoted in "Jessie Armstead Retires a Giant," *Wutang.com*, June 15, 2007, www.wutang-corp.com/forum/showthread.php?t=38235 (accessed June 23, 2013).

Chapter 23

1. Andy Robustelli, quoted in "Carl Ford (Spider) Lockhart," *FindaGrave.com*, January 8, 2013, www.findagrave.com/cgi-bin/fg.cgi?page=gr&GRid=103293004 (accessed May 26, 2013).

2. Robustelli, quoted in "Carl Ford (Spider) Lockhart."

3. Frank Gifford, quoted in "Carl Ford (Spider) Lockhart."

4. Tucker Frederickson, quoted in "Carl Ford (Spider) Lockhart."

5. Tucker Frederickson, quoted in "Carl Ford (Spider) Lockhart."

Chapter 24

1. Mark Haynes, quoted in Frank Litsky, "Silent Strength of Giants' Mark Haynes," *New York Times*, August 23, 1982, www.nytimes.com/1982/08/23 /sports/silent-strength-of-giants-mark-haynes.html (accessed June 11, 2013).

2. Fred Glick, quoted in Litsky, "Silent Strength of Giants' Mark Haynes."

3. Glick, quoted in Litsky, "Silent Strength of Giants' Mark Haynes."

4. Beasley Reece, quoted in Litsky, "Silent Strength of Giants' Mark Haynes."

5. Haynes, quoted in Litsky, "Silent Strength of Giants' Mark Haynes."

6. Haynes, quoted in Litsky, "Silent Strength of Giants' Mark Haynes."

7. Mark Bavaro, quoted in Litsky, "Silent Strength of Giants' Mark Haynes."

Chapter 25

1. Frank Gifford, quoted in Richard Goldstein, "Alex Webster, Giants Star and Coach, Dies at 80," *New York Times*, March 4, 2012, www.nytimes.com /2012/03/04/sports/football/alex-webster-giants-star-and-coach-dies-at-80.html? _r=0 (accessed May 13, 2013).

2. Al DeRogatis, quoted in *Giants Forever: History of the New York Giants* (NFL Films Video, 1988). VHS.

3. Al DeRogatis, quoted in Andy Barall, "Remembering Alex Webster, Giants Star and Coach, *New York Times*, March 5, 2012, http://fifthdown.blogs.nytimes .com/2012/03/05/remembering-alex-webster-giants-star-and-coach (accessed May 13, 2013).

4. Frank Gifford, quoted in Goldstein, "Alex Webster, Giants Star and Coach."

5. Frank Gifford, quoted in Ralph Vacchiano, "Giants Great Alex Webster Dies at Age 80," *New York Daily News*, March 4, 2012, www.nydailynews.com/blogs /giants/2012/03/giants-great-alex-webster-dies-at-age-80 (accessed May 13, 2013).

6. John Mara, quoted in Vacchiano, "Giants Great Alex Webster Dies at Age 80."

7. Al DeRogatis, quoted in *Blue Diamond: 75 Years of New York Giants Football* (NFL Films, 1999). VHS.

Chapter 26

1. Joe Morris, quoted in Bob Hill, "Giant Steps: He's Only 5 Feet 7, but Joe Morris Has the Giants Head and Shoulders above the Crowd," *Sun Sentinel* (Fort Lauderdale, Florida), December 30, 1986, http://articles.sun-sentinel.com /1986-12-30/sports/8603190925_1_giants-defense-giants-safety-joe-morris (accessed June 12, 2013).

2. Kevin Lamb, *Giants: The Unforgettable Season* (New York: Macmillan, 1987), 52.

3. Brad Benson, quoted in Hill, "Giant Steps."

4. Joe Morris, quoted in Hill, "Giant Steps."

5. Maurice Carthon, quoted in Hill, "Giant Steps."

6. Chris Godfrey, quoted in Hill, "Giant Steps."

7. Kenny Hill, quoted in Hill, "Giant Steps."

8. Kenny Hill, quoted in Hill, "Giant Steps."

9. Lamb, *Giants: The Unforgettable Season*, 52.

10. Lamb, *Giants: The Unforgettable Season*, 52.

11. Lamb, *Giants: The Unforgettable Season*, 52.

12. Lamb, *Giants: The Unforgettable Season*, 52.

13. Lamb, *Giants: The Unforgettable Season*, 52.

Chapter 27

1. Y. A. Tittle, quoted in John Fennessy, "Rote, William Kyle, Sr.," *Texas State Historical Association*, June 15, 2010, www.tshaonline.org/handbook/online/articles/frodf (accessed May 2, 2013).

2. Frank Gifford, quoted in Sam Farmer, "Kyle Rote, 74; Was Record-Setter as a N.Y. Giant Receiver," *Los Angeles Times*, August 16, 2002, http://articles.latimes.com/2002/aug/16/local/me-rote16 (accessed May 2, 2013).

3. Wellington Mara, quoted in Richard Goldstein, "Kyle Rote, a Top Receiver for the Giants, Dies at 73," *New York Times*, August 16, 2002, www.nytimes.com/2002/08/16/sports/kyle-rote-a-top-receiver-for-the-giants-dies-at-73.html (accessed May 2, 2013).

4. Mara, quoted in Goldstein, "Kyle Rote, a Top Receiver."

5. Sam Huff, quoted in Farmer, "Kyle Rote, 74; Was Record-Setter."

6. Y. A. Tittle, quoted in Farmer, "Kyle Rote, 74; Was Record-Setter."

7. Gifford, quoted in Farmer, "Kyle Rote, 74; Was Record-Setter."

8. Kyle Rote, quoted in Farmer, "Kyle Rote, 74; Was Record-Setter."

Chapter 28

1. Wayne Millner, quoted in Don Smith, "Tuffy Leemans: A Real Tuffy," *Professional Football Researchers Organization* 7, no. 1 (1985), www.profootballresearchers.org/Coffin_Corner/07-01-213.pdf (accessed May 1, 2013).

2. Wellington Mara, quoted in Smith, "Tuffy Leemans: A Real Tuffy."

3. Cliff Battles, quoted in Smith, "Tuffy Leemans: A Real Tuffy."

4. Mel Hein, quoted in *Blue Diamond: 75 Years of New York Giants Football* (NFL Films, 1999). VHS.

5. Tuffy Leemans, quoted in Smith, "Tuffy Leemans: A Real Tuffy."

Chapter 29

1. Grantland Rice, quoted in Bob Carroll, "Ken Strong," *Professional Football Researchers Organization* 1, no. 9 (1979), www.profootballresearchers.org /Coffin_Corner/01-09-015.pdf (accessed April 29, 2013).

Chapter 30

1. Jim Terzian, *New York Giants: Great Teams' Great Years* (New York: Macmillan, 1973), 32.

2. Terzian, *New York Giants: Great Teams' Great Years*, 171.

3. Frank Gifford, quoted in Nate Hale, "In from the Cold," *Former Spook*, February 4, 2008, http://formerspook.blogspot.com/2008/02/charlie-conerly -would-understand.html (accessed May 17, 2013).

4. Allie Sherman, quoted in *Blue Diamond: 75 Years of New York Giants* (NFL Films, 1999). VHS.

5. Wellington Mara, quoted in Dave Anderson, "Charlie Conerly, 74, Is Dead; Giants' Quarterback in 50's," *New York Times*, February 14, 1996, www.nytimes .com/1996/02/14/sports/charlie-conerly-74-is-dead-giants-quarterback-in-50-s .html (accessed May 17, 2013).

6. Frank Gifford, quoted in Anderson, "Charlie Conerly, 74, Is Dead."

7. Allie Sherman, quoted in Anderson, "Charlie Conerly, 74, Is Dead."

Chapter 31

1. Jim Terzian, *New York Giants: Great Teams' Great* Years (New York: Macmillan, 1973), 140.

2. Allie Sherman, quoted in Ed Valentine, "Giants by the Numbers: 55 Is for . . . ," *Big Blue View*, June 21, 2010, www.bigblueview.com/2010/6/21/1524809/giants -by-the-numbers-55-is-for (accessed May 10, 2013).

3. Pat Summerall, quoted in Richard Goldstein, "Ray Wietecha, Key to Giants' Glory, Dies at 74," *New York Times*, December 22, 2002, www.nytimes.com /2002/12/22/sports/ray-wietecha-key-to-giants-glory-days-dies-at-74.html (accessed May 10, 2013).

4. Terzian, *New York Giants: Great Teams' Great Years*, 140.

5. Ray Wietecha, quoted in Goldstein, "Ray Wietecha, Key to Giants' Glory."

6. Terzian, *New York Giants: Great Teams' Great Years*, 140.

Chapter 32

1. Wellington Mara, quoted in Don Amore, "Jim Katcavage Dies: Played for Giants," *Courant* (Hartford, Conn.), February 23, 1995, http://articles.courant .com/1995-02-23/sports/9502232732_1_jim-katcavage-linemen-giants (accessed May 4, 2013).

2. Andy Robustelli, quoted in Robert McG. Thomas Jr., "Jim Katcavage, 60, Giants Star of '56 Championship Team, Dies," *New York Times*, February 23, 1995, www.nytimes.com/1995/02/23/obituaries/jim-katcavage-60-giants-star -of-56-championship-team-dies.html (accessed May 4, 2013).

3. Jim Katcavage, "There's No Backing In for Giants," *Blade* (Toledo, Ohio), December 9, 1963, http://news.google.com/newspapers?nid=1350&dat= 19631209&id=MgJPAAAAIBAJ&sjid=PwEEAAAAIBAJ&pg=6205,6922966 (accessed May 4, 2013).

Chapter 33

1. Kevin Lamb, *Giants: The Unforgettable Season* (New York: Macmillan, 1987), 50.

2. Lamb, *Giants: The Unforgettable Season*, 50.

3. Lamb, *Giants: The Unforgettable Season*, 51.

4. Bill Parcells, quoted in *Giants among Men: The 1986 New York Giants from Opening Day to the Super Bowl* (NFL Films Video, 1987). VHS.

5. George Martin, quoted in *Giants among Men*.

6. Lamb, *Giants: The Unforgettable Season*, 51.

Chapter 34

1. Pro Football Hall of Fame, quoted in David Eskenazi, "Wayback Machine: Weinmeister's Dash to Canton," *SportsPressNW.com*, February 12, 2013, http:// sportspressnw.com/2146259/2013/wayback-machine-weinmeisters-dash-to -canton (accessed May 8, 2013).

2. Ray Flaherty, quoted in Eskenazi, "Wayback Machine."

3. Arnie Weinmeister, quoted in Eskenazi, "Wayback Machine."

4. Weinmeister, quoted in Eskenazi, "Wayback Machine."

5. Weinmeister, quoted in Eskenazi, "Wayback Machine."

6. Ed Strader, quoted in Eskenazi, "Wayback Machine."

7. Dante Lavelli, quoted in Richard Goldstein, "Arnie Weinmeister, 77, a Giants Star in the 50's, Is Dead," *New York Times*, July 7, 2000, www.nytimes .com/2000/07/07/sports/arnie-weinmeister-77-a-giants-star-in-the-50-s-is-dead .html (accessed May 8, 2013).

8. Buck Shaw, quoted in Goldstein, "Arnie Weinmeister."

9. Tom Landry, quoted in Goldstein, "Arnie Weinmeister."

10. Roosevelt Brown, quoted in Goldstein, "Arnie Weinmeister."

11. Weinmeister, quoted in Eskenazi, "Wayback Machine."

Chapter 36

1. Dick Lynch, quoted in "Giants Greatest Defensive Backs," *TheGiantsBeat.com* forum, http://mbd.scout.com/mb.aspx?s=64&f=1871&t=1739976 (accessed May 9, 2013).

2. Dick Lynch, quoted in Bill Gallo, "A Friend's Fond Farewell to Dick Lynch, Whose Giant Heart Will Never Be Forgotten," *New York Daily News*, September 24, 2008, www.nydailynews.com/sports/football/giants/friend-fond-farewell-dick -lynch-giant-heart-forgotten-article-1.320841 (accessed May 9, 2013).

3. Dick Lynch, quoted in "Giants Greatest Defensive Backs."

4. Bob Papa, quoted in Bruce Weber, "Dick Lynch, Giants Star Who Became a Broadcaster, Dies at 72," *New York Times*, September 25, 2008, www.nytimes .com/2008/09/25/sports/football/25lynch.html?_r=0 (accessed May 9, 2013).

Chapter 37

1. Osi Umenyiora, quoted in Ralph Vacchiano, "Osi Umenyiora Makes Peace with NY Giants GM Jerry Reese before Joining Atlanta Falcons," *New York Daily News*, March 28, 2013, www.nydailynews.com/sports/football/giants/osi-peace -reese-leaving-giants-article-1.1301481 (accessed June 30, 2013).

Chapter 39

1. Jeremy Shockey, quoted in "Jeremy Shockey," *Jockbio.com*, www.jockbio.com /Bios/Shockey/Shockey_mysay.html (accessed July 15, 2013).

2. Shockey, quoted in "Jeremy Shockey."

3. Shockey, quoted in "Jeremy Shockey."

4. Jim Fassel, quoted in "Jeremy Shockey Is Living Large," *New York Magazine*, August 18, 2003, http://nymag.com/nymetro/news/sports/features/n_9090 /index1.html (accessed July 15, 2013).

5. Jeremy Shockey, quoted in Toni Monkovic, "You've Been Outcoached," *New York Times*, September 25, 2006, http://fifthdown.blogs.nytimes.com /2006/09/25/youve-been-outcoached (accessed July 15, 2013).

6. Amani Toomer, quoted in Michael David Smith, "Amani Toomer on Jeremy Shockey: 'Bad Teammate, Worse Person,'" *NBC Sports*, March 15, 2012, http:// profootballtalk.nbcsports.com/2012/03/15/amani-toomer-on-jeremy-shockey -bad-teammate-worse-person (accessed 15 July 2013).

Chapter 40

1. Alex Webster, quoted in http://news.google.com/newspapers?nid=1350 &dat=19701109&id=ZOhOAAAAIBAJ&sjid=xgEEAAAAIBAJ&pg =5324,3963200 (accessed May 28, 2013).

2. Fran Tarkenton, quoted in http://news.google.com/newspapers?nid=1350& dat=19701109&id=ZOhOAAAAIBAJ&sjid=xgEEAAAAIBAJ&pg =5324,3963200 (accessed May 28, 2013).

3. Ron Johnson, quoted in http://news.google.com/newspapers?nid=1350& dat=19701109&id=ZOhOAAAAIBAJ&sjid=xgEEAAAAIBAJ& pg=5324,3963200 (accessed May 28, 2013).

4. Jim Terzian, *New York Giants: Great Teams' Great Years* (New York: Macmillan, 1973), 113.

Chapter 41

1. Fran Tarkenton, quoted in http://giantsfans.net/index.php?option=com _content&view=article&id=89:homer-jones-a-football (accessed June 1, 2013).

2. Fran Tarkenton, quoted in *Blue Diamond: 75 Years of New York Giants Football* (NFL Films, 1999). VHS.

3. Homer Jones, quoted in http://giantsfans.net/index.php?option=com _content&view=article&id=89:homer-jones-a-football (accessed June 1, 2013).

Chapter 42

1. Elroy Hirsch, quoted in Setshot, "Del Shofner," *BaylorFans forum*, January 28, 2008 www.baylorfans.com/forums/showthread.php?t=143362&page=1 (accessed May 14, 2013).

2. Y. A. Tittle, quoted in Brad Oremland, "Best Wide Receivers Not in the HOF: 1960s," *Sports Central*, March 6, 2012, www.sports-central.org /sports/2012/03/06/best_wide_receivers_not_in_the_hof_1960s.php (accessed May 14, 2013).

3. Frank Gifford, quoted in *Blue Diamond: 75 Years of New York Giants Football* (NFL Films, 1999).

4. Del Shofner, quoted in www.oldestlivingprofootball.com/delbertmdelshofner .htm (accessed May 14, 2013).

Chapter 43

1. Justin Tuck, quoted in John Robinson, "The Freak Talks Notre Dame, the Draft, and Madden," *IGN Entertainment*, March 29, 2005, www.ign.com /articles/2005/03/30/justin-tuck-interview (accessed July 1, 2013).

2. Justin Tuck, quoted in *New York Post*, www.nypost.com/p/sports/giants /item_eUAPUduyU6jszaZsg9cVKJ;jsessionid=9977D8DBCC800C3DC37D 74079265C0B5 (accessed July 1, 2013).

Chapter 44

1. Red Grange, quoted in "Red Badgro, Multi Sports Star Dies," *Dead Ball Era .com*, July 13, 1998, http://thedeadballera.com/Obits/Obits_B/Badgro.Red.Obit .html (accessed August 18, 2013).

2. Red Badgro, quoted in "Red Badgro, Multi Sports Star Dies."

Chapter 45

1. Allie Sherman, quoted in Dave Anderson, "Sports of the Times: This Was a Football Player," *New York Times*, February 8, 1989, www.nytimes.com /1989/02/08/sports/sports-of-the-times-this-was-a-football-player.html (accessed August 16, 2013).

2. Sherman, quoted in Anderson, "Sports of the Times."

3. Wellington Mara, quoted in "Joe Morrison, 51, Former Giant," *New York Times*, February 6, 1989, www.nytimes.com/1989/02/06/obituaries/joe -morrison-51-former-giant.html (accessed August 16, 2013).

Chapter 46

1. Eli Manning, quoted in "Victor Cruz: What They Say," *JockBio.com*, www.jock
bio.com/Bios/V_Cruz/V_Cruz_they-say.html (accessed July 17, 2013).

2. Tom Coughlin, quoted in "Victor Cruz: What They Say."

3. Shaun O'Hara, quoted in Dan Salomone, "NFL Network: Is Victor Cruz an
Elite WR?" *New York Giants.com*, www.giants.com/news-and-blogs/article-1/NFL
-Network-Is-Victor-Cruz-an-Elite-WR/6bf9248d-42a1-43a7-b71a-93abcc16a75f
(accessed July 17, 2013).

Chapter 47

1. Butch Davis, quoted in Ralph Vacchiano, "Giants First-Round Pick Hakeem
Nicks Grabs Comparison to Michael Irvin," *New York Daily News*, May 6, 2009,
www.nydailynews.com/sports/football/giants/giants-first-round-pick-hakeem
-nicks-grabs-comparison-michael-irvin-article-1.412178 (accessed July 16, 2013).

2. Davis, quoted in Vacchiano, "Giants First-Round Pick Hakeem Nicks."

3. Davis, quoted in Vacchiano, "Giants First-Round Pick Hakeem Nicks."

Chapter 48

1. Michael Bloomberg, quoted in *New York Post*, www.nypost.com/p/news
/regional/item_w3djOf7EFrNI4 AvXYxv7AL;jsessionid=4A66560E27470A6AEF
3FE31B35006806 (accessed July 18, 2013).

Chapter 49

1. John Mara, quoted in Dave D'Alessandro, "Road to the Super Bowl: Bob
Tucker, Lonely Light from Giants' Dark Times, Still Shines," *New Jersey On-Line*,
January 30, 2012, www.nj.com/giants/index.ssf/2012/01/road_to_the_super
_bowl_bob_tuc.html (accessed May 27, 2013).

2. Bob Tucker, quoted in D'Alessandro, "Road to the Super Bowl."

3. Tucker, quoted in D'Alessandro, "Road to the Super Bowl."

Chapter 50

1. Jerry Reese, quoted in Mike Garafolo, "Giants Brass Comments on First-Round Draft Pick Jason Pierre-Paul," *New Jersey On-Line*, April 22, 2010, www.nj.com/giants/index.ssf/2010/04/giants_brass_comments_on_jason.html (accessed July 2, 2013).

2. Kevin Patrick, quoted in "A Giants Project Is Paying Off," *Jason Pierre-Paul website*, February 25, 2011, http://jasonpierrepaul.com/2011/02/25/a-giants-project-is-paying-off (accessed July 2, 2013).

3. Jerry Reese, quoted in Garafolo, "Giants Brass Comments on First-Round Draft Pick."

4. Reese, quoted in Garafolo, "Giants Brass Comments on First-Round Draft Pick."

5. Jason Pierre-Paul, quoted in "Jason Pierre-Paul: My Say," *JockBio.com*, www.jockbio.com/Bios/J_Pierre-Paul/J_Pierre-6. Paul_my-say.html (accessed July 2, 2013).

BIBLIOGRAPHY

BOOKS

Lamb, Kevin, *Giants: The Unforgettable Season*. New York: Macmillan, 1987.
Terzian, Jim, *Great Teams' Great Years: New York Giants*. New York: Macmillan, 1973.

VIDEOS

Blue Diamond: 75 Years of New York Giants Football. NFL Films, 1999. VHS.
Giants among Men: The 1986 New York Giants from Opening Day to the Super Bowl. NFL Films Video, 1987. VHS.
Giants Forever: History of the New York Giants. NFL Films Video, 1988. VHS.
Greatest Ever: NFL Dream Team. Polygram Video, 1996. VHS.
LT: Lawrence Taylor. NFL Films, 1993. VHS.
Sports Century: Fifty Greatest Athletes—Lawrence Taylor. ESPN, 1999. Broadcast, Season 1, episode 11.

WEBSITES

Biographies, online at Hickoksports.com
(hickoksports.com/hickoksports/biograph)

Biography from Answers.com
(answers.com)

Biography from Jockbio.com
(jockbio.com)

CapitalNewYork.com
(capitalnewyork.com)

CBSNews.com
(cbsnews.com)

ESPN.com
(sports.espn.go.com)

Giants.com
(giants.com)

Hall of Famers, online at profootballhof.com
(profootballhof.com/hof/member)

Inductees from LASportsHall.com
(lasportshall.com)

LA Times.com
(articles.latimes.com)

Ledger Giants from BlogNJ.com
(blog.nj.com)

Newsday.com
(newsday.com)

NYDailyNews.com
(nydailynews.com/new-york)

NYTimes.com
(nytimes.com)

The Players, online at Profootballreference.com
(pro-football-reference.com/players)

Pro Football Talk from nbcsports.com
(profootballtalk.nbcsports.com)

SpTimes.com
(sptimes.com)

StarLedger.com
(starledger.com)

SunSentinel.com
(articles.sun-sentinel.com)

TwinCities.com
(twincities.com)

YouTube.com
(youtube.com)